ARCHITECTURE
IN THE UNITED STATES

CAPITOL, WASHINGTON, D.C. 1793–1865
Roman Revival
Photograph: Author's Collection

Dr. William Thornton, advised by
Benjamin Latrobe and Charles Bulfinch, 1793–1829
Robert Mills, 1836–1851
Thomas U. Walter, wings and dome, 1851–1865

ARCHITECTURE IN THE UNITED STATES

A Survey of Architectural
Styles Since 1776

RALPH W. HAMMETT

**Professor of Architecture, Emeritus,
University of Michigan**

A WILEY-INTERSCIENCE PUBLICATION

JOHN WILEY & SONS, New York • London • Sydney • Toronto

Library of Congress Cataloging in Publication Data:

Hammett, Ralph Warner.
  Architecture in the United States.

  "A Wiley Interscience publication."
  Bibliography: p.
  1. Architecture—United States—History. 2. Neo-classicism (Architecture)—United States. 3. Architecture, Modern—19th century—United States.
4. Architecture, Modern—20th century—United States.
I. Title.

NA705.H33   720′.973   76-4917
ISBN 0-471-34721-3

Printed in the United States of America

10 9 8 7 6 5 4 3 2 1

To the many students who
passed through my classes
and listened to my lectures
during my forty-five years
of active teaching

PREFACE

This book has been in the process of being written for a number of years. As a professor of architecture and lecturer in the history of architecture at the University of Michigan from 1931 until retirement in 1965, except for two years as officer in charge of Monuments, Fine Arts and Archives for all of France, Belgium, Holland and Luxemburg during World War II. I gathered many notes. However full-time teaching duties and an architectural practice, as well as civic duties, kept me away from the fulfillment of this project until recently.

It has been my aim to treat the subject in a popular manner, and I have listed only typical and outstanding examples of each style of architecture as representative of the society of each era. Although much scholarship has gone into this text, it was prepared primarily for the undergraduate student and for the layman, with the idea of giving an overall picture of the American architectural heritage. I have tried to be objective, and the outline was developed from my own observations. Generally this outline follows that of most authorities; however I have deliberately made some deviations. The picture as herein unfolded is as I have seen it.

For denoting the relative importance of the various architectural examples, an old cliché from Baedeker has been used: the use of asterisks to signify importance. Two asterisks are used to mark outstanding examples, one asterisk for very good ones, and no asterisk for those examples worthy of mention but less important. Most of the illustrations are of double-asterisked examples.

There has been no attempt to write a social history of the United States, and only those societal influences that have affected architecture are pointed out. Neither has the importance of architects and designers been stressed, except that of such a special leader, as Frank Lloyd Wright; however even he designed within the framework of his society of its technology.

Much of the material was gathered from magazine articles—architectural magazines in addition to *Life, Time, U.S. News & World Report,* and newspapers Sunday supplements. A bibliography of books is given at the end of this book, and some of the material in this text can be found in those books. However the material herein deals with history, which in general is the common property of all people. This book attempts to present a history of the evolution of architecture in the United States.

The reader may question why some buildings were passed over and others given prominence. There was no special reason except that I was trying to make certain points and draw certain conclusions; therefore I chose obvious examples of the architectural style of each era. The book does not include a compilation of all outstanding buildings of each era; otherwise it would be twice to three times as voluminous. It does contain a description of the architectural style of each period.

I am indebted to several people for their help in securing photographs and for their criticism. Particularly deserving of mention is Mrs. Constance Sanchez, now retired, who was for many years in charge of photographic slides at the Architectural Library, University of Michigan. Also to be acknowledged is Robert C. Metcalf, Dean of the College of Architecture and Urban Planning, for the help that he gave, and Herbert W. Johe, Assistant Dean, for his patience in answering many questions and providing references to much valuable material.

Furthermore, I wish to give special thanks to William Dudley Hunt, FAIA, architectural editor for John Wiley and Sons, and who lives in Virginia. He gave special advice and council in the preparation of the manuscript, and spent many hours outside the call of duty, criticizing and editing the copy.

Also, I must mention my dear wife who has stood by me in this enterprise, prodding me when I was inclined to let down, and reading the manuscript and proofs for corrections in spelling which I was often careless in making.

RALPH W. HAMMETT

Ann Arbor, Michigan
March 1976

CONTENTS

ARCHITECTURE
IN THE UNITED STATES

1

ARCHITECTURE AND FREEDOM
1776–1860

The American colonies underwent a political and social reaction against
the monarchial system, followed by war. There was also an architectural
reaction in Europe against the lavish Baroque and Rococo architecture
of the seventeenth and eighteenth centuries, and a growing trend toward
plain walls and simple classic forms.

It was not until 1790, after a 15 year period of very little building,
that architectural construction slowly started in the United States. After
1790 the predominant architectural style continued to be Georgian,
which had been popular in colonial America; although the states were
politically separate from England and George III, the culture remained
English. It was not until after the War of 1812 that the citizenry felt
themselves completely divorced from the mother country, and sought a
cultural identity of their own. The small amount of building that was
done in the years from 1790 to 1812 followed the Late Georgian style of
England and carries the same name, though also called *Early Federal*.

The most influential proponents of this style in seventeenth and
eighteenth century England, were Christopher Wren and James Gibbs,
both disciples of the sixteenth century Italian architect Andrea Palladio.
Gibbs' London Church, St. Martin's in the Fields, became the model for
many American churches.

The so-called *Palladian motif*, a popular architectural cliché of Late
Georgian architecture in America, consists of a round arch resting on
classic piers or columns and flanked by rectangular openings on each
side. Although it had also been used in the colonial period, it became
increasingly popular in Late Georgian work.

After the War of 1812 Americans began to ask for an architectural
style that would reflect the taste of the new republic. Thomas Jefferson,

in addition to being a lawyer, a farmer, and third President of the United States, was a talented architect. He advocated that the new republic adopt the architecture of Republican Rome. At first this Roman phase, which may be called Phase Two, was contemporary with Late Georgian, and in fact these two styles were often combined. However, the Roman Revival, as it was called, lasted longer, until 1860, the time of the Civil War.

Phase Three, the Greek Revival, started about 1820. Books on Greek architecture were published and every architect, carpenter, and, in fact, men in all walks of life became conversant with Greek Classic forms. It was all very Romantic, and whereas a few years before people were talking in terms of Roman Republican, now they talked about Greek Democracy, its form and customs. Roman styling did not end, but Greek styling superceded it, or was combined with it, up until the Civil War.

After the War of 1812, people began to live more comfortably, and wealth was accumulated in the principal cities, as well as in the plantations of the Southern states. The wealthy sent their sons to college, and historical sophistication was the mark of a gentleman. Architecture therefore followed historical styling, and Greek Revival became very popular, even for pioneer homes in the then new Middle West.

The question may be asked, "What about the log cabin?" It was used, but usually only for a few years, until the pioneer family could build a more permanent and more stylish home having wood floors and plaster walls, as well as white painted siding for the exterior walls. The log cabin was not considered to be architecture and will not be so treated here, even though some were lived in for up to a hundred years.

It is interesting that just when Greek styling reached the height of its popularity (about 1840), another historical style was revived and gradually became popular: Gothic. During the nineteenth and twentieth century, up to the present, styles have changed about every generation, or about every twenty years. When the older style of the moment became common, youth tried to supplant it with something new; however, something new meant another historical style. Starting in 1836, Sir Charles Barry and Augustus Welby Northmore Pugin designed the new Houses of Parliament in London. This great block of buildings surrounded the medieval Westminster Hall and was just back of Westminster Abbey and the famous Chapel of Henry VII. Barry and Pugin completed the picture by doing the new Parliament Buildings in Perpendicular Gothic. This magnificent piece of work soon became the talk of the Western World. Gothic Revival, Phase IV, became popular in the United States, particularly for churches, but also for residences; and continued until the Civil

War. The style was taken up again after the war and has since been named Victorian Gothic for the later period and expression.

The introduction of Gothic styling was actually the introduction of Eclecticism, the choosing of style, which became thoroughly implanted in sophisticated America as well as in the Western World as one of the primary considerations of architecture. Would the court house being built after 1840 be designed in Roman Republican, Greek, or Gothic? At this time another set of styles was being introduced by the École Polytechnique of Paris, under the leadership of Professor J. N. L. Durand. He was the advocate of the free use of all historical styles, and Paris by this time was the style center of the world. *Rundbogenstil,* the German word for Eclectic styling, was under Durand's influence and was quite the rage in Germany and Bavaria; it was also becoming popular in England. (Note the Traveler's Club on Pall Mall, London, in Italian Renaissance style, by Sir Charles Barry, and the Königsbau of the Royal Palace in Munich which is almost a replica of the Pitti Palace in Florence, Italy.) From this there was a broadening of the horizon from Roman, Greek, and Gothic to include Renaissance and Baroque, sometimes Moorish and even Egyptian. Perhaps this introduction of Eclecticism to America about 1840 should be noted as Phase 5; at least it was the beginning of a trend among the Academic Romanticists that led to the "battle of the styles" in the period that followed the Civil War (1860–1920).

PHASE 1. LATE GEORGIAN (EARLY FEDERAL) STYLE, 1776–1840

The Late Georgian style was a carry-over of the pre-Revolutionary Georgian style, popularly called *Colonial,* which was distinctly English, as was the social order. Late Georgian, which is quite indistinguishable from the architectural style before the Revolution, also has the name of Federal or Early Federal, as it dates from that period and blends with the Roman Republican style of Thomas Jefferson. However, it was more English Renaissance than Roman, and followed the dictums of Sir Christopher Wren and James Gibbs. Some of the churches were almost plagiarisms of the latter's work.

Many of the fine antebellum period plantation houses of the Southern States that have the style popularly known as *Southern Colonial* are

Late Georgian, and some were built as late as the 1850s. General characteristics of this style are hipped roofs with cornices carried around the four sides; colonnades around the house, or at least on three sides; balustrades immediately above the columns, often of thin spindles and Chinese Chippendale in character. Fan lights were used over the main entrance doorways, and the Palladian window was frequently present. Elaborately detailed central hallways with grand stairs were quite the mode, and fireplace mantels and wall panelings often had Louis XVI designs. It must be remembered that after the War of 1812 the country was becoming prosperous and could afford luxuries that were popular in the pre-Revolutionary period.

Religious Buildings

*UNITED CHURCH, New Haven, Connecticut, 1813–1815, designed by David Hoadley, is a typical example of Late Georgian, and is rated as one of the finest Georgian churches in New England. It has an Ionic templelike porch, a beautiful cupolalike belfry topping the tower, and a lovely interior.

**CENTER CONGREGATIONAL CHURCH, New Haven, Connecticut (Figure 1.1), 1812–1815, designed by Ithiel Town, a native son, stands next to the United Church, both face the Green. It has a Wrenlike spire and a beautiful interior. These two churches are so much alike, it is as though they were competing, one with the other, or were twins. The outstanding exterior difference is that the top of the tower of the United Church is topped by a cupola, whereas the Center Church has a spire.

FIRST CONGREGATIONAL CHURCH, Milford, Connecticut, 1832, was also designed by David Hoadley, and is another fine example of Late Georgian.

FIRST CONGREGATIONAL CHURCH, Lyme, Connecticut, 1815, was designed by an unknown architect. The original church was destroyed by fire in 1907, but the present church is an exact replica. It is also rated as one

Figure 1.1 Center Congregational Church, New Haven, Connecticut, 1812-1815; Ithiel Town, Architect; Late Georgian style. Photograph by Ralph W. Hammett.

of the most beautiful of the Late Georgian churches in New England; certainly it is more individual.

PARK STREET CONGREGATIONAL CHURCH, Boston, Massachusetts, 1819, was designed by Peter Banner. Standing on one corner of Boston Common and marking a large subway station underneath, it is distinguished for its beautiful Wren-like spire. The meeting hall is on the second floor with entrances at the ground level at the two front corners. There is no temple portico.

**ST. PHILIP'S EPISCOPAL CHURCH, Charleston, South Carolina (Figure 1.2), 1835–1838, was designed by Joseph Hyde, and is the third church to occupy this site. The parish was founded in 1670, and both earlier churches were destroyed by fire, the second in 1833. The exterior, of a gray sandstone, features a magnificent spire similar to that of St. Martin's in the Field, London, by James Gibbs. It is not too different from the spire of St. Michael's, also Georgian, only a few blocks away. St. Philip's spire, though designed by Joseph Hyde, is a later addition and was built between 1848 and 1850 by E. Blake White, a local architect and parishioner.

The narthex under the tower is entered on three sides by porches of the Tuscan order. The interior, which is one of the finest of its type, features Corinthian columns, also after St. Martin's in the Field. Arches spring from square entablatures of these columns and support a barrel-vaulted ceiling over the nave. The altar end, with a vaulted chancel and coffered niche, is very Roman in proportion and detail. Here one sees Roman Classic and Georgian combined to form a beautifully congruous composition.

Residences

PIERCE–NICHOLS HOUSE, Salem, Massachusetts, 1785, was designed and built by Samuel McIntire, architect, builder, furniture maker, and wood carver. It is a large, square, three-storied house, noted for its Classic exterior detail, although the house is Georgian in character. There are Doric pilasters, one at each corner, a small portico at front and side portals in careful Doric detail, and also a beautiful Classic balustrade at the roofline. The interior is noted for its refined carved detail and splendid furniture.

*OCTAGON HOUSE, 1735 New York Avenue, N.W., Washington, D.C., 1800, was designed by Dr. William Thornton for Colonel John Tayloe, a wealthy Virginia planter who spent a great deal of time in Washington and used this as his home when he was in residence there. Despite its name, it is actually hexagonal, but fits its nonrectangular corner very well. It has an interesting brick exterior with a simple two-columned classic entrance as the outstanding feature. This juts out from a circular bay at the sharp-angled intersection of New York Avenue and 18th Street. The interior has fine detail and beautiful furnishings.

Figure 1.2 St. Philip's Episcopal Church, Charleston, South Carolina, 1835–1838; Joseph Hyde, Architect; E. Blake White, designer of the spire; Late Georgian style. Photograph donated by St. Philip's Church.

After the executive mansion was destroyed by fire during the War of 1812, this house was used by President Madison and his family as the official residence while the White House was being rebuilt. The Treaty of Ghent was ratified here on February 17, 1815. The president and his wife, Dolley, entertained many of the notables of the day in this house.

It is now owned by the American Institute of Architects, and is a showplace in front of the Institute's national offices, which occupy part of the original garden area.

*HARRISON GRAY OTIS RESIDENCE, Beacon Hill, Boston, 1795, was designed by Charles Bulfinch for H. G. Otis, a wealthy civic leader of the time. This was the first of three fine residences built for and occupied by the Otis family. The exterior, that of a typical city residence on crowded Beacon Street, is of red brick with a nice and refined formal entrance. The interior has beautiful Adam detail, particularly the dining room, whose fireplace mantel simulates Wedgwood refinement. This house, now the headquarters of the Society for the Preservation of New England Antiquities, is open to the public.

**GORE HALL, Waltham, Massachusetts (Figure 1.3), 1805–1806, by Jacques Guillaume, Architect, was originally the home of Christopher Gore, lawyer, diplomat, and Governor of the state. It is a large brick country mansion with symmetrical flanking wings. In the interior is a beautiful spiral staircase and an impressive banquet hall with an elegant chandelier. The parklike setting is a country estate of many acres. It is one of the more impressive residential showplaces in New England.

NICKELS–SORTWELL HOUSE, Wiscasset, Maine, 1807–1808, is a three-storied, square, Georgian-type house of wood. It has a beautiful entrance portico of Corinthian columns and the doorway has both a fanlight and side lights. All of the detail is ultrarefined, in the tradition of the Adam brothers. Over the entrance portico is a Palladian window, and over that a remarkable half-round fan window of delicate detail. Also on the front of the house, the three central bays of the second and third floors are tied together by a treatment of Corinthian pilasters. The interior, which is furnished with fine furniture of the period, is equally fine in classic detail.

Figure 1.3 Gore Hall, Waltham, Massachusetts, 1805–1806; Jacques Guillaume, Architect; Late Georgian style. Photograph by Jeremy Cole, Watertown, Mass.

*RUGGLES HOUSE, Columbia, Maine, 1818, is often rated as the finest Georgian house in Maine. The interior hallway is especially noteworthy for its divided stairway, which is unsupported between floors. It is a remarkable piece of cabinetwork, as well as beautiful in proportion and detail. Other detail in the house is equally attractive for its refined Adam character.

*MANIGAULT HOUSE, Charleston, South Carolina, 1800–1803, was designed by the architect Gabriel Manigault for his brother, Joseph. It is a red brick, three-storied mansion with double-tiered porch on the front, and is surrounded by a small, formally designed garden. The interior is noted for its exquisite Adam detail. Features include the unsupported circular stairway in the front hallway, and the large ball room on the third floor. It is now owned by the Charleston Museum and is being restored.

NATHANIEL RUSSELL HOUSE, Charleston, South Carolina, 1807–1811, is a plain-fronted, three-storied house of red brick. The interior, which is entered by a very beautiful fanlighted and carved portal, has a free-floating staircase like the Manigault House, and has exquisite panelings and mantels of Adam detail. This house, now the headquarters of the Charleston Historical Foundation, is beautifully preserved and restored.

PHASE 2.   ROMAN REVIVAL STYLE, 1776–1860

The revival of the Roman Republican style had some overtones of Georgian, and the interiors often had exquisite carvings and the type of refined Classic detail devised by the Adam brothers of England. The style is often called *Federal* because it was popular in the Early Federal period, or *American Empire* because it paralleled the Imperial Roman styling used in France at the time of Napoleon. However, particularly when the style was adapted to furniture, American Empire, though Roman, was not as ostentatious as in France. American copies of Empire furniture were heavier and usually lacked the gold-plated metal ornaments that were popular in France.

American use of the style was led by Thomas Jefferson, who had learned it from books and from his travels while America's Minister to France (1785–1789). In Nîmes, in Southern France, he studied the Maison Carrée, a Roman Corinthian temple built during the time of Augustus Caesar. Most buildings of this style had templelike porches using one of the Roman orders.

Public Buildings

*STATE CAPITOL, RICHMOND, VIRGINIA, 1789–1791, designed by Thomas Jefferson, is an adaptation of the Maison Carrée. The exterior design was used without much change, but of course, the cella walls had to be punched with windows, and because of cost, the Corinthian capitals of the portico were changed to Ionic. Although wings were later added to the building, these wings have enhanced the central portico, not detracted from it.

**THE CAPITOL, Washington, D.C. (frontispiece); 1793–1865, had as original architect William Thornton, who was followed by Benjamin H. Latrobe (1803–1817), Charles Bulfinch (1819–1829), Robert Mills (1836–1861), and Thomas Ustick Walter (1851–1865). A competition held in 1792 for the design of the capitol was won by a doctor of medicine, William Thornton. Among the 17 competitors, was Thomas Jefferson, then Secretary of State. The prize was a city lot and $500. The corner-stone was laid on September 18, 1793, by President George Washington, and construction began under Stephen Hallet, who collaborated with William Thornton. The north wing was built first, and Congress met there in November, 1800.

Meanwhile, James Hoban, who had won the competition for the President's house, was put in charge of the construction with Stephen Hallet as his assistant. In 1803, Benjamin Latrobe was appointed Surveyor of Public Buildings by Jefferson, then President, and took over the supervisory work. He completed the south wing in 1807.

On August 24, 1814, during the War of 1812, Admiral Cockburn of the British Navy set fire to the building, which was greatly damaged. Work was soon resumed, but in 1817 Latrobe was forced to resign because of a feud that developed between him and William Thornton.

In 1819, Charles Bulfinch took over, and the domical link between the two wings was completed under him in 1829. For the first time, the building was complete; that is, the two original wings were joined by a central bay with a dome. However, since by midcentury the building was too small for the rapidly growing nation, in 1850 Congress authorized a competition for the design of two greatly enlarged wings, one to house the House of Representatives and its appendages, and the other for the Senate and its offices. The winning design, by Thomas U. Walter, included a greatly enlarged central dome.

In 1857 the House wing was completed, and in 1859 the Senate moved into its wing. In 1863, during the Civil War, the present dome was completed, and on December 2 of that year, the statue of Freedom by Thomas Crawford was placed on top.

The dome is made up of two trussed shells of cast iron and rises from a drum based on the design of St. Peter's in Rome. It all rests on the supports of the original dome, and the interior rotunda was not changed. The dome rises 285 feet above the eastern plaza, where inauguration ceremonies are held every four years. There are 36 columns in the drum, one for each state at that time, and 13 in the lantern, one for each of the original states. The entire dome, including all of the columns, cornices, and bases, is of cast iron painted to resemble marble. The dome, which is actually Renaissance in design, completes a beautiful ensemble and was certainly needed aesthetically to dominate the greatly enlarged composition. It has been criticized in recent years because it has no particular function other than the aesthetic one, and because it is a fake of cast iron painted to resemble marble. This is also true of a number of domes built in Europe during this period, and the criticism has some validity; however, it is a mighty composition, and its aesthetic and symbolic value cannot be underestimated. It is particularly effective at night, when it is floodlighted.

The original building was constructed of local cream-colored sandstone. The new wings are of white marble, so to tie the composition together, the original stone was painted to simulate marble. Because the sandstone is rather soft, crumbling has caused problems throughout the years. Even paint could not stop the disintegration, so in 1959–1960, under the direction of George Stewart, the east front of the central portion was reproduced in white marble and set forward 32 feet. Although the project was excessively costly, approximately 100 rooms were added, a deeper base for the dome was provided, which further enhanced the composition. It is said that Thomas U. Walter suggested this change 100 years before, but that money could not be granted at that time.

In 1966, a similar replacement was proposed for the west front—the only original facade remaining, and said to be crumbling badly. The American Institute of Architects, as well as the National Park Service, which is in charge of the preservation of historic buildings, lobbied against it, and the Senate voted against it in 1972. The project will probably come up again after 20 years or more.

Steam heat was installed in the Capitol building in 1865, and elevators in 1874. The interior has been decorated with beautiful murals showing meaningful allegorical scenes, and the building is an appropriate symbol of a great nation. Appendages such as Senate and House office buildings, and the Library of Congress have been located in the neighborhood and only connected underground, by electrically operated subways. Thankfully, they do not interfere with the composition of the capitol.

*FIRST BANK OF THE UNITED STATES, Philadelphia, 120 S. Third Street, 1794–1797, is the oldest bank building in the United States. The architect, Samuel Blodgett, designed a Corinthian-styled temple front having six columns, with singles in the middle and doubles on each corner. This excellent example of Roman Revival no doubt set the bank style in this country for 150 years. The bank was opened in 1791 in temporary quarters in nearby Carpenter Hall, and moved into this specially built building in 1797. However, its national charter expired in 1811, and in 1812 the building was purchased by Stephen Girard, who operated a private bank there until his death in 1831. The bank was then chartered as the *Girard National Bank,* which is its present name.

*MASSACHUSETTS STATE HOUSE, Beacon and Park Streets, Boston, 1795–1798, was by Charles Bulfinch. Although it is in the Romantic Classical style, it is not as Roman as Jefferson's work in Virginia. The main source of inspiration was Somerset House in London. The building has a beautiful setting on Beacon Hill overlooking Boston Common, the public park near the center of the city. The copper-covered dome is without exterior ribs and is usually bright with goldleaf, which glistens brilliantly in the sun. The interior rotunda and central hallway with circular stairway are beautiful in proportion and detail. Here the influence is definitely Adam.

Like the State Capitol of Virginia, this building has been enlarged with wings, but here also these do not detract from the original center portion.

**NEW YORK CITY HALL, between Broadway and Park Row, New York City, 1803–1811, was designed by Joseph François Mangin with

Figure 1.4 New York City Hall, New York City, 1804–1818; Joseph F. Mangin and John McComb, Jr., Architects; Roman Revival style with French Renaissance influence. Photograph by J. S. Johnston, New York, 1894. Courtesy of Bettmann Archive.

John McComb, Jr., as a result of a national competition. It is French Classic in style—Louis XVI—more after Gabriel's designs than the Jefferson tradition. The building is two stories in height, and each story is strongly marked by classic orders and pilasters. There is a central motif of five bays and side wings forming a shallow U-shaped court. A small baroquelike cupola, which caps the center, is topped by a small dome with sculptured figure holding a flagpole. The lobby features a self-supporting marble stairway, which was considered quite wonderful at the time it was built. This is a beautiful building, and has a nice setting in City Hall Park, though it looks diminutive now among its skyscraper surroundings. Although later office buildings in back of the building now house most of the city's business, this building still contains the mayor's offices and the council chambers, and is considered the official city hall.

Built entirely of marble, it was originally considered too extravagant by Boston and Philadelphia, who scrutinized it with envy and criticized it as surpassing the Federal Capitol in Washington, which for lack of money was in a very unfinished state at the time, and not very elegant in its yellow sandstone exterior.

OLD CATHEDRAL OF BALTIMORE, Church of the Assumption, Baltimore, Maryland (Figure 1.5), 1806–1818, by Benjamin Latrobe, has been called *North America's most beautiful Classic Revival building.* The central motive is a large dome on pendentives, much like Soane's interior of the Bank of England, London. The church is fronted by a Roman templelike porch using the Ionic order—added in 1838—in a design similar to that of the original, except that Latrobe's design used the Corinthian order. The two bulbous terminations of the western towers are later additions, which do not add to the otherwise Roman character.

The whole composition is quiet and dignified, and since it was cleaned and renovated in 1964, it presents an almost new appearance. It is hard to believe that this building is more than 150 years old.

LIBRARY, "ROTUNDA," University of Virginia, Charlottesville, Virginia (Figure 1.6), 1822–1826, by Thomas Jefferson, is a half-scale adaptation of the Pantheon of Rome. Here he used native red brick for the walls, and added windows for necessary interior lighting. The colonnade in front has six columns instead of eight, and are white; however, they have well-carved Corinthian capitals. Although a rotunda does not adapt itself very well to library usage, in the Romantic composition of the University, it is a very fitting aesthetic accent at the head of a classic court of honor.

Figure 1.5 Old Cathedral of Baltimore, "Church of the Assumption," Baltimore, Maryland, 1805–1818; Benjamin Latrobe, Architect; Roman Revival style. Photograph furnished by the Basilica of the Assumption.

The original parts of this University, which were built by Thomas Jefferson and given to the State, are most interesting; for when we say "built," we mean exactly that. He designed the entire complex; he and his slaves laid out the foundations, made the brick, hewed and planed the lumber, and put it all together. Like Monticello, he put his very life into it.

In 1912 the New York architects McKim, Meade and White renovated the Rotunda, added a grand flight of steps in front, and built a large wing onto the rear to make it much more usable as a modern university library.

BASILICA OF ST. LOUIS (OLD CATHEDRAL), St. Louis, Missouri, 1834, by George Morton and Joseph Laveille, is built entirely of stone and of simplified classic design that is Roman in character. It has a four-columned templelike front using the Tuscan order, and a belfry

Figure 1.6 Library "Rotunda," University of Virginia, Charlottesville, Virginia, 1822–1826; Thomas Jefferson, Architect; Roman Revival style. Photograph by University of Virginia, Photographic Division.

and spire of bold but well-proportioned design. The interior, which is quite ornate, has a shallow vaulted ceiling over the nave and Tuscan columns separating the nave from the side aisles.

*CUSTOM HOUSE, Charleston, South Carolina, begun in 1853, was not finished until after the Civil War. Distinctly Roman in character, the building was originally designed by Ammi B. Young, but was finished by E. Blake White, who made some minor alterations. This large, imposing building has a T-shaped plan, with a six-columned Corinthian porch at the end of the T. A broad flight of steps leads to the portico of the building, which sits on a high podium of granite. The superstructure is entirely of white marble from Georgia.

Residences

*MONTICELLO, near Charlottesville, Virginia, 1770–1775, remodeled 1796–1808, was the home of Thomas Jefferson. It was planned in a formal courtlike composition with the main house, its portico, and dome, as the central feature. It is built of red brick with white wooden trim, and, like the University of Virginia, all materials, even including the bricks, were fabricated on the site. About it Jefferson himself wrote, "Architecture is my delight, and putting up and tearing down one of my favorite amusements." This accounts for the dates given above; for over a period of 30 years, he put up, tore down, and remodeled Monticello many times. The interior is interesting for its various gadgets and for its hexagonal bedrooms. Also of interest is the master bedroom suite, which has a six foot wide bed that fills an opening separating Jefferson's room from that of his wife—half is in his room and half in hers. Though most of the house appears to be one story in height, there is a second floor, but no grand stairway for access. The stairs are hidden from view for private use only. Most of the dependencies and grounds are laid out in a formal arrangement, but most of the outbuildings are at lower terrace levels to the rear and are not at first recognized. When all of the rooms are counted, Monticello takes on palatial proportions, and the Jeffersons often entertained as many as 50 houseguests at one time.

Monticello, long neglected and partially dismantled, has now been restored and is gradually being refurnished with original Jefferson furniture as it can be located and repurchased. The estate is now in the hands of a private foundation, the Jefferson Memorial Fund, which operates the building and grounds as a museum, and collects funds for its complete restoration and perpetual care.

**THE WHITE HOUSE, 1600 Pennsylvania Ave., N.W., Washington, D.C. (Figure 1.7), 1792–1829, was also designed by the winner of a competition, James Hoban, an architect from Ireland who practiced in Charleston, South Carolina. For winning the competition, he was awarded a $500 gold medal. The design is said to have been inspired by Leinster House in Dublin and by details from the Petit Trianon at Versailles. It does show French influence and is more Renaissance than Classic Roman.

Construction began immediately under Hoban, but the building had not been completed when the government moved from Philadelphia in November, 1800. In 1807 Latrobe, in collaboration with President Thomas Jefferson, added the low terrace pavilions on each side of the main building. Then, during the War of 1812, the British set fire to the building, and the interior was almost entirely burned out at that time (August 1814). It was saved from total destruction by a violent thunderstorm, which quenched the flames.

Figure 1.7 The White House, Washington, D.C., 1792–1829; James Hoban, Architect; Roman Revival style (Early Federal). Photograph by Ralph W. Hammett.

In 1815 Hoban reproduced the original building, and the exterior sandstone was painted white to cover charring by the fire. It has been called the *White House* ever since. The semicircular South Portico was added by Hoban in 1824 from designs said to have been drawn by Latrobe for Jefferson's consideration in 1807, and in 1829 the North Portico, also from Latrobe's design, was finished. Those porticos gave the building its Roman Classic appearance.

In 1902 McKim, Mead and White extensively remodeled the interior of the building and restored it to its original character. During the years 1850 to 1900 each president had decorated and rearranged the interiors to suit his own liking and that of his wife, even to the point of removing fire place mantels when stoves were installed. Minor changes were made here and there when gas lighting was installed in 1848, plumbing and bathrooms in 1878, and electric service and lighting in 1890, so that by 1900 the interiors had lost much of their dignity and beauty. The East Gallery and the executive office wing, which has now been further extended into the old State, War and Navy building, were added in 1902.

During the years 1949 to 1952, the White House was found to be structurally unsound. The interior construction was mostly of wood, and dry rot had set in during the installation of plumbing, wiring, and other amenities. Many of the original joists and supports had been cut and weakened. The entire inner structure had to be removed and replaced with fireproofed materials. Nevertheless, the original paneling, trim, and decorations were either saved and reinstalled or perfectly reproduced. Lorenzo Winslow was the architect for this restoration.

**HOMEWOOD, Johns Hopkins University, Baltimore, Maryland (Figure 1.8), 1798–1801, was built by Charles Carroll, a signer of the Declaration of Independence, as a wedding gift for his son. The center section, a story and a half high, is of pink brick and features a delicately detailed four-columned white portico. This center section is flanked by lower symmetrical wings. The building has beautiful Adam detail throughout, and is one of the more noble and refined examples of domestic architecture on the Eastern Seaboard.

Figure 1.8 Homewood, Johns Hopkins University, Baltimore, Maryland, 1798–1801; Architect unknown, may have been Benjamin Latrobe; Roman Revival style. Photograph by Johns Hopkins University.

The house, which has risen on the grounds of the estate, now serves as the office of the president of Johns Hopkins University.

*FARMINGTON, Bardston Road, Louisville, Kentucky, 1810, has been mistakenly ascribed to Thomas Jefferson because it has a certain character that is reminiscent of Monticello. It is a one and a half story, red-brick house with a central pedimented portico of slender, white-painted Doric columns. The interior, which has oval rooms flanking the central hall, is similar to that of "The Woodlands" in Philadelphia and other Early Federal houses. The house was built for John Speed, an important citizen. His two sons were friends of Abraham Lincoln, who was a house guest here in 1841, long before he became politically important.

**TAFT HOUSE, Cincinnati, Ohio (Figure 1.9), 1820, designed by Benjamin Latrobe, is one of the finest Federal houses west of the Allegheny Mountains, if not in the entire United States. It certainly compares favorably with Homewood, and in fact, the two are strikingly similar. In front the exterior appears to be that of a high-basement, one-storied house, however the rear, which appears to be two stories high, partially surrounds a paved terrace and formal garden. The front has a beautiful central portico of fine Adam detail, flanked by two very long side wings.

Figure 1.9 Taft House, Cincinnati, Ohio, 1820; Benjamin Latrobe, Architect; Roman Revival style. Photograph by the Taft Museum.

This was the home of one of Ohio's most illustrious families. William Howard Taft, the twenty-sixth President of the United States, was born and raised here, and two United States Senators claim it as their ancestral home. It now serves as the Cincinnati Institute of Fine Arts, and contains a fine collection of old Master paintings, as well as fine furnishings, most of which belonged to the Taft family.

ARLINGTON, Natchez, Mississippi, 1816, was by James H. White, who moved there from New Jersey. It is a red-brick house with four tall, white Tuscan columns that form a templelike entrance porch. Like all Natchez mansions and most Southern plantation houses, it is surrounded by a beautiful garden. The interior, which has much of the original furniture, silver, china, and crystal, boasts a library of over 8000 rare books of English printing.

GREENWOOD, about 35 miles North of Baton Rouge, Louisiana, 1830, is Greco-Roman in style. This large, square house has 28 Roman Doric columns and surrounding entablature. It epitomizes the wealth and luxurious living of the antebellum period. It is said that 700 slaves were required to build this mansion. The interior is well preserved and furnished.

OAK ALLEY, near Vacherie, Louisiana, 1836, is one of the few remaining fine plantation homes that used to line both sides of the lower Mississippi River. Each decade sees the demise of one or more until there are now only a few left. This Classic Revival mansion, which is 70 feet square, is surrounded by 28 Greco-Roman Doric columns. The exterior is of brick stuccoed to look like stone. The main portions are painted pink with white columns; iron railings and shutters are turquoise. The building stands in large grounds noted for a great avenue of ancient live oaks.

**THE HERMITAGE, Donalson, near Nashville, Tennessee (Figure 1.10), 1834–1838, was designed by Joseph Rieff for President Jackson and his wife, Rachel; however Mrs. Jackson died before the house was finished. It is a large, square structure with six fluted, two-storied Doric columns forming a porch across the front. This dignified and spacious residence is furnished and cared for by a local group of ladies.

Figure 1.10 The Hermitage home of Andrew Jackson, near Nashville, Tennessee, 1834–1838; Joseph Rieff, Architect; Roman Revival style. Photograph by Ada Whisenhunt, furnished by Ladies Hermitage Society.

*RATTLE AND SNAP, near Columbia, Tennessee, 1845, attributed to William Strickland, was built for George Knox Polk, a cousin of the eleventh President of the United States. It is said that the owner won the land in a dice game with the governor of North Carolina, and gave the mansion its peculiar name because of the incident. (The *rattle* of the shake of the dice, and the *snap* as they were thrown onto the table.) This grand house, rated by some as the finest mansion in Tennessee, is a large, square edifice fronted by 10 Corinthian columns of carved marble. It has exquisite interiors with ceiling medallions and mantel pieces of extreme delicacy. The furnishings also are of the best of the period.

*SHREWSBURY HOUSE (1844) and the **LANIER HOUSE** (1849), both in Madison, Indiana, were designed by Francis Costigan, a very talented carpenter, architect, and wood-carver who lived in the area at this time. Both houses are spacious mansions that have most successfully blended Georgian, Roman, and Greek elements. The houses are quite individual, but both have Classic Roman exteriors, with magnificent Greek detail and carvings inside. Both houses have self-supporting spiral stairs—flying stairs—in the central hallways, and the one in the Lanier house ascends to a cupola that commands a magnificent view of the Ohio River valley.

DUNLEITH, Natchez, Mississippi, 1848, has been the home of five generations of the Carpenter family since it was built. The architect is not known. This large, square, white house with 26 columns forming a peristyle is a splendid example of antebellum living by the wealthy slave owners of this city. This house could be classified as Late Georgian as it has many characteristics of that style, particularly its peristyle surmounted by a surrounding classic entablature.

**STANTON HALL, Natchez, Mississippi (Figure 1.11), 1852–1857, was built at the direction of the cotton broker Frederick Stanton, the first Natchez millionaire. This is the most sumptuous house in the city; the owner even chartered a ship to bring materials and furnishings directly from Europe for this residence. The house, which boasts 20 palatial rooms, is fronted by a templelike porch with four grand Corinthian col-

Figure 1.11 Stanton Hall, Natchez, Mississippi, 1853–1857; Architect unknown; Roman Revival style. Photograph by Mabel Lane.

umns of stone. In keeping with the scale of the house, a drawing room and music room can be opened up to form a grand ballroom 72 feet long with ceilings 22 feet high. The house boasts Italian marble mantels carved with flowers and cherubs, bronze and crystal chandeliers from France and Austria, and solid silver hardware from England.

It is now the headquarters of the Natchez Garden Club Pilgrimage, which takes place through March each spring, and which is the finest of the many house and garden tours throughout the United States. Stanton Hall is also used as a hostelry for distinguished guests of the city.

BELLE MEADE, near Nashville, Tennessee, 1853, was designed by William Strickland for John Harding, who came from Virginia in 1796 and by 1850 had become one of the wealthier men in the state. This mansion has a two-storied, square-columned porch extending across the front, and a most gracious and beautiful interior. The mansion of a large plantation, on John Harding's death it passed to his daughter and her husband, and then became one of the more famous horse-breeding farms in the nation.

*MONTEIGN, Natchez, Mississippi, 1855–1859, is another one of the more than 20 fine mansions of Natchez that belong to this period and style. It is a most impressive pink stucco house with white columns and trim. The interior is particularly noted for its beautiful hallway, which has a black and white marble checkerboard floor and delicately detailed staircase. This house, now beautifully restored, was the last of the fine mansions built in Natchez before the holocaust of the Civil War. During the city's occupation by Union soldiers, horses were stabled in its palatial first floor rooms.

PHASE 3.   THE GREEK REVIVAL STYLE, 1820–1860

About 1820 the Western world became very interested in ancient Greek history, art, and architecture. The Greek War of Independence from Turkey (1821–1831) was closely watched, and most Western Europeans and Americans sympathized with the Greeks, whom they saw as the founders of democracy.

A few years before people had spoken in terms of the Roman Republic; now they talked of Greek Democracy, its form and customs. Books on Greek architecture were published, and every architect, carpenter, and gentleman became conversant with Greek classic forms. Roman styling continued to be used, often in combination with Greek, but Greek forms predominated.

There was little difference between the Greek and Roman Revivals. During both periods temple fronts with columns were used, but from about 1820 onward most builders preferred the Greek orders: Doric, Ionic, and Corinthian. Greek Revival style was used for courthouses, city halls, and residences. The following statement, quoted by Aristabulus Bragg in James Fenimore Cooper's *Home as Found* (1828), shows the sophisticated taste of the time.

> The public sentiment just now runs almost exclusively and popularly into the Grecian school. We build little besides temples for our churches, our banks, our taverns, our court houses and our dwellings. A friend of mine has just built a brewery on the model of the Temple of the Winds in Athens.[1]

Public Buildings

*SECOND BANK OF THE UNITED STATES (OLD CUSTOM HOUSE), Chestnut Street near 4th Street, Philadelphia, Pennsylvania, 1819–1824, by William Strickland, was the first of many Parthenon adaptations. It has Parthenon-like front and rear porches with carefully detailed Doric columns and entablatures. The interior banking room is a barrel-vaulted, basilicalike space running across the width of the building and bordered by Ionic columns. The bank's national charter was revoked in 1836, and for 90 years thereafter the building was used as the Philadelphia Customs House.

DISTRICT OF COLUMBIA COURT HOUSE (OLD CITY HALL), 4th and D Streets, N.W., Washington, D.C., 1820–1830, designed by George Hadfield, is a very dignified stone building with a hexastyle

---

[1] The American Institute of Architects, Washington Metropolitan Chapter, *A Guide to the Architecture of Washington, D.C.*, 1965, p. 53.

Ionic temple front. Although it stands on a high podium of Roman character, it is typical of the Greek Revival as copied and used a hundred times throughout the nation.

*MERCHANTS' EXCHANGE, Third and Walnut Streets, Philadelphia, 1832–1834, by William Strickland, is an interesting building on a triangular lot bordered by Third, Walnut, and Dock Streets. The main entrance facade, on Third Street, features a high ground story base under a Greek temple front with six Corinthian columns. However, the main feature of the building, at the apex of the triangle at the intersection of Walnut and Dock Streets is a semicircular colonnade of Corinthian columns and a tower inspired by the Choragic Monument of Lysicrates in Athens. In back of this tholoslike colonnade is a large circular room, 35 feet high, which originally served as the library.

This building has gone through many changes and some abuse in its time, but has recently been acquired by the Historic American Buildings Survey (HABS), under the Park Service of the U.S. government. No doubt it will be meticulously restored and given the best of care from now on.

**FOUNDER'S HALL, Girard College, Corinthian and Girard Avenue, Philadelphia (Figure 1.12), 1833–1847, by Thomas U. Walter, is the central building of this unique college, which was endowed with a $6,000,000 bequest in the will of Stephen Girard, a Philadelphia banker and philanthropist. The school was founded to educate orphaned boys from 6 to 16 years of age, and Girard, though a Catholic, stipulated that there should be no sectarian teaching. Clergymen of all denominations are barred from the campus. This hall is a beautiful white marble, peripteral Greek temple that, like the Merchant's Exchange, adapts the Corinthian order from the Monument of Lysicrates. The interior rooms are vaulted in masonry in an attempt to produce a permanent fireproof building.

*OLD CUSTOMS HOUSE (SUBTREASURY BUILDING), now known as the Federal Hall National Memorial, Wall and Nassau Streets, New York City, 1833–1841, was designed by Ithiel Towne and A. J. Davis. The building is located in Lower Manhattan, in the heart of the financial district, on the site of the first Federal Building, where much early history took place. Washington delivered his farewell address from here.

Figure 1.12 Founder's Hall, Girard College, Philadelphia, Pennsylvania, 1833–1837; Thomas U. Walter, Architect; Greek Revival style. Photograph by Thomas C. Walsh, courtesy of Girard College.

The present building, in the style of an amphiprostyle Greek Doric temple in the manner of Strickland's Bank in Philadelphia, has been completely redesigned. A statue of George Washington stands on a pedestal on the front steps. The interior rotunda, which has been restored, is very beautiful. It was first a customs house, then a subtreasury, and now a museum of early Federal history.

*OLD ILLINOIS STATE CAPITOL, Springfield, Illinois (Figure 1.13), 1837–1839, was designed by John F. Ragus, who won a competition for the design, including a prize of $300. It is a not-too-large rectangular structure of two stories with evenly spaced Doric pilasters and a four-columned, Greek Doric templelike porch on one of the long sides. It is topped by a small dome on a tholoslike drum of Corinthian columns.

In 1876 the capitol was moved to a larger building, and this building was turned over to Sangamon County as its courthouse. In 1899 the entire structure was raised 11 feet, and a new first floor was inserted. The

Figure 1.13 Old Illinois State Capitol, Springfield, Illinois, 1837–1839; John F. Ragus, Architect; Greek Revival style. Photograph by Ralph W. Hammett.

interior was completely altered at that time. In 1964 the building was returned to the state, and the Springfield firm of Ferry and Henderson, Architects, was hired to restore it to its original condition. The 1899 first floor was removed, and the building was lowered to its original level. It now belongs to the Illinois State Historical Library and contains Americana, particularly articles belonging to the time of Lincoln. The restoration, including the furniture of the time, has been very well done.

NATIONAL PORTRAIT GALLERY (OLD PATENT OFFICE), 7th, 9th, and G Streets, N.W., Washington, D.C., 1836–1840, by William

Elliot and Robert Mills, has a templelike, octastyle Doric portico that was copied from the Parthenon of Athens. It now stands on a high podium and is entered by five ground-floor doorways; originally there was a grand flight of steps in front, and entrance was by way of the second floor. It is built of Virginia freestone, which has been beautifully cleaned and given a cement wash on the outside. The interiors have been restored and changed to accommodate its new use as a gallery. This is an interesting building to visit.

*TREASURY BUILDING, 1500 Pennsylvania Avenue, N.W., Washington, D.C., 1838–1842, by Robert Mills and Thomas U. Walter, is a large, white marble, rectangular building with 38 Greek Ionic columns on the east side along Pennsylvania Avenue. This colonnade is terminated by templelike pavilions each using two Ionic columns in antis. On the end facades of the building are templelike porticoes of six Ionic columns. This well proportioned building is the oldest departmental building in Washington.

Sadly however it is not well placed next to the White House, and cuts off the view from the Capitol to the White House that was intended in the original plan by L'Enfant. Pennsylvania Avenue must make a sharp angle to go around this building before reaching the Executive Mansion. The story is told that when the architects were planning this building, they asked Andrew Jackson, then President, where the building was to be placed, and that without reference to the L'Enfant plan he said, "Build it here." So here it was built.

**OHIO STATE CAPITOL, Columbus, Ohio (Figure 1.14), 1839–1861, was designed by Henry Walters, an Ohio architect who received the commission as the winner of a national competition; however at the insistence of the legislature, the final design was reworked by Walters and incorporated many ideas from other competitors. The building is a two-storied structure composed in a rectangle and surrounded by heavy Doric pilasters. The center of the main facade is featured by an indented porch fronted by eight Doric columns in antis. Instead of a dome the building is capped by a cylindrical topping of severe pilaster design. This feature was said to have come about as an addition to the original design because the legislators insisted on a dome or some sort of central roof feature. The whole design is quiet but has great dignity.

*COURT HOUSE, St. Louis, Missouri, 1839–1862, was the scene of the famous Dred Scott case, which helped to arouse the northern states so

Figure 1.14   Ohio State Capitol, Columbus, Ohio, 1839–1861; Henry Walters, Architect; Greek Revival style. Photograph courtesy of the Secretary of State of Ohio.

violently against slavery. Henry Singleton was the architect of the original building, which was Greek Cross in plan, with a low dome in the center. The four ends were fronted by six-columned, Greek Doric pedimented porches. It was very similar to the original Boston Customs House, which was finished eight years later. Between 1851 and 1857 Robert S. Mitchell was the architect, and he added wings at each of the north and south ends; however he kept the rhythm and detail of the design so that the composition was not destroyed, but in fact enhanced. In 1862 the dome was capped by a Renaissance exterior shell designed by Thomas Lanham, and contemporary with the dome of the National Capitol by Thomas U. Walter.

*CATHEDRAL OF ST. PETER IN CHAINS, Cincinnati, Ohio, 1840–1846, designed by Henry Walters, is a basilica with a Greek hexastyle portico of the Corinthian order. Instead of the usual triangular pediment, Walters designed plinthlike receding steps as a base for a Wren-like spire. The exterior is of Dayton, Ohio, limestone. The interior, more Renaissance than Greek in spirit, has deeply coffered ceilings in the nave and side aisles, although the columns separating the nave from the side aisles are of Greek Corinthian detail. Though a mixture of Greek and Italian Renaissance detail, the design is excellent and unified; also quite individual and not a stylistic plagiarism.

**OLD CITY HALL (Municipal Museum, now known as Gallier Hall), New Orleans, Louisiana (Figure 1.15), 1845–1850, designed by James Gallier, Sr., is a beautiful example of Classic temple design. The main facade, which faces Lafayette Square on St. Charles Street, uses a doubled six-columned Ionic porch on high pedestals. At the opposite end is a four-columned Ionic porch. The building is three stories high, counting the high basement. The upper portion is of white marble from New York State; the basement story is of Quincy granite from Massachusetts. Beautiful tympanum sculpture over the front porch denotes Justice attended by Commerce and Industry. This building served as the city hall for over a hundred years; now it is used as a municipal museum for miscellaneous shows.

*LE VIEUX CARRE, New Orleans, Louisiana, the French Quarter, is the original New Orleans, which was founded about 1718, almost 100 years before the Louisiana Purchase (1803) made it part of the United States. This rectangular area measures seven city blocks in width from the river to Rampart Street on the northwest, and thirteen blocks in length from Canal Street on the southwest to Esplanade on the northeast. Canal Street is now the central street of the modern city. New Orleans was French, then Spanish, before 1803, then French again, and the city still retains a great deal of French–Spanish influence. It is the home of many descendants of these early citizens, some of whom still live in the French Quarter.

Jackson Square, the old parade ground—Place des Armes, in the center edge of the Quarter and opening out toward the river—is now landscaped as a park with a statue of General Andrew Jackson in the center. On the northwestern side of the Square are two matching buildings, the *Cabildo* (1795–1799) and the *Presbytere* (1795–1840), which flank each side of St. Louis Cathedral (1789–1794). These buildings are Spanish and French in character.

On each side of the square are the *Pontalba Apartments,* 1849–1850, designed by James Gallier, Sr., for the Baroness Pontalba as an invest-

Figure 1.15   Old City Hall, now known as Gallier Hall, New Orleans, Louisiana;
1845–1850; James Gallier, Sr., Architect; Greek Revival style. Photograph
courtesy of City of New Orleans.

ment, and to supply New Orleans with large and beautiful apartment
residences flanking the square. These apartments occupy the second and
third floors of identical buildings, a city block in length, on each side of
the square. The main floor level, which is the second floor, one flight up,
has filagreed iron porches; shops, car parking, and servant quarters

occupy the ground floor. These buildings were renovated and modernized in 1940, and are again occupied by the very elite.

In back of the cathedral and running parallel with the river is Royal Street, one of the more important streets of the quarter. Here are three-storied buildings principally famous for the cast- and wrought-iron filagreed work that decorates the balconies of the two upper stories. These balconies are supported by small iron columns at the outer edge of the sidewalk. Thus these balconies, which are usually continuous from one building to another, covered the sidewalks throughout much of the quarter. Some of these buildings have shops on the ground floor fronting onto Royal Street—antique shops, delicatessens, and other service conveniences. All have driveway entrances guarded by solid doors that open onto paved courtyards. Originally these courts were used for carriages, and some had stables located on the back lot line. Along the side of the courtyard were the kitchen and quarters for the domestic slaves. Now most of these courtyards are landscaped. The main buildings are residences occupying two or three floors, with the main living rooms one flight up and bedrooms on the third floor. Vertical circulation was generally by an open staircase in one corner of the courtyard, and some of the residence court facades have balconies here similar to those on the street side. These buildings date from between 1806 and 1860, and some have Greek Revival detail; however they are distinctive for their filagreed ironwork, which is so typical of New Orleans that they are almost in a style by themselves. Although similar ironwork is occasionally found throughout the southern states, most of it can be traced to New Orleans.

One block northwest of Royal Street, and running parallel to it, is Bourbon Street. The architecture here is similar to the rest of the Quarter, but the street floors are now occupied by bars, jazz orchestra dance halls, striptease and go-go girl joints. It has always tended to be that way, although before the Civil War a certain gentlemanly decorum was followed. Then young blades with their mulatto or quadroon mistresses might meet at the Old Absinthe House for drinks and music, or to gamble away a few dollars. Most gambling, however, was done only by the men, at the Old Coffee House on the riverfront.

New Orleans was a brilliant cultural city during this era. Annual balls were held during the social season, ending with the Mardi Gras at the beginning of Lent. The famous New Orleans Opera boasted a brilliant season in its opera house, which stood in the French Quarter but has been destroyed now for many years. In those days, before New York had an opera, New Orleans rivaled Paris and heard many of the great singers of the day, many from Europe. Madame Adeline Patti, the toast of Paris,

London, and Rome, as well as New Orleans, occupied a house on Royal Street.

OLD UNITED STATES MINT, 400 Esplanade Avenue, New Orleans, 1835, is a stone building having a Doric temple front typical of the Greek Revival style.

Residences

It is interesting how popular Greek styling became for residences. Every citizen, whether professional man, urban dweller, or farmer, aspired to live in a building that looked like a Greek temple or one that at least had Greek detail. Many of their plans were Georgian with center doorway, central hall and stairway, and rooms on each side. In the temple types, however, a new plan was evolved with entrance doorway at one side. Thus the main stairway was more or less in the corner of the plan. Across the remainder of the front was a parlor, and in back of this, reached from both the parlor and the front hallway, a large living room that stretched across the width of the house. Behind this were the dining room and kitchen, with other appendages to the rear. In the Georgian-type plans the ridge of the roof ran lengthwise to the house, with ends at the sides, whereas in the temple types the ridge ran perpendicular to the front. If the house boasted a temple front, the roof was accommodated to the triangular tympanum; however the low pitch of Greek roofs became the style and rule of all Greek Revival houses regardless of whether they boasted a columnar portico.

Small houses for working men and their families were one or one-and-a half stories in height, and though they seldom had Greek colonnades, they always had a simplified entablaturelike frieze and cornice, and sometimes simplified classic pilasters at the corners. Most of these houses were of wood siding—a few were of brick—but the trim was of white-painted wood. At the gable ends of the house, the frieze and cornice lapped around the corner and returned on itself so that as the cornice ran up the slope of the roof, it formed a broken pediment in effect. This was a universal detail that all carpenters used whether the house was a cottage or a palatial residence.

*ARLINGTON HOUSE, Custis–Lee Mansion, Arlington, Virginia, 1812–1820, was designed by George W. P. Custis and George Hadfield and remodeled to its present Greek form in 1830 by L. M. Leisenring. It stands on a hill overlooking Arlington National Cemetery and beyond to the City of Washington. The house is noted for its great central portico made up of six Greek Doric columns. These columns are very heavy in proportions, and this templelike front is said to have been inspired by the Temple of Neptune at Paestum, Italy, an example of the heavy Archaic Greek form.

The estate on which this house was built originally occupied 6000 acres, which were purchased by the Alexander family for six hogsheads of tobacco. George Washington's stepson, John Parke Custis, bought 1100 acres of the tract, and his son, George Washington Parke Custis, built the original house. His daughter Mary, who became the wife of Robert E. Lee, inherited the house and remodeled the central portion to its present form in 1830. It is said that this house introduced the Greek Revival style to America; however we know that the Old Customs House, in Philadelphia, and the old City Hall, in Washington, D.C., were built 10 years before this home. The house has been restored and furnished as it was when occupied by the Lee family.

ANDALUSIA, the Biddle mansion, Philadelphia, Pennsylvania, 1834, was remodeled by Tomas U. Walter, who added a Parthenon temple form that encloses an earlier house. This was the home of Nicholas Biddle, the wealthy banker who had traveled in Greece and was an enthusiast of the Greek Revival style. Probably he more than Walter designed this temple shell, and also he, as trustee of Girard College, who insisted on the temple design for its Founder's Hall.

*SAILORS' SNUG HARBOR, north end of Staten Island, New York City, 1831–1833, was the work of Martin E. Thompson, architect. This is a row of five Greek Revival buildings, three of them with two-storied temple fronts using the Ionic order. They were built as dormitory homes for retired seamen, and have housed around 800 mariners at one time. Snug Harbor is now being closed and is being purchased by the City of New York to be used as a Staten Island museum.

Snug Harbor, founded in 1801 by Captain R. R. Randall, has been supported by the income from the original 21-acre Randall estate in Greenwich Village. Snug Harbor embraces an area of 100 acres and has the appearance of a seminary campus, very sedate and dignified.

Staten Island has many Greek Revival edifices of the midnineteenth century, when it was favored as a summer spot for wealthy New Yorkers and Southern planters. It is still a great place for cool breezes off the ocean. The old *Planter's Hotel,* ca. 1835, originally a most fashionable hotel, now is dilapidated and abused, but is still standing. Nearby is the old *Family Court House,* 1830, with fine Doric columns, and the remains of Temple Row, which originally included 10 Greek Revival temple houses. Now all are destroyed except for two, *Columbia Hall* and *Brooks House,* both built in 1835.

*GREENFIELD VILLAGE, Dearborn, Michigan, the best-attended open-air museum in the United States, includes over 200 acres planned to show the development of American customs, institutions, and industry, with particular reference to the nineteenth century. Near the entrance to the village is the Ford Museum of Industry and Mechanical Arts, with the world's finest collection of antique vehicles and household artifacts of all kinds, including furniture, china, glass, and silver. The entrance to the museum is through a tower portal that is a replica of the entrance and tower of Independence Hall in Philadelphia.

The streets of the village are lined with mills, shops, a church, a one-room school, and a hostelry, Clinton Inn. The residential buildings are actual homes that have been moved here and restored. Many of these are the homes of important nineteenth century American personages: Stephen Foster, Luther Burbank, Noah Webster, and others. Here also are Henry Ford's birthplace and boyhood home, and the workshop of Thomas Edison in which he invented the electric light and phonograph. Most of these buildings are Greek Revival and American Midwest, however Mr. Ford also brought here a watch factory from London, a couple of sixteenth century cottages from the Cotswold district of England, and an old Dutch windmill. The village also has an old, wooden, covered bridge properly placed over a small stream that meanders through the village, an original small-town railway station, and a small paddle-wheel river boat that circles a small millpond.

It will be noticed that in this survey of Greek Revival Residences in the United States, the scene has moved from New York state to the Midwest. Many good examples in the east—in New England, Pennsylvania, Virginia, West Virginia, Ohio, Kentucky, and points south—have been omitted, principally to avoid repetition. However the East and Southeast were pretty well settled by this time, and it was to Michigan and the Midwest that new settlers were going and building new homes. The opening of the Erie Canal in 1825 led to a rush to the Midwest. The most popular route was via the Erie Canal to Buffalo, then by boat across the length of Lake Erie to Detroit, and thence overland through Michigan to Chicago and west to the Mississippi River. Settlers took up government land claims all along this route, particularly in Michigan. They built Greek Revival houses, large and small, urban dwellings as well as farmhouses.

BOTTSFORD INN, Grand River Avenue, Detriot, Michigan, 1835, an old landmark purchased and restored in 1924 by Henry Ford, is leased and operated as an inn. The taproom and old hearth are as they were in the days of stagecoaches. *Clinton Inn* from Clinton, Michigan, now in Greenfield Village, is a similar hostelry of the midnineteenth century; as well as *Wayside Inn* at Wayland, Massachusetts, near Concord, which has been restored by Henry Ford, and is also typical of this time.

LONG WINDOWS, Grosse Ile, Trenton, Michigan, 1845, is a large, square, wooden house overlooking the Detroit River. The interior is noteworthy for its entrance hallway with flying stairway, not quite as daring as that of Shrewsberry in Madison, Indiana, but similar. The double parlors have nice Greek detail. The house was carefully restored in 1967, and a modern kitchen and bathrooms were installed for modern living. Since restoration the owner, Mrs. Fred Glover, a descendant of the original owner, has rented the house to the nearby St. James Episcopal Church for $1.00 per year, for use as a manse.

**WILSON–WAHR HOUSE, Ann Arbor, Michigan (Figure 1.16), 1840, by an unknown architect-builder, was built for Judge Wilson, a prominent citizen of the time. This four-columned, Ionic Greek temple of stately proportions is rated by some as the finest Greek Revival house in the state. The detail, both inside and out, is well executed, and the house is furnished with fine nineteenth century heirlooms. It has been lived in by Mrs. Wahr-Sallade, the daughter of George Wahr, a local bookseller and publisher. He purchased the house in the 1870s. Mrs. Wahr-Sallade lived in the house until her death in 1975. The house is now for sale. The furnishings have been distributed.

*REVEREND GUY BECKLEY HOUSE, 1425 Pontiac Street, Ann Arbor, Michigan (Figure 1.17), 1842, was built for the Reverend Guy Beckley, a Methodist minister and ardent abolitionist, who published a

Figure 1.16 Wilson–Wahr House, Ann Arbor, Michigan, 1840; Architect unknown; Greek Revival style. Photograph by Eck Stanger, Ann Arbor.

small but nationally distributed antislavery magazine, *The Signal of Liberty.* The house was used as the Ann Arbor station of the Underground Railroad for runaway slaves on the last lap of their journey to Canada. This rectangular two-storied, yellow-painted, brick house of New England Georgian type has a one-storied rear wing for kitchen and carriage house. A small front portico, which has been restored, has fluted Ionic columns. The house was purchased and restored by the author of this book in 1933; modern amenities such as plumbing and heating were added at that time, as was also the templelike side porch. The Hammett family occupied the house for 22 years.

JUDGE DEXTER MANSION, Dexter, Michigan, 1842, the largest mansion in Michigan in the latter half of the nineteenth century, was built for Judge Dexter, a prominent lawyer and country squire. Orig-

Figure 1.17 Reverend Guy Beckley House, Ann Arbor, Michigan, 1842; Architect unknown; Greek Revival style (Georgian type). Photograph by Ralph W. Hammett.

inally a farmhouse of an extensive estate, it sits on a hill commanding a fine view. The exterior has been restored, but the interior has been gutted and remodeled into several apartments. It is now owned by the University of Michigan. The house boasts a two-storied, columnar templelike portico with huge square Doric columns. It has the appearance of a Southern colonial mansion, and is often so called by the natives of the community. It is said that in its heyday the house boasted some beautiful furniture and was well appointed; however the detail of the house both inside and out was poor and did not possess the elegance of most houses of the period. The most that can be said for it is that it is large and commanding.

KEMPF HOUSE, Ann Arbor, Michigan (Figure 1.18), 1854, was built by H. D. Bennett, one time Secretary of the University of Michigan. It is designed like a small Greek temple with four square columns in front,

Figure 1.18 Kempf House, Ann Arbor, Michigan, 1854; Architect unknown; Greek Revival style. Photograph by Eck Stanger, Ann Arbor.

and very refined detail in the entablature. Among the several features are the cast iron grilles, which are set in the frieze and in front of the half windows that light the sloped ceilings of the second-floor bedrooms.

In 1890 the house was purchased by Mr. and Mrs. Reuben Kempf as a residence and music studio. Both were professional musicians, educated in Germany, who taught piano and voice. They occupied the house for 65 years. The house, now owned by the City of Ann Arbor, was renovated and restored in 1970 under the direction of the author of this book. It contains Victorian furniture of midcentury and after, much of which belonged to the Kempf family, including their Steinway opera-grand piano of 1880. The house is open to the public on Saturdays and Sundays.

*STONE HALL, Marshall, Michigan, 1837, and the *Fitch–Brooks House,* 1840, across the street, are both on commanding corners and were built from the same plans by Richard Upjohn of New York City. Stone Hall, built for a wealthy land speculator from New York by the name of Hays, is now owned by Louis E. Brooks, and the Fitch–Brooks House by Harold C. Brooks, brothers. Both houses are of yellowish local stone, and both have five-columned temple fronts. They are entered by small porticoed side entrances. The earlier house is fronted by the Roman Tuscan order, and the Fitch House by the Ionic order of beautiful proportions and detail. Both houses are furnished with fine antiques.

In antebellum days the city of Marshall seemed destined to be the capitol of the state, but politics ruled otherwise, and the capitol was moved to Lansing, a more central location. The city contains many Greek and Gothic Revival houses as well as an old *Stage Coach Tavern* and the *City Hall,* which has been remodeled but in beautiful character.

PIKE HOUSE, now the Art Gallery, Grand Rapids, Michigan, 1840, is a small two-storied, templelike building of wood with four fluted Greek Doric columns forming the front porch. Symmetrical side wings on the first story also have porches using the Doric order. A residence until 1922, it was given to the city by the Pike family to be used as an art gallery. It has since been gutted and remodeled into galleries which, together with a new rear building, houses a fine collection.

One may traverse the roads of southern Michigan, pass through Niles, which has several fine houses, and through Wisconsin, passing Milwaukee with its *Kilbournetown House,* and even continue to Green Bay which was a thriving port before Milwaukee or Chicago were thought of; and then through Illinois passing Rockford with some charming examples along the roadside to Galena on the Mississippi River. This city in pre-Civil War days was a booming river port that owed its prosperity to lead mining as well as shipping. For a number of years it was the home of Ulysses S. Grant, victorious general of the Union forces in the Civil War, and later President of the United States.

ELIHU WASHBURN HOUSE, Galena, Illinois, 1832–1834, architect unknown, was built for Eilhu Washburn, who later became U. S. Minister to France. It is a handsome and imposing Greek Revival house, situated on a large plot of ground. In 1861 General Grant helped drill Galena's company of volunteers on the lawn.

GENERAL JOHN W. SMITH HOUSE, Galena, Illinois, 1845, was built for John Smith, a jeweler who later became a staff officer for General Grant. The one-storied red brick house with high stone basement on the front stands on a sloping site. A high flight of steps leads to a four-columned, templelike porch of the Ionic Order. It is nicely proportioned and has good classic detail.

Buildings in the Southern States

Although Greek styling became very popular in opposition to Republican Roman, the overall picture did not change a great deal. Some houses that were prized as being "true Greek copies" actually used pseudo-Greek instead of Roman detail on Georgian plans and compositions. In some houses there is a mixture of details; the interior may be quite Greek while the exterior is more Roman.

The entire southeastern half of the United States is dotted with stately mansions, mostly of the antebellum Greek Revival type. The landowners of the south were wealthy at that time, and prided themselves on their magnificent plantation homes. Many of these have disappeared for lack of money to maintain them during Reconstruction days, but many still stand. Georgia, particularly Athens, Washington, Milledgeville, and Macon, seems to have more than its share. However, throughout the South, one can find examples here and there: from Virginia to Louisiana and from Tennessee to Florida.

**GOVERNOR'S MANSION, Milledgeville, Georgia (Figure 1.19), 1838, was originally built as the governor's mansion of the state before the capitol was moved to Atlanta, and served as the home for eight successive governors. It now serves as the president's house for Georgia State College for Women. It is a 60-foot-square masonry house fronted by a high porch of four Ionic columns. The masonry structure and columns are stuccoed to look like smooth stone. The interior features a central rotunda lighted by an eye at the top of a plaster-coffered and gold-ornamented dome, a large ballroom, and a basement kitchen with original cooking hearth and brick bake ovens.

COWLES–BOND HOUSE, Macon, Georgia, ca. 1840, was designed and built by Alexander Elam, one of the outstanding architects of the state.

Figure 1.19 Executive Mansion, Milledgeville, Georgia, 1838; Architect unknown; Greek Revival style. Photograph courtesy of the Milledgeville Chamber of Commerce.

This beautiful Greek Revival mansion is of Georgian form and might be classified as such, but the detail is Greek. The colonnade surrounding the house has a fine classic cornice and balustrade circling the roof. The house stands on lovely grounds and presents a most gracious appearance.

*PRESIDENT'S HOUSE, University of Georgia, Athens, Georgia, 1854, was designed by an unknown builder. In 1869 Senator Benjamin Harvey Hills, a post-Civil War patriot who tried to urge his constituents to accept defeat of the Southern States as inevitable and to take up reconstruction, purchased the mansion for his home. This great white house of wood with a peristyle of 16 two-storied Corinthian columns has a most beautiful interior having decorative plaster ceilings and cornices, magnificent crystal chandeliers, and fine furniture. As the name implies, it is now the residence of the president of the University of Georgia.

**LOUISVILLE WATER COMPANY PUMPING STATION, Louisville, Kentucky (Figure 1.20), 1858–1860, designed by Theodore R. Scowden, Chief Engineer, with Charles Herman, Assistant Engineer of the company, is located about 3 miles upriver from the city. It is composed of an engine room in the form of a Corinthian Temple with side wings, and a 169-foot standpipe in imitation of a Roman triumphal column. This standpipe triumphal column, the *pièce de résistance* of the ensemble, is a beautifully proportioned Doric column with a wraparound grouping of nine Corinthian columns at the base. Each column is topped

Figure 1.20   River Road Pumping Station, Louisville, Kentucky, 1858–1860; H. R. Scowden, Chief Engineer; Charles Herman, Assistant Engineer; Classic Revival style. Photograph by Ralph W. Hammett.

with a piece of Classic sculpture representing a Roman god: Neptune, god of waters, rivers, lakes, and the sea; Mercury, god of gymnastics and physical fitness; Vesta, goddess of the home; Hebe, Goddess of Youth; Flora, goddess of flowers; Pomona, goddess of fruits and vegetables; Ceres, goddess of grain and the harvest; and Diana, goddess of the hunt. Some of the figures are of cast iron, some of terra-cotta. Another figure among this group has caused some controversy: an Indian, 6 feet 6 inches in height. Whether this Indian was among the original figures or a replacement after a tornado in 1890 blew down most of the figures and severely damaged many, is an unanswered question.

Residences in Natchez, Mississippi

The magnificent mansions for which the Southern states are noted were built by the wealthy cotton planters during the antebellum period, at the height of "King Cotton" affluence. Most of these belong to the period between 1830 and the Civil War, and are a combination of the three classical styles of the time: Late Georgian, Roman Revival, and Greek Revival.

It will be noted that Arlington, Dunleith, Stanton Hall, and Monteigne of Natchez have been listed under Roman Revival, although all three have details that belong to other related styles. Here are to be found beautiful Georgian fanlighted doorways, baroque fireplace mantels, crystal chandeliers, and gold mirrors and elaborate gold window valences reminiscent of the French rococo. Some have distinct Greek Revival features, such as exterior Greek columns.

*AUBURN, Natchez, Mississippi, 1816, architect unknown, is quite distinctly Roman Revival. It is a square, red-brick house with Roman Ionic portico. The plan is of the central hallway, Georgian type, and the interior has a beautiful spiral self-supporting stairway.

*ROSALIE, Natchez, Mississippi, 1820–1823, is Georgian in style with a Roman Doric classic porch. The body of the house is of red brick. During the occupation of Natchez by the Union army after the Civil War, this house served as Union headquarters, and General Grant slept here. General Gresham, the military governor of Natchez, and his wife occupied the house, where they entertained those of Natchez who would accept their invitations. They were among the few Union military governors who ingratiated themselves to the proud residents and helped in the Reconstruction.

RICHMOND, Natchez, Mississippi, belongs to three different periods. The central portion is Spanish; the left wing is Greek Revival, 1832; and the right wing is Roman Classic showing influence of the French Napoleonic Empire style, 1859.

MELROSE, Natchez, Mississippi, ca. 1840, is a sturdy, square brick house with Roman Doric templelike portico. It is in a perfect state of preservation and boasts an outside two-storied kitchen, smokehouse, dairy, and other typical outbuildings.

*DEVEREUX, Natchez, Mississippi, 1840, a large, square house with six Greek Doric columns across the front, also retains its outside kitchen with servant quarters on the second floor, and other outbuildings. It is in an excellent state of preservation, even to its gardens, which, though not as fine as originally, are still beautiful. Henry Clay was often a guest in this house, and many brilliant balls were given in his honor. This house has often been chosen by the motion-picture industry for scenes of Southern romance.

LANSDOWN, 1852, and **HOMEWOOD,** 1854, Natchez, Mississippi, were built by a wealthy planter and slave owner as wedding gifts for his two daughters. They are both magnificent houses, complete with original furnishings, fine silver, and imported china. The outbuildings of Landsdown include not only a kitchen and servant quarters, but also a separate building for billiards, a children's school, and play quarters.

PHASE 4.   GOTHIC REVIVAL STYLE, 1840–1860

About 1840, just when Greek styling reached the apex of its popularity, another historical style was revived and gradually became popular—Gothic. It is true that styles change about every generation—every

20 years. The older style of the moment becomes common, and the young men of the time try to supplant the style of their parents with something new: in this case, Academic Gothic.

Gothic styling was primarily an English importation occurring about 1830, although Benjamin Latrobe had suggested its use as an alternate scheme for the Cathedral of Baltimore in 1805, and Maximilien Godefroy had built a Gothic Chapel for a girls' seminary in Baltimore in 1807. Also from 1809 to 1812 Joseph Francois Mangin, one of the architects of the New York City Hall, designed and built the first St. Patrick's Cathedral in Lower Manhattan, New York City, in pseudo-French Gothic; and in 1822 James O'Donnell of New York designed the Gothic-styled church of Notre Dame in Montreal, Canada. However Gothic styling did not become popular until people began talking about the magnificent new Houses of Parliament in London by Sir Charles Barry and Augustus Welby Pugin, designed in 1836 as the result of a competition.

Books such as those by Pugin, imported from England, gave examples of Gothic detail and arguments that tried to prove that Medieval church design is the only true and meaningful architecture, particularly for churches. Later, in 1852, John Ruskin came out with his several books that profoundly argued that Gothic ornament is Christian, true and beautiful. All of these books presented Romantic approaches to the style, and dealt with decoration and ornament rather than the underlying structure.

It was not until the 1840s that a few architects actually started to take the Gothic styling seriously, and that Richard Upjohn was able to introduce archaeologically correct structure and detail in New York's Trinity Church begun in 1839. Then followed James Renwick, a young architect of great sensitivity and ability, and the style took hold, particularly for churches.

It developed and remains, however, a style based on the picturesque and romantic—revivalistic backgrounds for dreams of Sir Lancelot and the Holy Grail, saints and medieval crusaders, knights and ladies. It reflects the literature and thinking of the time, especially the romantic poetry of Tennyson and the novels of Sir Walter Scott.

Public and Religious Buildings

**TRINITY CHURCH (Episcopal), Broadway at Wall Street, New York City (Figure 1.21), 1839–1846, by Richard Upjohn, is a beautiful Gothic church in English curvilinear style. The brown sandstone struc-

Figure 1.21   Trinity Church, New York City, 1839–1846; Richard Upjohn, Architect; Gothic Revival style. Photograph by Ralph W. Hammett.

ture, with its single tower with spire on the west front, is now dwarfed by the skyscrapers of New York's financial district; however it is in good scale, and its interior is a refreshing and quiet relief from the rush and bustle of the world outside. The interior is beautifully vaulted with well-composed detail throughout. It has excellent stained glass windows, some made in England and some in France.

It is probably the wealthiest church in the world: the land on which it stands alone is estimated to be worth at least $25,000,000, and it owns large portions of Lower Manhattan by a 1705 land grant of Queen Anne. This land is leased by the church on hundred-year contracts.

Many illustrious Americans of early United States history are buried in the churchyard, among them Alexander Hamilton and Robert F. Fulton, inventor of the steamboat.

*GRACE EPISCOPAL CHURCH, 800 Broadway, New York City, 1843–1846, was designed by James Renwick, who gained the commission by winning a competition when he was a young man of only 23 years. It is a fine composition of English curvilinear style with a single richly detailed spire on its west front, and compares favorably with its contemporary, Trinity Church by Upjohn. It forms a beautiful composition with the attached parish buildings, which were built later but were also designed by Renwick. The interior is of vaulted design, although here the vaults are of lath and plaster. It contains beautiful stained glass windows, most of them memorials.

**ST. PATRICK'S CATHEDRAL (Catholic), Fifth Avenue between 50th and 51st Streets, New York City (Figure 1.22), 1853–1858, was dedicated in 1879. It was designed by James Renwick, a Protestant, under the authority of Archbishop John Hughes. During the design and construction period a very close friendship arose between the Archbishop and Renwick, and the architect was sent to Europe at church expense to visit and make notes on the great cathedrals, particularly Chartres, Amiens, and Cologne. He is said to have been particularly inspired by Cologne, and as a result this church is definitely Continental rather than English in character.

The building, of a light gray, almost white, crystalline marble quarried at Pleasantville, New York, is of excellent proportions and scale. It is of true European cathedral proportion and size. The cathedral is 336 feet in overall length, not counting the Lady Chapel, which was added later, and 185 feet wide at the transepts. The central front portal is 70 feet high and 33 feet wide, the two western spires are 336 feet high, and the interior vaults are 110 feet high from floor to ceiling. The interior is especially beautiful and well detailed with magnificent ribbed vaulting. The vaulting is not of stone in any way structural; it was cast and molded of papier-mâché.

Figure 1.22 St. Patrick's Cathedral, New York City, 1853–1858; James Renwick, Architect; Gothic Revival style. Photograph furnished by St. Patrick's.

The story of Archbishop Hughes' promotion of this great building is interesting and gives particular insight into the stature and foresight of this great man. Work was suspended several times due to exhaustion of money, the Civil War, and two severe financial depressions. During the Civil War, Archbishop Hughes was sent to France by President Lincoln to plead the Union cause. He also visited Ireland and was most successful in both cases. He died in 1864 before the edifice was completed. However he had said, when he broached the idea in 1849, that he did not expect to live to see the finished cathedral.

The cornerstone laying on August 15, 1858, on the Feast of the Assumption, was a great citywide event, and more than 50,000 people assembled for it. A great two-storied platform was erected for church and city dignitaries on the top level, and a large band of musicians and choir on the lower level. The festivities, which started at 11:00 AM, lasted a large part of the afternoon, and included processions, music, speeches, and the consecration.[2]

The building was finally completed for dedication in 1879. Since then, the spires were finished in 1888, and subsequently the Lady Chapel, the elaborate high altar, and other memorials. The center of Catholicism in New York, now the seat of a Cardinal, is a place where charwomen and millionaires meet and rub elbows at all services.

*SMITHSONIAN INSTITUTION, Jefferson Drive, between 9th and 12th Streets, N.W., Washington, D.C., 1850–1852, designed by James Renwick, is in a free Tudor Gothic style with many towers and spires. The writings and published drawings of Augustus Welby Pugin and Andrew Downing probably influenced Renwick and also his mentor, Robert Owen, Congressman from Indiana. Owen argued that this building had honest functional qualities and that it represented "the true National Style of Architecture." It did influence the acceptance of High Victorian Gothic in the following decades, but had little effect on later buildings of the Capitol City. Some years later Renwick himself chose French Renaissance in designing the Corcoran Gallery. Additions to the original ensemble in 1881 followed the Victorian Gothic style.

ST. MARY'S CATHOLIC CATHEDRAL, Natchez, Mississippi, 1844–1851, designed by Robert Carey Long, Jr., is a brick structure trimmed with stone. The church, a hall type with side aisles the same height as

---

[2] Burton, Katherine, *The Dream Lives Forever*, Longmans, Green and Co.

the nave, has a central portal accenting a front tower and spire. It is Germanic in composition, though the detail is English, no doubt from Pugin's books. The interior has lath and plaster vaulting under a roof that is supported by wooden trusses. It is not an impressive edifice, but is interesting because it shows the Gothic Revival in Natchez, a stronghold of Roman and Greek Revival in the antebellum period.

*ST. MARK'S CHURCH, 1625 Locust St., Philadelphia, Pennsylvania, 1848–1852, designed by John Notman, is rated as one of the best examples of Gothic Revival church architecture in the United States. It is of English Decorated style, of brown sandstone with a beautiful spire at one side. The interior has wood trusses and is well proportioned. This church is rather overlooked in Philadelphia because of the many Federal and Greek Revival buildings, particularly those of historical importance, such as Christ Church, Independence Hall, and those in the Society Hill section.

HOLY TRINITY EPISCOPAL CHURCH, 157 Montague St., Brooklyn, New York, 1849–1853, was designed by Minard Lafever. It is less authentically Gothic than the churches of Upjohn and most other architects of the time, but for that reason is more original and more American. Minard Lafever was ranked as one of the leading designers of the style in that day.

FIRST PRESBYTERIAN CHURCH, Baltimore, Maryland, 1853–1856, by Nathan S. Starkweat, is an outstanding example of Gothic Eclecticism. Its highly traceried west front spire of stone was not finished until 1874; however it followed the original design and was placed over an intricate cast iron frame that had been constructed in 1856. The tracery used throughout this edifice is very florid, complicated, and overdone, but is nevertheless quite magnificent. The interior also is very ornate, with detail that almost defeats itself.

FORT STREET PRESBYTERIAN CHURCH, Detroit, Michigan, 1855, by Albert and Oscar Jordan, is a buff sandstone building in English Perpendicular style. The ornate tower, which has Perpendicular traceried openings, is topped by a very high and pointed spire. This spire almost overbalances the rest of the building, and is in itself a distinctive landmark. It has a fine west window of Curvalinear tracery. The Parish Hall, which was added in 1885, forms a harmonious composition with the original building.

Residences

American houses of the Gothic Revival style were not as ambitious as some in England or on the Continent. There were a few pseudo-medieval castles or large baronial estates in the United States before the Civil War; however, as in the classical styles, the movement was romantic, with the attempt to create a picture and a mood.

Soon a type was developed, known in the Midwestern states as Hudson River Gothic, as several houses of this type—now destroyed—were built upriver on the Hudson. They were characterized by steep gables, bay windows, and porches with thin clustered columns. The structures were usually of brick or stone, and trimmed with carved and scroll-sawed bargeboards, sometimes painted but usually stained brown or of the dark gray color of oak allowed to weather. Some houses were even designed with half-timber effects in the gable ends.

In 1855 and after books on the Gothic Cottage style, written in America by Andrew Downing, popularized the Gothic cottage as picturesque and most appropriate for rural adaptation. These books show plans and details of buildings, replicas of which are to be found throughout the United States, particularly in the Midwest, east of the Mississippi.

GARDENER'S CASTLE, also known as The Oaklands, Gardener, Maine, 1835–1836, was designed by Richard Upjohn for his first important commission. English manor house in style and built of stone, it is not too well proportioned, and the crenolations are scaled too small; however it is a Romantic attempt, and noteworthy as first of the few mansions in the United States to turn to the Gothic style.

KINGSCOTS, Newport, Rhode Island, 1841, by Richard Upjohn, is another large stone house of baronial proportions. It was done over in 1885, and is noted for its beautiful dining room, which was added by Stanford White at that time. However its original parts have good Gothic detailing and decoration.

*CEDARHURST, Holly Springs, Mississippi, 1857, architect unknown, is an ornate house of red brick and white wooden trim that was sawed and carved in the English Gothic manner. The house has many gables—three across the front, and a decorative thin-columned veranda. It was built for Miss Sherwood Bonner, a popular writer of Southern dialect stories at the time, who was at one time secretary to Henry Wadsworth Longfellow.

Two other Gothic Revival houses in Holly Springs are *Grey Gables,* 1830, and *Magnolias,* 1850; however, although both of these have Gothic Revival exteriors, their interiors are Classic.

*FOWLER HOUSE, Lafayette, Indiana, 1851–1853, architect unknown, is a plain stone house with elaborately carved wooden trim, beautifully detailed windows, and a porch of thin, clustered columns. It is well composed with fine detail throughout, quite in the style of the gabled English manor house, even to leaded-glass, diamond-shaped windows.

**LYNHURST, Tarrytown, New York (Figure 1.23), 1838, was designed by Alexander Jackson Davis for General William Paulding, a congressman from New York and mayor of New York City. He and his son used the house as a country retreat. The house was enlarged in 1865 by Davis for a second owner, George Merritt, and in 1880 was acquired by Jay Gould, a famous New York financier. In the style of an English baronial manor house, it possesses many fine rooms and is surrounded by a beautiful English garden having a special coach house that houses a fine collection of horse-drawn coaches. In 1965 the house and grounds were given to the National Trust by Anna Gould, Duchess of Talleyrand-Perigord.

*MACK–RYAN HOUSE, Division and Ann Streets, Ann Arbor, Michigan (Figure 1.24), 1850 and doubled in size in 1867, was designed by Gordon W. Lloyd, an architect of Detroit. It is an excellent example of Hudson River Gothic. It is of red brick trimmed with stone, and the steep gables of wood are beautifully scroll sawed and carved in English Gothic detail. The house has bay windows and thin, clustered columns on the side and front porches. It is quite large and pretentious, overly so for the corner lot on which it is located. It was built by Dr. Alonzo Palmer, who came from New York State and was the first professor of medicine at the University of Michigan.

Figure 1.23 Lynhurst, Tarrytown, New York, 1838, enlarged 1865; Alexander Jackson Davis, Architect; Gothic Revival style. Photograph Library of Congress.

RING LARDNER HOUSE, Niles, Michigan, ca. 1860, architect unknown, is one of several Gothic Revival residences in that small city on the old Post Road between Detroit and Chicago. It is a sizable English type with carved and scroll-sawed bargeboards on the gable ends. An original front porch of thin clustered columns has been removed. Ring Lardner, famous American wit and writer, was born and spent his boyhood in this house.

WILLIAM LEDUC HOUSE, Hastings, Minnesota, 1860, architect unknown, is a 15-room residence of English manor-house type. The exterior is of deep cream-colored, local limestone with carved and scroll-sawed wood detail. The interior is rich in native cherry and black walnut woodwork.

Figure 1.24   Mack–Ryan House, Ann Arbor, Michigan, 1850–1867; Gordon W. Lloyd, Architect; Gothic Revival style. Photograph by Eck Stanger, Ann Arbor.

PHASE 5.   EARLY ELECTICISM, 1840–1860

During the first 75 to 80 years of the Republic of the United States of America (from 1780–1860), it should be evident that there was an unseen force that seemed to control the philosophy of the time: a romanticism that looked back into history for its expression. Society wanted to be sophisticated, to be academic, to show its respect for ancient Rome and Greece, and for medieval Europe, with Roman Revival, Greek Revival, and later with Gothic Revival. But why stop there? J. N. R. Durand of the Ecole Polytechnique of Paris was advocating the free use of all historical styles, and Bavaria and England as well as Paris, the style center of the world, were responding with examples of Italian Renaissance, Baroque, Romanesque, and other styles.

The United States gloried in its nationalism; however culturally it was dependent on Europe. Most of the styles and fashions of each gen-

eration followed the patterns of England, although France and Germany
also exerted a strong influence.

PHILADELPHIA COUNTY PRISON (MOYAMENSING PRISON),
Tenth and Reed Streets, Philadelphia, Pennsylvania, 1832–1835, was designed by Thomas U. Walter, who adapted the medieval castellated style
for the main building, which was several stories high and gave the
appearance of an English castle keep. However the design of the main
portal of the debtor's wing was Egyptian in style.

THE TOMBS, New York City Prison, New York, 1836–1840, by John
Haviland, was similar in plan to Eastern Penitentiary in Philadelphia.
The exterior design was Egyptian in style, and the main gate was reminiscent of the ancient Nile tombs. This resemblance gave the prison the
popular name by which it became known. The building was demolished
in 1897.

GROVE STREET CEMETERY GATE, New Haven, Connecticut, 1845,
designed by Henry Austin, is another example of copying and adaptation
of Egyptian styling.

*ATHENAEUM CLUB, Philadelphia, Pennsylvania, 1845–1847, by
John Notman, was no doubt inspired by the several clubs of London by
Sir Charles Barry. It is a very refined palacelike building in the Italian
Renaissance style.

*CATHEDRAL OF STS. PETER AND PAUL (Catholic), Philadelphia,
Pennsylvania (Figure 2.1), 1846–1860, was originally designed by Fathers
Maller and Tornatore; however John Notman was commissioned to
translate the designs into workable drawings, and he designed the Palladian facade and dome. The building's exterior is of stone and is completely Baroque in character. The interior is almost a riot of Baroque,
though in good taste and color.

It can be correctly deduced here that John Notman was the leading
early eclecticist in America. He started as a protégé of William Strickland and received a solid background in classic design. Later he became

Figure 1.25 Cathedral of Sts. Peter and Paul, Philadelphia, Pennsylvania; 1846–1850; John Notman, Architect; Early Eclectric (Baroque) style. Photograph by Sibre Photography, Philadelphia, Pennsylvania.

an academician of the Gothic, Romanesque, Italian Renaissance, and Baroque styles.

CHURCH OF THE HOLY TRINITY, Philadelphia, 1857–1859, was designed by John Notman in the Norman Romanesque style. Built of brownstone, which was so very popular at this time and later, it is a good example of Norman detail. The tower top was originally intended to have had a Norman spire, and the exterior design consequently suffers from its lack.

GENERAL D. M. FROST RESIDENCE, St. Louis, Missouri, 1858, was designed by George I. Barnett, the leading architect of the city at that time. It is a very refined, palacelike city residence of stone in the Italian Renaissance style.

*PROBASCO–NAGLE MANSION, Clifton Hill, Cincinnati, Ohio (Figure 2.2), 1852–1863, was designed by William Tinsley for Henry Probasco, a wealthy trader. It is in the Norman Romanesque style, built entirely of yellow limestone, and looks like an H. H. Richardson Romanesque design of 20 to 30 years later. Entrance is through a fine stone porch having triple Norman arches. On the northeast side is a Norman-like porte cochere. The main entrance leads through a 15 by 70 foot grand hall, baronial in appearance, having a heavy beamed ceiling and a staircase off to one side. The parlor, or reception room, immediately to the right on entrance, is in French Renaissance style; the library has German flavor. The dining room originally had walls hung

Figure 1.26 Probasco–Nagle Mansion, Cincinnati, Ohio, 1852–1863; William Tinsley, Architect; Early Eclectic (Romanesque) style. Photograph donated by present owners.

with Flemish tapestries. All of the woodwork is of cherry or walnut, and is heavily molded and carved.

The house once possessed one of the finest libraries outside of Europe, with rare and valuable early editions of the Bible and illuminated manuscripts. The vast grounds, now subdivided, were dotted with sculpture and planted with rare evergreens collected from Europe, Asia, and the Rocky Mountains.

NINETEENTH CENTURY DESIGN AND CONSTRUCTION, 1800–1860

Structures

During this period the usual building materials were wood, brick, and stone. The type of framing for most buildings evolved from European half-timber construction, at least for the skeleton frames, which were made of hand-hewn timbers. Structural sills were about 10 by 12 inches and made of oak or other hard woods that were not too susceptible to rotting. These sills were laid on foundations of fieldstone, made fast with lime mortar, to form a basement or crawl space under the building. The sills were notched into one another at the corners, and cross beams were doweled in where major partitions were to be located on the floor above. Rooms were usually twelve feet wide or larger. Spaces between the beams were set in with joists, which were hand sawed and approximately 2 by 8 inches or 2 by 10 inches in dimension. The joists were notched into the beams so as to be level with the beams on top. Only the top halves of the joists were notched into the beams; the lower halves were cut away and butted against the supporting beams, so that only the top halves of the joists supported the floors. Over these joists a 1 inch floor of clear poplar, gumwad, or tulipwood was laid. This flooring, generally of varying widths, was tongued and grooved, and nailed to the joists with square, wrought iron nails. As the building was being finished, the flooring was sanded, then either stained and waxed or painted a medium tan or walnut brown.

At the corners of the building, and at the ends of the interior beams, 8 or 9 foot hewn uprights were set in to hold the second floor beams, which matched the sills of the first floor. The second floor was framed on top of this in the same way as the first floor, or the roof was framed with "A" trusses. All of the heavy beams and trusses were doweled to fit together and pinned with heavy wooden pegs driven solidly into the joints. Partitions and outside walls were framed of hand-sawed two-by-fours set approximately 16 inches on center. Windows and doors were framed much as they are today. Over this, lapped siding was nailed on the exterior, and lath and plaster on the interiors and ceilings. Various trims were used around windows and doors, and classic pilasters were often used at exterior corners. If the outside walls were of masonry, they were usually solid, with beams used for the interior framing only.

Journeymen carpenters were very adept in the use of tools. They could use hand tools to shape ogee, cyma, and cove moldings. For this work they used straight-grained, soft woods, such as white pine, poplar, and even basswood, which were then painted and enameled. All doors were handmade and paneled, some with two long vertical panels, some with four or six. Many exterior doors had six panels, the two nearest the top being small squares that were set in with panes of glass. All windows were handmade, with muntins separating the glass. At the beginning of the century, the panes of glass were small, 6 inches by 10 inches, but the size increased as the technique of glassmaking advanced over the years. By the 1840s the standard glass size was 8 inches by 14 inches, most overall window sizes were 28 inches by 62 inches, and both upper and lower sashes were three panes wide and two high. Occasionally windows had a lower sash that was four panes wide and three high, for a total dimension of 36 inches by 76 inches. However such sashes were heavy and rather clumsy to handle. Only the lower sash was allowed to slide, although it was not counterbalanced, as are present day windows, and had to be held open by a stick. During the seventeenth century windows were mostly the swinging sash, casement type, with small diamond-shaped pieces of glass mounted in leaded frames. The double-hung window was introduced about 1700, and, improved but little changed in appearance, continues to be used in homes. Glassmaking remained rather crude until the middle of the nineteenth century. Glass often contained bubbles and was not too clear; some was quite green in color.

Fireplace mantels and exterior columns were handmade and carved, often of wood but sometimes of marble. Wooden column capitals were carved from large blocks, and great care was taken in the proportions and detail. Toward the middle of the century some capitals were cast of gesso—a combination of sawdust, plaster, and glue that could be pressed into plaster forms and that, after it was thoroughly dried and painted, was quite impervious to weather.

Cast iron was often used for ornamental features such as exterior over-window trim and attic window grilles. Columns and their capitals were often cast in iron and then painted white to look like the other trim, whether wood or marble. (Note the columns at the base of the dome of the Capitol in Washington, D.C.) Decorative storefronts were completely fabricated in cast iron before the time of the Civil War until the end of the century.

Construction was not always very scientific, as for example the notching and cutting away of the joists. Generally this was very carefully done, and a wide factor of safety kept the buildings safe enough. However even the poorest carpenter seemed to be sensitive to proportion and beautiful detail, and as stated before, the modern viewer can be amazed at the fine carving, beautiful moldings, and fine plaster work, sometimes with set-in cast-plaster ornaments and refined plaster moldings and coves at the ceiling line. Wide-banded door and window trim carried to the floor was usually painted with white enamel, most of which was imported from Holland.

Interior Furnishing and Decorating

Good taste was usually displayed in the interior furnishing and decoration. Walls were often painted or calcimined in an off-white or subdued color, or covered with printed wallpaper imported from France; brocaded patterns and colorful toiles were used. Chandeliers hung with crystal prisms from France or Czechoslovakia, quite the rage for the wealthy, were generally a feature of the dining room. Oriental rugs were used in the parlors and best rooms, along with flowered Aubusson rugs from France or homemade hooked rugs of similar design. Wall-to-wall carpeting from Belgium and the Netherlands was introduced for bedrooms and small living rooms. Mahogany furniture made in Philadelphia and other eastern cities copied eighteenth century designs from Europe. New designs, such as those by Duncan Phyfe of Philadelphia, were introduced, and a simplified version of Napoleonic Empire also belonged to the period.

Colored imported brocades were used as overdrapes at the windows of principal rooms and were drawn at night. These were hung on rings threaded on brass or wooden poles that were mounted on the window trim behind elaborate valences. These valences were often of wood covered with gold-leafed gesso ornament, or of the same brocade, lavishly draped and festooned. The overdrapes extended to the floor and were tied back. Machine-made lace curtains were usually hung behind the overdrapes next to the sash. Fine sheer cotton curtains with ruffled edges, used for bedroom and other windows, were similar to the cotton tieback curtains of today.

Of course there were pioneer homes in the West and Midwest, and simple homes of laborers who could not afford the luxuries listed above. Nevertheless a man's home was his castle, and even the small cottage was usually not lacking in good taste. The Swedish, German, or English emigrant generally brought with him a refined culture.

Sanitary Elements

There was no indoor plumbing at this time. Water was carried in from an outside pump which was dug or drilled to an underground source of pure water, or attached to a cistern that gathered rainwater from the roofs. Generally rain water was used for washing clothes or for the Saturday baths dispensed in washtubs set up in the kitchen. Water for drinking and cooking was from a pure source as close at hand as possible, or from cistern water that had been boiled on the kitchen range or in a kettle hung in the kitchen fireplace.

Human wastes were taken care of indoors by means of chamber pots and slop jars, which were carried out-of-doors by the housewife or chambermaid in the morning. There they were disposed of in the ever-nearby privy or between the rows of the vegetable garden. Once in a while there was a mild epidemic of cholera, typhoid fever, or diarrhea, but generally these people were healthy and had high standards of sanitation within practical means.

Heating and Cooking

Heating was by fireplaces, which were located in all principal rooms, or by Franklin stoves distributed about the house or public building. Cooking was done over wood fires in large kitchen hearths, where iron or copper pots were hung on chains from wrought iron cranes that could be swung over or away from the fire. Baking was done in large, brick ovens built into the kitchen hearth, or sometimes in ovens in an outbuilding near the house. These were heated up as necessary—usually once a week—for baking the family supply of bread, cakes, and pies. In the southern states these baking kitchens often supplied an entire plantation or a small community.

Lighting

This was by candles, singly or in multiple groups in chandeliers, candelabra, or wall sconces. Usually each family had its own candle molds, which they used to make candles from tallow fat saved from the roastings of lamb or mutton. On the eastern seaboard there were a few open-type oil lamps that burned whale oil or various substitutes, but except for the wealthy, who could afford many candles, most people went to bed soon after dusk and got up with the dawn.

2

THE INDUSTRIAL REVOLUTION

The Age of Cast Iron

1800–1860

PHASE 1. EARLY FUNCTIONAL ARCHITECTURE, 1800–1860

In addition to political revolutions bringing newfound freedoms, there was an industrial revolution in the making. The Industrial Revolution was the replacement of hand labor by machinery, which was powered by man, horse, water, or, later, by steam. Far-reaching new methods were being introduced. One machine could do the work of many laborers, and each machine could be guided by a single operator. There were improved methods of smelting cast iron, and from this product new machines and new engines were invented. This revolution started about 1780 in England and proceeded slowly enough at first. It began to be felt in the United States 20 years later, and the discovery of iron and coal deposits in the Allegheny Mountains helped speed the industrialization.

The making of textiles, among the first of the crafts to be industrialized, was first mechanized in England before the processes were imported to New England. New Hampshire and Massachusetts in and around Lowell had plenty of water power. In England the spinning jenny was patented in 1767, and the mechanical shuttle, known as the *flying shuttle,* was worked out and patented in 1784. These were followed by the power loom in 1785. In the United States Eli Whitney invented the cotton gin in 1793. This machine, which removed the seed from raw cotton, made this material a pliable and cheap commodity. New Hampshire and Massachusetts in and around Lowell had sufficient water-power to run the new machines, and within a few years textile making was organized into special mills. Textile mills were built in the form of fenced-in compounds with dormitories for the workers, mostly young women.

The steam boat was invented by Fulton in 1793 and perfected for commercial use by 1807. In 1814 Stevenson in England introduced an improved locomotive, and by the 1830s railroads were being built in the United States and throughout Western Europe. Bridges had to be built over rivers that had been previously forded. By the middle of the century passenger- and freight-carrying vessels powered by steam were plying the oceans and rivers in and around the United States and the world. Horse-drawn vehicles were also improved, and better roads to accommodate them had to be built. Steep grades were eliminated whenever possible.

It was an exciting time, helped greatly by protective patent laws in England and in the United States. There were many patents and discoveries such as the paper machine (1809), the sewing machine (1830), phosphorus matches (1831), and the magnetic telegraph by Morse in the United States in 1832.

It was natural that these changes should bring on new types of buildings and new structural solutions. Factories required new forms. Long-span bridges of cast iron in compression were invented and built, and long-span suspension bridges of wrought-iron chains were introduced. Railroads demanded train sheds of wide dimensions, and large market areas were covered. Conservatories for growing tropical plants and flowers during winter months were fabricated from cast iron and glass, and in 1851 England opened its great Golden Jubilee Exhibition in the Crystal Palace, London.

England and France led the way in developing these new types of buildings; however these structures were usually not thought of as architecture nor designed by architects. They were designed by a new class of technical constructionists known as *engineers*. Architects often worked with the engineers but with a different function: that of exterior decorator. Engineers laid out the building and designed its structure to fit its function the architect then designed exterior facades in one of the historical styles, often with the intent to camouflage and cover the structure as much as possible.

Examples in England and France

A few of the buildings of England and France are listed here because they were of world importance and greatly influenced contemporary functional architecture in the United States.

**THE CRYSTAL PALACE, London, England, 1850–1851, was designed by Joseph Paxton, heretofore a gardener and handyman in the employ of the Duke of Devonshire, owner of a great residence at Chatsworth. There Paxton designed and built a large conservatory that was the prototype for the Crystal Palace. This great palace was completely prefabricated in mills throughout England and put together within a period of four months. This milestone in construction was entirely detailed and scheduled by Paxton with the backing and daily help of Prince Albert. It contained over a million square feet of space including the side balconies, and covered more than 750,000 square feet of ground. Built mostly of cast iron and glass like a greenhouse, the structure was 1851 feet long and 408 feet wide. A 72 foot high nave with large galleries on each side ran the entire length of the building. An arched transept that cut through the center gave a total height of 108 feet and spanned over several large trees that the Jubilee committee had asked to be saved.

The exhibition itself, a great triumph for England and its far-flung empire, brought before the world the importance of industry and glorified the Industrial Revolution. Millions of people attended.

After the Golden Jubilee the Crystal Palace was unbolted, disassembled, and moved out to Sydenham, a suburb of London, where it was reerected and used for exhibition purposes for 84 years. It was destroyed by fire in 1936.

During the decade following the Golden Jubilee, iron and glass exhibition halls of varying sizes and importance were erected in most of the principal cities of the world: *Dublin, Ireland,* 1852, by Sir John Benson; *New York City,* 1853, by C. J. B. Carstensen of Copenhagen, Denmark; *Munich, Bavaria,* 1854, by August von Voit; *Amsterdam, Holland,* 1856, by Cornelius Outshoorn; and, greatest of all, the *Paris Exposition, France,* 1855, with a Hall of Machines having 160 foot span and 4000 foot length. Thus the Age of Cast Iron reached its greatest climax in 1860, just as steel entered the construction field.

Other great European buildings of the period that influenced the world included the following:

*LES HALLES, Paris, France, 1852–1858, was designed by Victor Baltard, architect, with the aid of a municipal committee that refused his first design—a pseudomedieval castlelike building that fronted a wide-span iron and glass structure. The finished structure was a great covered market made up of three buildings joined together so that they contained a continuous area of over three city blocks. The buildings, which were fabricated of cast iron and wrought iron, were supported with light cast-iron columns. Streets and unloading spaces dipped under to the basement level so that the area on the ground level where the market stalls were located was free from vehicular traffic.

With the advent of frozen foods and household refrigerators, this set of buildings became obsolete by 1965 because of newer methods of merchandizing. The market was demolished in 1970.

BIBLIOTHÈQUE STE. GENEVIÈVE, Paris, 1845–1850, and *Bibliothèque Nationale,* Paris, 1862–1868, both designed by Henri Labrouste, introduced many new structural ideas as well as new efficient ways to catalog, distribute, and store books. These libraries also provided large reading spaces having overhead daylight.

GALLERY D'ORLEANS, Paris, 1829–1831, consisted of two stories of fashionable shops on each side of a public passageway that was roofed over with iron and glass. Now destroyed, it was for many decades the meeting place for the socially elite of Paris, who went there to promenade and shop. It was adjacent to the Royal Palace, occupied at that time by the Duc d'Orleans, who promoted it and gave it its name.

England had a number of bridges such as the ***SUNDERLAND BRIDGE,** near New Castle on the North Sea, 1793–1796, which was designed by Thomas Paine, the American engineer, noted for his patriotic writings in the Colonies during the Revolutionary War. This bridge was of cast-iron bars fitted together to form a supporting series of huge arches in compression. It had a clear span of 236 feet high over the Wear River so that sailing vessels could pass underneath.

*STRAITS OF MENAI BRIDGE, northern Wales, 1819–1824, by Thomas Telford, engineer, was the first suspension bridge of great size, with a clear span of 570 feet. It was built of wrought-iron bars linked together as chains, a design patented in 1796 by James Finley, an American engineer.

Other important buildings of the time were large train sheds, some of which are still in use, like *Paddington Station, London,* 1852–1854; the Great Western Hotel attached to it; and *Palm Stove, Greenhouse, Kew Gardens, London,* 1845–1847.

Factories and Mills, 1830–1860

During the early years of the Republic, the United States was not able to compete in trade with England or the Continent because of economic conditions. It was not until after the War of 1812–1814 that the United States began to catch up to, and eventually surpass Europe in technical discoveries, machine patents, and commercial innovations. The 40 years between 1820 and 1860 was a feverish period of financial and physical expansion to the West. The Erie Canal was built (1817–1825), linking the Great Lakes to the Hudson River and New York City. That city became a world port on a level with London. The Ohio–Mississippi River system, linking Cincinnati, Louisville, St. Louis, and Minneapolis–St. Paul to New Orleans, became as busy as the Rhine. After 1836 railroads expanded the traffic from New York, Boston, and Philadelphia to Chicago and St. Louis. However the country was increasingly divided between the industrial North, with paid labor, and the fuedal agrarian South, dependent on slaves. The two philosophies were opposed economically and morally. The issue was finally resolved by the Civil War (1861–1865), which left the economy of the South in ruins for close to 100 years.

Then came steel. The Bessemer process of steel making was discovered in 1856, and this was closely followed by the open hearth process. With the availability of an economical iron product having tensile as well as compressive strength, there was almost another industrial revolution as steel replaced cast iron for use in construction and became the foremost commercial product of the age. The year 1860 can be set as the end of the cast iron and water power era and the beginning of the Age of Steel and Steam.

By the 1830s factories were being built in the United States, particularly in New England, where water power was plentiful and transportation relatively easy. As in England mill construction was used, and the manufacturing processes as well as the factory designs were adapted from the mother country. Among the important factories were *Stone Mill, New Market, New Hampshire,* 1835; *Lippit Woolen Mills, Woonsocket, Rhode Island,* 1836; *Hamilton Mills, Lowell, Massachusetts,* 1846; *Governor Harris Factory, Harris Rhode Island,* 1851; and a very ambitious one on the Ohio River in Indiana.

These mills were constructed of masonry walls with timber construction inside. A double row of wood timber or cast iron columns formed an aisle through the center. All timbers were usually hand hewn, and all were morticed and doweled together. The clear spans were not more than 12 feet on the average, and the structures were three spans wide, for a total inside width of 36 to 40 feet. The timbers were about 12 × 16 inches. Each bay was about 12 feet wide, and purlins were set in between approximately 4 feet apart. These purlins, averaging 6 × 8 to 10 inches, were notched into the beams. Over this a plank floor about 2 inches thick was laid, sometimes tenoned and grooved.

The masonry walls varied in thickness from 24 inches on the first story to 16 or 18 inches on the second, to 12 inches on the third. The trusses and purlins for the roof were also of hewn timbers, morticed and doweled together. This method of construction for mills and loft buildings persisted throughout the nineteenth century. It was known as Mill Construction.

*CANNELTON COTTON MILL, Cannelton, Indiana, 1849–1850, on the Ohio River, was designed by Thomas Tefft of the office of Tallman and Busklin, architects, of Providence, Rhode Island, under the direction of Brigadier General Charles T. James of Providence, who had had experience in cotton milling as a director of the Newburyport Mills, Massachusetts. This building is of stone, 225 feet by 45 feet, and three stories plus attic in height. The front is distinguished by twin towers, which flank the central entrance and are reminiscent of Tefft's design for the Union Station in Providence.

Train Sheds and Railway Stations, 1830–1860

Although railways were built rapidly throughout the eastern half of the United States, station and train shed design was 20 to 30 years behind that of England and the Continent. Perhaps this was because passengers in the States were not as accustomed to physical comforts as were those of the older countries; the stations that were provided were little more than ticket offices with maybe a small waiting space around an iron stove. In many small settlements no such buildings were provided until after the Civil War. Trains were scheduled to stop and depart on a street, and nearby local taverns were the only sheltered places where passengers could wait. Sometimes houses parallel to the tracks were designated and used as stations, or, a nearby building was adapted for use. In Washington, D.C., the Baltimore and Ohio Railway took over a three-storied brick building in 1835, and with slight remodeling used it as its passenger station for 15 years.

The stations that were built in small cities were generally of wood, about 24 by 50 feet, with wide, overhanging eaves to give some protection for passengers waiting outside for the trains. A company engineer provided the plans for these simple buildings. However as railway traffic grew, some architectural attempts were made in the larger cities.

NEW YORK CENTRAL STATION, Syracuse, New York, 1838, was designed by Daniel Elliot, architect. This two-track shed built across the street in downtown Syracuse completely blocked the street down which the railroad had usurped the right-of-way. The building was pseudo-Greek with a smoke vent on the ridge of the roof in the form of a small Ionic temple. Although the tracks were under cover, there was little space for offices and waiting rooms. The building was destroyed in 1869 by popular demand.

*UNION STATION, Providence, Rhode Island, 1848, designed by Thomas Tefft, was a large brick building at the terminal end of tracks that made a large loop as a turnaround. The building had for an entrance feature a center section flanked by two high towers, in turn flanked by long wings with arches, arcades, and terminal motives, all of brick in well-adapted German Romanesque style. In 1885, when it was 37 years old, it was voted among the 20 most beautiful buildings in the United States. Unluckily it was destroyed by fire the next year.

Whether this building or the *Kneeland Street Station*, Boston, Massachusetts, 1847, by Gridley J. F. Bryant, was the first to furnish the traveling public with the amenities is not known; but from this time on, most stations were equipped with smoking rooms for men, restaurants, lavatories, barber shops, and newsstands.

UNION STATION, Harrisburg, Pennsylvania, 1850, designed by an unrecorded architect, was a twin station for two railroads. The twin sets of two tracks each ran through the station and were separated by a huge clock tower. Passage between the two stations was by way of a second-story common room, but each side had its separate waiting spaces and services. Although the building was styled in nondescript Baroque, it was well proportioned and was one of the outstanding buildings of the city.

THE PHILADELPHIA, WILMINGTON, AND BALTIMORE STATION, Philadelphia, 1851–1852, was noted for its 150 foot span train shed. This was designed by a bridge engineer who used Howe trusses of cast and wrought iron. A train shed of similar proportions was designed by Otto Matz, a German, for the old *Great Central Station*, Chicago, 1855–1857, but it seems not to have been until the next era, with the use of steel, that a great clear span was attempted in the first *Grand Central Station*, New York City, 1869–1871.

Cast Iron Commercial Buildings, 1830–1860

A great deal of experimentation took place in the use of cast iron. Probably the first structure having a cast iron facing was a triumphal arch in St. Petersburg (now Leningrad), Russia, in 1815. However the first commercial building built entirely of cast iron was a three-storied 27 by 50 foot prefabricated flour mill, which was cast in England for the Turkish government in 1839–40. This mill, made by William Fairbairn in London, was assembled and opened for public display at Millwall, a suburb of London, then disassembled and sent to Istanbul. Cast-iron beams and columns carried the structure and roof, which was of corrugated iron sheets. The exterior was of cast iron of uniform prefabricated sizes.

The dome of the National Capitol in Washington, D.C., was designed and built by Thomas U. Walters, the architect in charge from 1851 to 1865, and is an outstanding example of the use of cast iron at that time.

In 1829 John Haviland designed the Miner's Bank, Pottsville, Pennsylvania, with a two-storied facade of cast iron plates made to look like masonry. When painted, the cast iron looked somewhat like stone. In 1842 Daniel Badger erected a cast iron storefront on Washington Street in Boston. However it was not until 1850 that cast iron was accepted as a suitable material for commercial buildings. From that time until 1890 cast iron, used with pseudoclassical styling in imitation of stone, became the most popular and economical material for storefronts and commercial buildings.

The person given most credit for fabrication and popularization of this material was James Bogardus, the owner of an iron-fabricating company in New York City. He advertised himself and his fabricated designs widely, and by 1858 supplied cast iron fronts to clients in New York, Philadelphia, and Baltimore, as well as in Washington, D.C., Chicago, San Francisco, and Havana, Cuba. By 1865, Daniel Badger, another fabricator of note, claimed to have executed 55 multistoried cast iron buildings and 550 single storefronts. Later foundries and fabricators were established in many cities throughout the states.

EDGAR H. LAING STORES, Washington and Murray Streets, New York City, 1849, had Bogardus cast iron details for the two four-storied corner facades and an interior framed with cast iron columns. The fronts are said to have been used also for the Bogardus Iron Factory, also four stories high, built later that year. This factory lasted only a decade and was dismantled by the owner for another site; however for some reason or other it was not rebuilt. The Laing Stores Building is still in use although it now has different occupants.

*SUN BUILDING, Baltimore, 1850–1851, was designed by R. G. Hatfield, architect. Bogardus used Hatfield's baroque-styled drawings to design and cast the exterior details. The five-storied building emphasized the four upper levels, which were designed in two double stages with arched windows capping each stage at the third and fifth stories. Strong vertical emphasis was gained by use of three superimposed orders on pedestals and entablature blocks, with cast caryatids at the fifth floor level. Extra-heavy brackets supported an overhanging cornice at the roof line.

HARPER AND BROTHERS, PRINTING HOUSE, New York City, 1854, was designed by John B. Corlies, architect, and James Bogardus, fabricator. Patterns from Hatfield's Sun Building in Baltimore were used, but the ground floor was redesigned and a much better proportioned crowning cornice was used. The building was razed in 1920.

*HAUGHWOUT BUILDING, 488 Broadway at Broome Street, New York City, 1857, was designed by J. P. Gaynor, architect, and fabricated by Daniel Badger with the aid of George H. Johnson, a young designer. This five-storied building for the Haughwout and Company Store was designed in Italian Renaissance style with superimposed Palladian arches framed in Corinthian columns and with a strong entablature marking each story. It was one of the first commercial buildings to use a passenger elevator, which had recently been patented by Otis (1852) and shown at the New York Exposition of 1853. This building is still standing, but is in neglected condition.

NEW YORK CRYSTAL PALACE, 1853, destroyed by fire in 1858, was designed by Karl Gildemeister and G. J. B. C. Carstensen, who was famous for the planning and layout of Tivoli Gardens, 1843, in his native city of Copenhagen, Denmark. The site for the New York Exposition was Reservoir Square (Fifth Avenue and 42nd Street), now occupied by the New York Public Library and Bryant Park. The building was a cast iron and glass edifice similar to the Crystal Palace in London, though not as large.

The design, which was the result of an international competition, was no doubt the most practical. The most innovative design, however, was one submitted by James Bogardus. His design called for an interior court, 400 feet in diameter, surrounded by a circular hall, 150 feet wide, whose outer circumference would have been 1200 feet. The center of the court was to have had an open, 13-storied, circular cast iron tower. The hall was to have been covered by a sheet iron roof suspended from linked chains supported radially by the tower. The outer and inner facades of the great circular tower were to appear like those of a four-storied building and were to have had shallow interior galleries. It is regrettable that this design was not accepted and built—it would have been the talk of the century.

As indicated by these descriptions of cast-iron buildings, several were for department stores. The largest of these was Wanamaker's Store, on Union Square and Tenth Street, New York City, which was destroyed by fire in 1957, just two years short of a century in age. At midcentury the department store was introduced in all large cities of the world. Each department represented a shop, and thus served to bring the town market indoors in a multistoried building under one roof and one owner.

Steel Bridges

Following the lead of England and Western Europe, America began to build steel bridges, which were made necessary by the rise of commercialism, the need for better roads to truck produce to markets and railroad centers, and the growth of the railroads. A means had to be found to transport heavy loads across the rivers and to avoid steep grades. In 1823–1824 a suspension bridge was built in Philadelphia, using Finley's patent; however this bridge has since been destroyed. It was not until 22 years later that another suspension bridge was built in the United States.

MONONGAHELA SUSPENSION BRIDGE, Pittsburgh, Pennsylvania, 1846, was designed by John Roebling, who became America's foremost bridge designer during the latter half of the century. This was the first long suspension bridge in the United States and carried two lanes of traffic.

NIAGARA RIVER GORGE SUSPENSION BRIDGE, Niagara, New York, 1851, by John Roebling, was for railway trains only and was known as the most daring suspension bridge of the age. Instead of chains Roebling used steel cables, known at that time as *wire rope*. He was among the first to manufacture wire and its products at a mill which he organized in Trenton, New Jersey, in 1849. However the populace greatly objected to this bridge because it was built immediately below the falls and blocked the view. They clamored for its removal, and 30 years after its building it was replaced.

3

THE INDUSTRIAL REVOLUTION IN FULL SWING

The Age of Steel and Steam 1860–1930

After the Civil War came an era of great change. Urban society expanded tremendously and London, Paris, New York, Philadelphia, and Chicago became cities of millions of people. Agrarian society became less influential, both numerically and economically. Factories were concentrated in the cities, where there were railroad and steamship terminals.

Industrialism fostered international trade and big business. There was a growing class of wealthy manufacturers, mill owners, bankers, realty speculators, and ship and railway owners. Millionaires were created within the space of a few years, and a new aristocracy of money came into being.

Great business combines—trusts and cartels—were formed. Labor formed into trade unions to protect itself and to advance its rights for adequate pay and proper freedom. Laws were passed to protect children and women laborers from being exploited and to promote better working conditions.

This was a great age, but a confusing one—it seemed to have arrived too fast. Most people worked and made their livelihood in one atmosphere: that of business and the machine; but lived with the culture of a previous era.

Many of the period's society leaders responded to the era by building palatial homes that rivaled those of the nobility of Europe. The William Vanderbilts built a palace in the French style of Francis I on upper Fifth Avenue in New York City; the decorative carving on the building even used the crest, crown, and salamander of that king. Richard M. Hunt

(1827–1895), the favored architect of the Vanderbilt family, did many residences for them. He designed The Breakers, an Italian Baroque palace that was built for Cornelius Vanderbilt, on the seashore at Newport, Rhode Island. George Vanderbilt founded and built Biltmore in the hills of North Carolina near Asheville. This palace, in the style of François Premier, was a clever copy of the chateaux of the Loire Valley in France. It is a beautiful and extravagant palace having a grand dining hall, spacious lounges, and extravagant terraced gardens. It is especially noted for its outside staircase, a copy of the famous staircase of the Chateau of Blois.

Although many of the newly rich had very little formal education, they were smart business people. They were not sophisticated, nor were they schooled in the humanities, fine arts, or architecture. They loved ornament, the more the better, and the many new machines made ornament easy to obtain. The new machines could turn out spindles and balls, and scroll saws could fashion the most intricate wooden grilles. Porch columns of wood could be turned with bulbous forms not possible in former times. Woodworking mills set up near the sources of supply merchandized their products throughout the country by means of catalogs distributed through lumber store chains.

The great Centennial Exposition, held in Philadelphia in 1876, and the great Columbian Exposition, in Chicago in 1893, were milestones for American architecture, particularly the Chicago exhibition, which was a marvelous extravaganza of classical eclecticism. Its colossal exterior of plaster and paint simulating marble fronted great halls of steel and glass that housed the products of the industrial age.

New commercial cities grew up on rivers where transportation or waterpower or both were available. Factories were built. Railroads were pushed through to service the factories, and laborers' tenements or houses were placed as near to the factories as possible. These were pedestrian cities. Tradesmen built their stores along Main Street, which paralleled the railroad tracks and the river, and all local business took place on this street.

Residences were spread out from there, but it was necessary that everything be within relatively easy walking distance. The pattern was not too different for the growing larger cities except that in the commercial areas the buildings were taller and closer together in an attempt to get as many people as possible near the center. Public transportation had to be developed before there could be further growth. Omnibuses and horse-drawn cars came first. Then the development of electric power brought electric streetcars in the 1890s.

Suburbs developed and were linked to the central areas by commuter trains; however the central cities were based on pedestrian traffic until 1920. Most buildings were placed within walking distance of each other, with factories and the depot, then hotels, stores, offices, residences, schools and churches. Public buildings such as city halls, police and fire stations, courthouses, and sheriff's quarters, which included the county jail, were also usually accommodated in the same area. Streets were generally ungraded; only Main Street might be paved. Most green areas such as parks were eliminated from the centers, though some towns had a city park located a mile or more up river from the factories and the raw sewage dumps below the main part of the city. An exception was the courthouse square, which often graced the center of the city and offered breathing space to the otherwise crowded center.

Thus cities were generally rather drab. Their architecture, like their people, was pseudosophisticated. The craftsmen of preceding eras who had schooled themselves to build were now replaced in large part by machines that could do wonderful things but without taste. Architectural styling became very confused. Ornament became synonymous with beauty, and machine-made ornament was easy to come by through the local lumberyard or the cemetery stone carver. So while technology was making great advancements, architectural taste was deteriorating.

Most present-day architects and builders are aware of the many changes that took place with the introduction of steel as the chief structural material for commercial work and with the development of many fireproof materials that are now common. Even such old materials as brick, stone, and wood underwent great changes because of machine methods of fabrication. The most important of the new materials was Portland cement, a by-product of steel manufacture. More and more building materials and parts were prefabricated, and delivered to the jobs, and then fastened in place. Prefabricated materials included, to name only a few, window units, wall panels, partitions, and prefinished floorings. Building materials the world over were reaching a sameness and standardization caused by the industrialism of the late nineteenth century. This did pose some limitations, but the advantages far outweighed the disadvantages. What would we do now if every cabinet had to be made on the job?

Great advances were made in the field of wood frame construction. Prior to this age all wood frame houses were fabricated on the job by carpenters and joiners who started with freshly cut logs. The frames were of large timbers fitted together by a method based on medieval half-timber. But the Age of Steel and Steam saw the development of the circular saw and the gang saw which could rip out hundreds of feet of lumber in a few hours. Soon lumber was made in standardized dimensions and graded in sizes from two-by-fours to two-by-twelves. Wood was machine planed into smooth siding and all manner of finished boards for doors, trims, and flooring.

Framing lumber, as well as the outside siding, sheathing, and roof boards was of white pine, most of it from Michigan. Rough flooring was of pine, as was sometimes the finished flooring of 6 inch wide tongue and grooved material. The finished flooring might be 3 inch tongue and grooved boards of yellow pine from the South, which was then oiled, or shellacked and waxed. Toward the end of the period hardwood flooring came into popular use; this was narrow boarding of tongue and grooved design securely nailed to the underflooring. This flooring was of northern maple, beech, or oak, carefully sanded on top and stained, shellacked, and varnished or waxed. Whereas softwood floors were usually carpeted with grosgrain carpeting or imported Brussels carpeting; hardwood floors were covered by large rugs with about 2 feet of the wood flooring showing around the edges or by a variety of small rugs—Oriental or domestic —scattered about.

Door and window interior trim, as well as doors, were of molded oak, native cherry, or walnut, sanded, stained and varnished.

With the development of steel wire came machines that could cut and form nails. Before this time wooden frames were doweled and morticed together and fastened with wooden pegs; nails were handmade of wrought iron and were very expensive. Steel spikes were practically unknown. But from 1870 onward steel nails and spikes could be purchased for as little as three cents per pound.

Balloon construction—2″ × 4″s 16 inches on center, covered with clapboards became very popular from 1870 onward, and soon supplanted timber framing, which had been used before the Civil War. It became the accepted method of rebuilding Chicago after its great fire in 1871. Complete doors and windows were soon purchased at the mill or lumberyard, and lath and plaster on the interiors often covered a multitude of carpenters' mistakes, as is true today.

Masonry construction followed older methods, but new backing materials such as hollow tile and later hollow cement block came onto the market. These were made in factories from washed sand and cement and used where weight was not a factor; lightweight aggregates such as cinders were used in other cases, especially after 1920. Brick remained a favorite material for many types of structures, and was often veneered over frame construction in houses.

Science has produced wonderful plumbing mechanisms and fixtures that can be placed in the uppermost story of a tall office building or in a mountain resort 500 miles from an urban center. How could modern man endure without the electrically driven centrifugal pump, which is the root of modern plumbing?

Science has also produced central heating and other fixtures of modern buildings; the important fact to remember is that most of these advances were developed in the period extending from the second half of the nineteenth century until World War I.

Practically all of this construction was sound and much more scientific than before. There was always the jerry-builder who cheated and built flimsy, weak structures, but there was not the waste of timber and other natural resources that there had been in the preceding, less scientific age. Testing of materials was started, and governments set up formulas and standards for building. Building codes and fire-protection laws came into being.

Five different categories of architecture used during this era can be identified. The different categories were not all developed at once, although during the latter years all five were used.

Phase 1. *Industrial Romanticism, 1860–1900.* This was the unsophisticated use of new machines: the turning lathe and scroll saw that affected the use of wood. Sheet steel could be pressed into many shapes. Profuse gingerbread ornament typified this phase.

Phase 2. *Eclecticism, 1860–1930.* This was the copying of historical styles and imitating of the Academic Revivalists of the previous period by the sophisticated citizenry.

Phase 3. *Functionalism, 1860–1930.* New types of buildings, new uses, and new materials called for new solutions: steel bridges, train sheds, covered markets, and skyscrapers.

Phase 4. *Art Nouveau, 1885–1910.* This style, originated by an avant-garde group of Europeans searching for a new style. It used forms based on flowers, vines, trees, and sinuous lines.

Phase 5. *Arts and Crafts Movement, 1890–1910.* This style was promoted by those who remonstrated against the machine and advocated that all art and architecture be based on handcraft.

PHASE 1. INDUSTRIAL ROMANTICISM:
GINGERBREAD ORNAMENT 1860–1900

During this period one segment of society, made up of industrialists, bankers, and merchants, ran the country, particularly in the Midwest and West. These newly rich and self-made people lived in smaller cities generally, but enjoyed life to the full and took their politics seriously.

Factories were pouring out a flood of merchandise. Machines could turn out hundreds of yards of "handmade" lace and printed silk. Wallpaper could be printed with allover intricate designs like those—at least almost like those—that only royalty could have affored a century before. Carpets could be woven and printed in floral and arabesque patterns for less than a dollar per square yard.

Furniture, of scrolled design, was ornamented with balls and knobs turned out by the lathe. Many a house had a corner fireplace with an ornamental cast iron grate and a front of fancy glazed tiles. Over this was a mantel of two or three different stained woods, scrolled, grooved, and ornamented with turned work. Often a heavily framed mirror was part of the fireplace composition, along with two or three shelves, one of which supported a heavily ornamented key-wind clock.

The architecture was an expression of *Industrial Romanticism,* and most of it was contrived by local builders. It was not professional architecture by architects, nor did it have a homogeneous style. The different variations were given names such as Victorian Romanticism; Eastlake, named for Charles Eastlake, who, more than any other man, popularized the style during the later years of Queen Victoria; Italianate; the General Grant style; the Queen Anne style, the Stick style, as described by Professor Vincent Scully, Jr., of Yale University; and the bizarre Steamboat Gothic style, which was patterned after the elaborate river steamboats of the time. There were some marked differences in form between some of these styles, but most had one characteristic in common: love of machine-made, overly rich ornamentation. This gave rise to the term "gingerbread ornament," a name that is applied to all of these variations. The era has been referred to as the "Mauve Decades," and its architecture as the "brownstone" style.

The Italianate Style

One of the unsophisticated styles that was popular immediately following the Civil War, was the Italianate style which vaguely resembled Italian Late Gothic and Early Renaissance. Italianate structures were usually built of fire-red brick, with light grey stone trim, and often sported a tower. The silhouette of this tower was often Italian in proportion and in a fog gave an impression of Italian derivation; however, the resemblance stopped there, as the tower usually used gingerbread detail.

*JEDEDIAH WILCOX HOUSE, Meriden, Connecticut (Figure 3.1), 1868–1871, was a mansion of 40 rooms built for Mr. Wilcox, a wealthy

Figure 3.1   Jedediah Wilcox House, Meriden, Connecticut, 1868–1871; Industrial Romantic (Italianate) style. Photograph by Allen E. Meyers; furnished by Meriden Chamber of Commerce.

manufacturer of carpetbags and hoopskirts. A newspaper of the time called it "Franco-Italianate Style," whatever that was supposed to mean. It was built of Milwaukee pressed brick and trimmed with carved Portland sandstone around the windows and doors. The yard was enclosed by an ornate cast-iron filagreed fence, and the entranceway was guarded by two crouching lions carved in stone. The interior was elegant, with a library, an ornate music room, and a dining room that could seat 30 people. The parlor was decorated in "Grand Duchess Style," which was indescribable but most elegant. The house boasted gaslights and indoor plumbing. It is sad to state that Jedediah Wilcox was caught in the financial crash of 1873 and forced into bankruptcy. The house was sold complete with furniture in 1875. Through the years it has had excellent care and was turned over to the city of Meriden as a museum only a few years ago. However a drive for money to support the museum failed, and the house was demolished in 1974. Details have been salvaged for the American Wing of the Metropolitan Museum in New York City.

*CENTRAL FIRE STATION, Ann Arbor, Michigan (Figure 3.2), 1882–1883, designed by William Scott, architect of Detroit, is an example of the Italianate Style. This two-storied red-brick building trimmed with gray cut stone has a corner tower whose shape is somewhat reminiscent of Italian towers of the Late Gothic, Early Renaissance period. Its entire cost at time of building was $10,004.45, which was $4.95 over the estimated cost. Now it would cost at least a quarter of a million dollars to build. The tower still holds the old bell that was used to call the volunteer firemen, though it rings no more. This old firehouse has seen the evolution of fire-fighting equipment from man-drawn to horse-drawn to mechanized trucks, but the building is now too small and obsolete to be a first-rate fire station. There is talk of saving it as a historical landmark and remodeling it into city offices. Certainly it is a landmark, not beautiful but a testament to the romantic industrial style of the late nineteenth century.

**CARSON MANSION (now the Ingomar Club), Eureka, California (Figure 3.3), 1885, was designed by S. and U. J. C. Newson for William Carson, a wealthy lumberman. It is an outstanding example of the Industrial Romantic style. Whether it can be classified as Italianate is questionable—in fact it cannot be classified in any one category. The house is wonderful in its extraordinary exuberance. It is almost a nightmare with turnings, fiagree, gables, bay windows, and a tower with bal-

Figure 3.2 Central Fire Station, Ann Arbor, Michigan, 1882–1883; William Scott, Architect; Industrial Romantic (Italianate) style. Photograph by Eck Stanger, Ann Arbor.

conies and decorative lunettes that are almost out of this world. It is hard to imagine that one house, even though large, could contain so many ornamental forms and details in one composition. The interior, of equal profusion and confusion, attests to the *nouveau riche* taste of that day. It has been an exclusive club since 1950.

Although Industrial Romanticism was well launched immediately following the Civil War, it received its big boost and acceptance from the

Figure 3.3 Carson Mansion (now the Ingomar Club), Eureka, California, 1885; S. and U. J. C. Newson, Architects; Industrial Romantic style. Photograph furnished by Ingomar Club.

Philadelphia World's Fair in 1876, the centennial of the United States. This vast industrial showing was housed in steel and glass pavilions that were fronted by elaborate compositions of towers in red brick and painted with light gray striped bands. False balconies were aflutter with red, white, and blue bunting and flags. Some of the buildings had Gothic flavor, others Moorish, but none were strictly eclectic.

In England, Charles Eastlake, the son of a prominent Gothicist architect, led the Industrial Romantic movement. His first designs were Gothic and stressed the picturesque; later he moved into the field of furniture design for urban dwellers who had to live close to the city centers, near the factories and commercial districts, often in crowded conditions. This furniture, which came under the heading of "patent furniture," was featured at the Philadelphia Centennial in 1876. Here were folding beds that could be closed up vertically into what looked like wall cabinets; chairs that folded into lounges; and swivel, rocking, and reclining chairs of various kinds. Although his designs were loaded with machine-made ornament, some of them were fresh and practical. They appealed especially to the unsophisticated.

In the 1880s Charles Eastlake was brought to Grand Rapids, Michigan, the then-growing furniture center of the United States, as the chief designer for one of the big furniture factories. There he greatly influenced architecture as well as furniture design throughout the country.

OLD MAIN, WOODBURN HALL, West Virginia University, Morgantown, West Virginia, ca. 1880, is like many other "old Mains" that were built throughout the northern states during this period. Many small colleges were established at this time. Some were state schools and universities; many were church schools financed by various denominations. The buildings, usually of red brick or brownstone with light gray stone trim, always had a central clock tower. Some were Gothic in a Smithsonian sort of way, some were Richardsonian Romanesque, but most were nondescript Industrial Romantic in style.

This style with its clock tower was also used for other institutional buildings—in fact it almost became a category in itself. It was used for county homes for the indigent and aged, mental hospitals, and normal schools (teachers' colleges). In fact it was hard to tell whether the building was for mental training or incarceration.

The General Grant Style

This style reached its height at the time of Grant's greatest popularity, and his home (1857) in Galena, Illinois, was in this style. This house and hundreds like it were square, usually two-storied buildings having wide eaves and cornices all around them. These wide eaves appeared to be supported by elaborate scrolled-wood brackets that had bed moldings of classic derivation. There was usually an attic story lighted by small windows in the frieze. The homes were planned around a central hall and stairway, with each floor having a room in each corner. Ceilings were high, 9 to 10 feet on every floor, and rooms were generally small. The windows were high and narrow in proportion, and each sash was divided into two vertical panes. Each window opening was topped with pedimented pseudoclassic caps of scrolled wood, or if the body of the house was brick, with light gray stone caps.

The rooms of this time were rather ungainly in proportion. The effect was definitely on the tall side, which was the mode of the time, although in decorating the picture molding was sometimes dropped a foot or more from the ceiling and a dado molding placed 30 inches from the floor.

*GENERAL GRANT HOUSE, Galena, Illinois, 1857, by an unknown architect, is furnished with original furniture and a complete set of china that the family used while in the White House. Its description follows that of the General Grant style. It is open to the public on most days.

The Queen Anne Style

Why Queen Anne's name is attached to this style has never been fully explained. It does sound sophisticated, and that is all that mattered at the time. These houses tended toward the picturesque in the use of gables and nondescript towers. Bay windows, balconies, and verandas across the front and sides were common. These verandas were usually very narrow and not too useful; however they were decorative, with wooden columns that were turned into a multitude of bulbous and cylindrical shapes. At the base these columns were spanned by balustrading whose spindles were also turned in intricate designs; at the top, echoing the balustrade, there might also be a band of grillwork of spindles, balls, and jigsawed patterns. Most of these houses were of wood and painted white, although it was not uncommon for them to be painted with the body of one color and the trim of another. Lumberyards stocked many patterns of porch columns, balustrade spindles, and intricate gable ends to fit standard roof angles. The new mail-order houses of Sears, Roebuck and Montgomery Ward showed a variety of stock items. Journeymen carpenters gloried in the possibilities of using so many different designs so easily arrived at and at reasonable prices.

Larger houses might have a porte cochere covering a side entrance for carriages; and many houses had a large plate-glass window surrounded by small panes of colored glass. Some had bay windows. The front yards of the more affluent residences sometimes had a cast iron deer painted in natural colors, or a fountain with a little girl and boy standing under an umbrella that trickled water from the top.

HARRY S. TRUMAN RESIDENCE, Independence, Missouri, 1865, the family home of the former President of the United States, has been in the family since it was built. A rambling, two-storied frame house that has a mansard-roofed third story, it is similar to thousands that once lined the streets of Midwestern cities before expanding commercialism caused their removal. This house has a veranda on two sides with the usual gingerbread ornament; however it is quite conservative, much more so than many homes of the period.

Octagonal and Round Houses, Domes, and Cupolas

Octagonal and round houses were popular at this time although they are awkward in plan and not very practical. This was a period in which people seemed to crave something different and often went to extremes to get it. Although some of these buildings were topped by domes, or bulbous cupolas which gave an oriental effect, they were not in a Moorish or other Oriental style.

*LONGWOOD, near Natchez, Mississippi, also known as "Nutt's Folly," 1859–1861, was designed by Samuel Sloan of Philadelphia for Mr. Haller Nutt, a wealthy plantation owner. A two-storied, octagonal house whose receding attic floor is topped by an Oriental-appearing, bulbous cupola, is an extravaganza of verandas, bracketed balconies, and ornamented cornices, not to mention the gorgeous onion-shaped dome. The mansion is the epitome of romantic architecture, and because it was never completely finished, it became known as "Nutt's Folly." It had reached the interior finishing stage when the Civil War broke out, where upon the workers dropped their tools on the attic (third) floor where they were working and departed for service in the armed forces. These tools amid sawdust are there to this day to be seen by tourists who visit the house. Because Haller Nutt died during the war, the house was never finished; however the family finished the ground floor and moved in. Most of Haller Nutt's fortune was swept away by this dreadful war, as were those of so many Southern plantation owners.

Public Buildings

Although red brick and gray stone have been mentioned as typical of the Italianate style, they were popular throughout the 1870–1920 era for all types of buildings. Red brick and gray stone were used for the buildings of the Philadelphia Centennial Exposition and in the work of Frank Furness, a famous Philadelphia architect of the period who was greatly admired by Louis Sullivan in his early years.

*ISAAC M. WISE TEMPLE CENTER, Cincinnati, Ohio, 1864–1866, was designed by James Keys Wilson under the direction of Isaac Wise, rabbi of the temple. It is of orange-red brick and trimmed with light gray sandstone and is in pseudo-Moorish style, with two minaretlike spires protruding from the roof at each side. An interesting mixture of Gothic and Moorish detail, the building seats approximately 1000 people. It is now used only on Jewish high holy days. It is famous as the center of the Reform Jewish Movement, which was lead by Rabbi Wise in the 1870s.

**PENNSYLVANIA ACADEMY OF FINE ARTS, Broad and Cherry Streets, Philadelphia, (Figure 3.4), 1871–1876, was designed by Frank Furness and is an excellent example of his style. Although it has Gothic overtones, its brownstone facade trimmed with light-colored sandstone and colored marble, as well as an exuberant cornice treatment, make it impossible to classify as other than industrial Romantic. Spots of sculpture in panels of marble are offset by cornice and roofridge crestings of pressed sheet iron. Certainly the exterior design is very original. The interiors are likewise interesting and serve their purposes exceedingly well.

ENTRANCE PAVILIONS, Zoological Gardens, Philadelphia, 1873–1875, by Frank Furness, were designed as twin gatekeeper lodges on each side of a pair of beautiful ornamental wrought iron gates. The houses of stone in three wide, contrasting-colored bands, have filagreed porches plus cornices and gables that enhance the steep roofs of polychrome slate.

Figure 3.4 Pennsylvania Academy of Fine Arts, Philadelphia, Pennsylvania, 1871–1876; Frank Furness, Architect; Industrial Romantic style. Photograph by City of Philadelphia Municipal Services Department.

*HORTICULTURAL HALL, Centennial Exposition, Philadelphia (Figure 3.5), 1876, was designed by Herman J. Schwarzmann, a little-known landscape designer of the time. A large greenhouselike structure of iron, glass, and colored brick, it had exterior walls of masonry in Saracenic style. It was the last large building that remained of the Centennial Exposition, and for almost 80 years it was one of the showplaces in Fairmont Park. The interior was particularly beautiful, with light iron members, great chandeliers, and magnificent tropical plants and flowers. It was torn down in 1955 after being damaged by a hurricane, even though it was not beyond repair.

PROVIDENT LIFE AND TRUST COMPANY, Philadelphia, 1879, by Frank Furness, is a small, two-storied office building showing similarity

Figure 3.5 Horticultural Hall, Centennial Exposition, Philadelphia, Pennsylvania, 1876; Herman J. Schwarzmann, Architect; Industrial Romantic style. Photograph by City of Philadelphia Municipal Services Department.

in style to the Fine Arts Academy. It is almost ponderous in scale but exemplifies the originality and masculinity of the designer. It has guts!

The Stick Style

This was a wood frame style that exposed the framing of the building in an attempt to make it part of the aesthetic design. It was an attempt to be rustic and is somewhat suggestive of medieval half-timbering. Vincent Scully, Jr., in his book *Modern Architecture,* calls it "Romantic Naturalism—a movement which started about 1840, and went through several phases down to the present time." It was not widespread in its use, and there are few examples. The Michigan pavilion at the Philadelphia Centennial was outstanding at the time because it was designed to draw attention to the lumber industry of the state, then at its height. Scully also gives as an example a large house in Middletown, Rhode Island (1872).

MICHIGAN STATE BUILDING, Centennial Exposition, Philadelphia (Figure 3.6), 1876, designed by Julian Hess, was a Stick style residential

Figure 3.6 Michigan State Building, Centennial Exposition, Philadelphia, Pennsylvania, 1876; Julian Hess, Architect; Industrial Romantic style. Photograph furnished by City of Philadelphia Municipal Services Department.

type, entirely of Michigan lumber. It was an excellent example of the style and had a tower flying a flag on top; however it was not beautiful and must have been considered somewhat of an oddity even in that day. After the fair it was sold, dismantled, and moved. The lumber was probably used for other purposes.

In Marshall, Michigan, there is an interesting house that has balustrading of Stick-type design; otherwise the house is an oddity of style and stands alone as an example of the Industrial Romantic Age.

HONOLULU HOUSE, Marshall, Michigan, 1857–1860, was built by the Honorable Abner Pratt, who had been Minister to the Hawaiian Islands under President Buchanan. The house, designed by Mr. Pratt, was inspired by his former home in Hawaii. This square-planned, wooden home is painted white and has a large, open, terracelike veranda all around it. The veranda is set about 4 feet above the ground, as is the first floor, and has balustrading of Stick-type detail.

Mr. Pratt was a distinguished lawyer in his day and later became Supreme Court Justice of Michigan. The house is now owned by the Historical Society of Marshall and is open to the public as a museum.

Pressed Sheet Iron

Besides the scroll saw and the turning lathe, which could do such wonderful things with wood, there was now pressed sheet metal, which could be painted to look like carved stone, cast bronze, or cast plaster. Pressed panels 18 by 18 inches were used on the ceilings of public buildings and retail stores; such ceilings were not only decorative, but also fire retardant. Moreover pressed sheet iron was very intriguing for use as an imitative sculptural material. Many a sumptuous courthouse or city hall in the Midwest and West had a dome or tower having sheet metal decorations and a topping of Justice or Liberty in pressed sheet iron painted to look like stone or bronze. The author remembers one such sheet metal figure of Justice atop a Midwestern courthouse. First she lost her scales of justice to rust, then her arms—poor thing—and was only removed by the authorities when her head tipped forward.[1] Harvard Yard also used to have a seated figure of **Benjamin Franklin,** which finally rusted out and had to be removed.

OCTAGONAL DOME, Irving, New York, 1860, as the name implies, is an octagonal, dome-shaped house. It has a filagreed veranda surrounding it on all sides and builds up to a third story at the base of the dome, which has a lookout cupola at the very top.

---

[1] This figure of Justice stood on the roof of the old Washtenaw County Court House, Ann Arbor, Michigan. The statue was removed about 1950, and the building was demolished in 1954 to make way for a new courthouse building.

The Ultimate in Gingerbread Ornament

Houses inspired by the Mississippi steamboats, which had overly rich ornament, are to be seen here and there along the levees of the great river.

*STEAMBOAT HOUSE, Sam Houston Memorial Park, Huntsville, Texas, 1858. As the name implies, this house was built by Sam Houston in the style of a Mississippi steamboat. It was the second house that he built and is across the street from the first house (1847), which is much larger. Huntsville, a suburb of Houston, was a major stagecoach stop in eastern Texas before the Civil War. In these early days it was noted for its taverns and hospitality. In addition to these two residences, the Memorial Park contains Houston's law office and the Sam Houston Museum, with memorabilia of his life from the Texas Revolutionary War period.

WEDDING CAKE HOUSE, Kennebunk, Maine, ca. 1865, is a four-square house built by a sea captain who made his home fashionable by adding a profusion of scroll-sawed pseudo-Gothic ornament all around. The house is of wood, painted yellow with white-painted trimming, its ornamentlike festooning does make it suggestive of a decorated wedding cake.

Mid-Victorian Theaters

**GRAND OPERA HOUSE, Wilmington, Delaware (Figure 3.7), 1871, was designed by Thomas Dixon and Charles L. Carson. Now being restored at a cost of $3,800,000 by private subscription, it will be reopened as the *Delaware Center of the Performing Arts.* It has become a statewide as well as a regional enterprise involving nearby Pennsylvania areas. It will be the home of the Delaware Symphony Orchestra and the Wilmington Opera Society.

The front, which is 100 feet in height, is divided into five bays, all of classic-styled French Second Empire executed in cast iron. It has three stories and a fourth floor that is a mansard attic in slate. It is undoubtedly the handsomest cast iron building on the eastern seaboard.

Figure 3.7 Grand Opera House, Wilmington, Delaware, 1871; Thomas Dixon and Charles L. Carson, Architects; Eclectic, French Second Empire style (Cast Iron). Photograph by Tom Sherman.

The building was originally built by the Masonic Lodge as a commercial enterprise and cast iron detail contains a number of Masonic symbols. The entire building is being renovated, and modern hallways, offices, and toiletrooms are being inserted. A new and enlarged lobby, new lighting, heating, and air conditioning are being installed. The lounge and dressing rooms are also being brought up to date.

Most attention, however, is being paid to restoring the 1200-seat auditorium, which will have a renewed interior with restored frescoed ceiling, new sidewall decorations, and a rearrangement and reduction in the number of box stalls. There will be new seats, reproductions of the original gaslight fixtures, and of course, new heating and air conditioning for the auditorium apart from the rest of the building.

The building is listed in the National Register of Historic Buildings. (See National Trust for Historic Preservation publication, *Preservation News*, April 1975).

*TIBBITS OPERA HOUSE, Coldwater, Michigan (Figure 3.8), 1882, typical example of the theater of the period, had a facade of red brick trimmed in sandstone. Balconies and cornices of pressed sheet metal in very intricate designs were painted, of course, to match the stone trim. Even the square dome that topped the center bay of the facade was of pressed metal and purely ornamental; it merely sat on the roof and had no relation to the interior.

Originally this theater billed the one-night-stand traveling companies of the period. After the advent of the cinema it was remodeled into a motion-picture theater, and the entire front was shaved off and covered with enameled iron. Since 1965, however, the interior of this theater has been in the process of being restored to its original design. The backstage has been entirely modernized and the interior decorated in original Victorian manner. Completely air-conditioned, it now books plays, concerts, and ballets from nearby large cities and universities, as well as performances by its own company of players. It is subsidized by local citizens.

Although the porcelain-enameled sheeting over the exterior has been removed, restoration of the gay facade is not being attempted. Its present exterior is of a tan, nondescript brick that is less than satisfactory.

FORD THEATER, Tenth Street between E and F Streets, Washington, D.C., ca. 1850, is where Abraham Lincoln was shot on the night of

Figure 3.8 Tibbits Opera House, Coldwater, Michigan, 1882; Architect unknown; Industrial Romantic style. Photograph courtesy of the Library of Coldwater.

April 14, 1865. It has recently been restored to its original appearance. Located on a commercial street and squeezed between commercial buildings, the exterior is not prepossessing; however the interior is of the usual horseshoe type, having a wide proscenium arch with boxes on each side.

OPERA HOUSE, Central City, Colorado, 1885, is an example of a late nineteenth century theater. It was built during the rich silver-mining days of Colorado, when culture was being spread from Maine to California, and Central City was not to be left out. This old mining town, which retains overtones of a boom town, is now a summer tourist attraction, and its summer theater presents famous guest stars on the boards. The Teller Hotel and its typical western saloon are famous for its "Face on the Bar Room Floor."

Summer Hotels and Spas

GRAND HOTEL, Saratoga Springs, New York, 1873, and the **UNITED STATES HOTEL,** Saratoga Springs, New York, 1882, were among the more elegant hotels of their day. Here Victorian society from New York City and as far west as Chicago used to congregate to "take the baths," watch and bet on the horses at the racetrack, gamble at cards, and dance. Both hotels advertized magnificent lobbies and ballrooms with crystal chandeliers, elegant dining rooms, and several bath and toilet rooms on each floor. Both hotels claimed to have the longest veranda, and each was filagreed with scroll-sawed ornament. It seems a pity that these grand old hostelries have been demolished, for in their time they were patronized by the Vanderbilts, the Goulds, and great opera stars, as well as by an occasional fortune-hunting nobleman from Europe. Although Saratoga Springs was never quite in the class of Europe's Baden-Baden, it tried.

TAMPA BAY HOTEL (now owned by the University of Tampa), Tampa, Florida, ca. 1880, was originally a lush hotel that is now serving as a university building. It has a great deal of Moorish detail and also boasts a long veranda of filagreed scroll-sawed ornament.

*GRAND HOTEL, Mackinac Island, Michigan, 1888–1890, is one of the few summer hostelries of this period that is still operating. It boasts the longest veranda in the world, which is probably true since most others have been destroyed. This very popular vacation spot caters to the many conventions that mix business with pleasure. The historical island, which has much to offer in the line of sight-seeing, has an ordinance prohibiting motor-driven vehicles on the island. Horse-drawn vehicles, riding horses, and bicycles can be rented.

Religious Buildings

This period saw the development of a new auditorium type of plan for churches as opposed to the straight-nave types of earlier days. Although Gothic and Colonial designs continued to be used, the fan-shaped auditorium having a sloping floor became popular, particularly for non-liturgical denominations such as Methodist, Congregational, and Presbyterian. The exteriors were freely designed, many of red brick with gray stone trim, some with pseudo-Gothic windows, and some suggestive of the Romanesque style through the use of towers offset from the main facade. Few used gingerbread ornament, although many had an industrialized appearance. Most of their interiors were finished with golden oak woodwork having a high-gloss varnish.

Mormon temple architecture may be introduced here as it was during this period that two of the greater ones were built. They are not Industrial Romantic in style and do not use gingerbread detail. These temples, built by hand by the Mormon followers, were designed and supervised by Brigham Young, the great Mormon leader.

*GREAT MORMON TEMPLE, Salt Lake City, Utah, 1847–1887, took 40 years to build. Fabricated of local white granite, it has six spires and buttresses that are remindful of Gothic. The temple is a mixture of round and pointed arches and has mansardlike cupolas and dormers. Revered by the Mormons as a very holy place, it is open only to professing Mormons of good standing.

THE MORMON TEMPLE OF MANTI, Utah, 1877–1888, like the Great Temple in Salt Lake City, has Gothic overtones. It is generally conceded to be of better design than the Great Temple, though it does not have the prestige of the mother temple.

PHASE 2. ECLECTICISM—BATTLE OF THE
HISTORICAL STYLES, 1860–1930

Although the United States grew to colossal size and strength during this period and became quite self-assertive politically, financially, and industrially, in cultural matters it continued to follow and imitate Europe. The socially registered society of the larger cities thought in terms of nobility and tried to copy the manners of the European courts. They lived in a make-believe age of grand monarchs and occupied sumptuous palaces in the style of Francis I or Louis XIV. Neither Marie Theresa of Austria nor the Medicis of Florence had it any better. The Vanderbilts led the parade in New York City, but others followed until Fifth Avenue from 45th Street to Central Park became almost solidly lined with classic palaces. The summer colony at Newport, Rhode Island, was one of grandeur and affluence.

Italian villas were built in Grosse Pointe, on the shores of Lake St. Clair; on Lake Michigan, along the shore north of Chicago; on Lake-of-the-Isles Boulevard, in Minneapolis, Minnesota; and elsewhere. The Potter Palmer family of Chicago built a medieval castle on North Michigan Avenue, and several French and Italian palaces were erected on Prairie Avenue on the south side of the city. Most middle class and laborer's dwellings were built without any particular style, or if owned by a sophisticated person, were in pseudo-Romanesque, Gothic, or watered-down Colonial. During the winter season some of the wealthy families went to Florida or to the French Riviera, but from October to the Lenten season, most of them stayed at home to participate in the social season, with its balls, dinners, theater, opera, and concerts.

Commercial buildings were generally built in one of the historical styles. Railway stations might be designed as great Roman basilicas or as the tepidarium of a great Roman bath, as was the now-demolished concourse of the Pennsylvania Station in New York City. Banks, following the lead of the Bank of England in London, were Roman in style. Even New York City skyscrapers used adaptations of classic Roman, Baroque, or Gothic styling with more or less success. Most of the departmental building in the national capital were Roman classic, and most state capitals followed this pattern. Churches were often Gothic or Romanesque, occasionally classic or Georgian.

Architectural styling moved in waves. During the first 20 years (1860–1880) the popular eclectic style was *Second Empire,* from France, which was contemporary with the popular reign of Napolean III until his downfall in 1870. America had the Italianate style, the General Grant style, and later a mansard-roofed style called Queen Anne. Then (1875–1895) popularity swung to Romanesque as introduced by Henry Hobson Richardson. This style, which became known as the Richardsonian style, was very strong and had marked individual character. Contemporary with it was the *Shingle style,* which was an adaptation of the stone-masonried Romanesque to wood frame construction using stained shingles as the exterior material. Throughout this period there coexisted a rather free interpretation of *Gothic Revivalism,* given the name of Victorian Gothic (1860–1890), and this was followed by a very eclectic, archaeological plagiarism of Gothic, particularly for churches, which lasted from 1890 to 1930. Leaders in this Gothic styling were Ralph Adams Cram and Bertram Goodhue.

About 1890 the Francis I style of France was introduced to the Vanderbilt family of New York City by their architect, Richard M. Hunt, and this style was used by high society throughout the United States. However it lasted only about five years and was supplanted after the Chicago World's Fair in 1893 by an outburst of Classic Eclecticism that ran the gamut of all of the classic and monarchial styles—from *Roman* to *Italian, Spanish, French,* and *English Georgian. Baroque* became very popular for theaters, and even Moorish was tried, along with ancient *Egyptian, Japanese,* and *Hindu.* This showed the architects' erudition and the clients' sophistication. It was truly a battle of styles, and it lasted through World War I to 1930, until it could no longer be afforded owing to the Great Depression, which started with the stock market crash in October, 1929, and lasted to 1937. By that time Eclecticism was pretty well dead.

The Second Empire Style, 1860–1880

This style from France became popular because of Napoleon III and his beautiful queen, Eugénie. Paris was the fashion capitol of the world, and nothing was more French than the style of the Louvre, which had recently been added to by Napoleon III.

OLD CITY HALL, Boston, Massachusetts (Figure 3.9), 1862–1865, by G. J. F. Bryant and Arthur D. Gilman, is a compactly planned building of masonry having a carved stone facade. Each exterior story is a series of arches framed by the classic orders, and the building is capped by a

Figure 3.9 Old City Hall, Boston, Massachusetts, 1862–1865; G. J. F. Bryant and Arthur D. Gilman, Architects; French Second Empire style. Photograph by Ralph W. Hammett.

mansard roof having French dormers. A central portion is one story higher. Hitchcock, in his book *Architecture, Nineteenth and Twentieth Centuries,* says that this building more than any other set off a nation-wide program of public buildings in the Second Empire style. At that time and continuing for a score of years, Boston was the artistic as well as the intellectual center of the country in succession to Philadelphia and prior to New York.

Since the new Boston City Hall has been built, this building has been renovated and continues to be used for government offices.

CITY HALL, Baltimore, Maryland, 1867–1875, was designed by George A. Frederick in the Second Empire style. This iron-structured building has outer walls and detail in masonry and is faced with white marble. It has high mansard roofs and a Baroque dome of cast iron. It was completely renovated in 1967.

OLD MAIN HALL, Vassar College, Poughkeepsie, New York, 1860–1862, by James Renwick, is a large U-shaped buildisg of elaborately pavilioned composition crowned by high mansard roofs of varying heights. The donor, Matthew Vassar, insisted that the style follow that of the Tuileries in Paris.

OLD STATE, WAR AND NAVY BUILDING (Executive Office Annex), Pennsylvania Avenue and 17th Street, N.W., Washington, D.C., 1871–1875, was designed by Arthur D. Gilman in association with Arthur B. Mullet, who was the architect in charge. It is a large, four-storied building on a high base and, like the City Hall of Boston by the same designer, is of gray granite. It is topped by mansard roofs with dormers, and though well proportioned and grand, it is a cold gray building, quite out of character with most of Washington, particularly the White House, which adjoins it.

*MICHIGAN STATE CAPITOL BUILDING, Lansing, Michigan, 1872–1879, was designed by Elijah E. Myers winner of a national competition. The architect was originally from Springfield, Illinois, but moved his offices to Detroit after winning the commission. The plan is remindful of that of the Capitol in Washington. It too has a high central dome, but there the comparison stops. The dome is slender and almost pointed. The buff sandstone exterior is in the pavilioned style of the Second Empire, although without the usual mansard roofs.

The interiors are rich with heavy walnut and marble details of the period. These should be cleaned and restored. The rotunda has fine allegorical paintings that should be preserved. Generally the building has not been greatly altered since it was built except for the addition of plumbing, electric lighting, and relatively new heating. The original building was lighted by gas, and many of the old fixtures remain in place.

Now the building has become so crowded and obsolete that something will have to be done. It is hoped that like the City Halls of Boston and Philadelphia, it will be restored and modernized for executive and legislative usage. Separate buildings can be constructed for legislative offices, as was done in Washington, D.C., so that this landmark can be preserved.

CITY HALL, Broad and Market Streets, Philadelphia, Pennsylvania (Figure 3.10), 1874–1890, designed by John McArthur, Jr., is a large and beautiful complex surrounding several courtyards and designed in a very well-done Louvre-like style. It is truly Second Empire in style and magnificent in scale. The building has recently (1959–1964) been repaired, refurbished, and completely cleaned at great expense. The exterior detail is fascinating in its variety, and some of the offices are lavishly ornate in Neobaroque style. Several grand staircases are elaborately done. The main feature of the building is a 500 foot tower topped by a 37 foot high statue of William Penn, done in 1894 by Alex M. Calder. A *tour de force* in concept as well as in style, this tower is a distinguishing landmark of the city, and its importance saved the building from destruction a few years ago.

At that time there was a movement by some well-meaning but misguided politicians to have the entire complex torn down and replaced by an "efficient steel and glass office building." How lucky for posterity that money was spent to renovate rather than to destroy and replace!

Many residences were built in the Queen Anne style during this lush period. Many courthouses and other public buildings were built throughout the country, but most of these have been torn down to make way for commercial expansion or more modern structures. Most of the remaining residences are now cheap rooming houses or offices in border areas awaiting urban renewal. Many hotels of the period adapted the Queen Anne and Second Empire styles, and the cast iron commercial buildings of the era were often travesties of the mode.

The Romanesque Revival Style, 1875–1895

This was also known by the name of the architect who introduced it, H. H. Richardson a famous Boston architect, scion of a wealthy Louisiana family, and Harvard graduate; also with a diploma from the École des Beaux Arts of Paris. He imported the style from the Auvergne region of France after winning a competition (1871) for Trinity Episcopal Church of Boston. The style became popular almost immediately and was adapted to all manner of buildings from churches to public buildings and even to opulent residences. It supplanted the Second Em-

Figure 3.10 City Hall, Philadelphia, Pennsylvania, 1874–1890; John McArthur, Jr., Architect; French Second Empire style. Photograph by City of Philadelphia.

pire style almost overnight. A massive, rough, brownstone style, it was handled with great strength and masculinity by Richardson, the master. Henry Hobson Richardson, born in 1836, died at the height of his fame in 1886.

**TRINITY CHURCH, Copley Square, Boston (Figure 3.11), 1873–1877, by H. H. Richardson, is often called his masterpiece. The plan is a Greek across with a great central tower over the crossing and a large semicircular apse for the chancel. The tower is suggestive of the old Cathedral of Salamanca, Spain, though bolder and heavier, and the front porch, which was added later by Shepley, Rutan and Coolidge, successors to Richardson's practice, is Provincial Romanesque of an archaeological correctness. The interior, though pseudo-Romanesque in form, was alive with color from the painted and stained glass by Burne-Jones and John LaFarge. Wall decorations and murals were also by LaFarge. The present chancel decorations, by Charles D. McGinnis, were done in the present century. However the entire interior has unity and looks as if it could have been done at one time under Richardson. The entire building shows the strength of the man.

WINN MEMORIAL LIBRARY, Woburn, Massachusetts, 1877–1878, by H. H. Richardson, was the first of a series of Romanesque-styled adaptations to small city library design. *Ames Memorial Library, North Easton, Massachusetts,* 1878–1879, and the *Crane Memorial Library, Quincy, Massachusetts,* 1880–1883, are other famous members of the series. The asymmetrical planning is very well worked out to satisfy function, and the great arched entrances and ribbon windows of the stack wings are beautifully integrated. The Crane Memorial Library introduced eyebrow windows on the roof, a clever design device that was strictly Richardsonian. Similar libraries were executed at Malden, Massachusetts, and Burlington, Vermont.

SEVER HALL, Harvard University, Cambridge, Massachusetts, 1878–1880, by H. H. Richardson, is a slight departure from his heavy Romanesque styling. Although this red-brick classroom building uses large squat arches of Romanesque inspiration, it somehow has a different character. Hitchcock calls these arches Syrian, and well they may be, for Syrian Early Christian architecture has strong similarities to the Romanesque

Figure 3.11 Trinity Church, Copley Square, Boston, Massachusetts, 1873–1877; H. H. Richardson, Architect; Romanesque Revival style. Photograph by Fay Photo Service, Boston.

of the West. The sweeping roof of this building is covered with red tile, which is another departure; usually Richardson's roofs were of slate.

THE LAW SCHOOL, Harvard, Cambridge, Massachusetts, 1881–1883, also by H. H. Richardson, is another of his freestyle Romanesque designs in rough brownstone.

**ALLEGHENY COUNTY COURT HOUSE AND JAIL, Pittsburgh, Pennsylvania, (Figure 3.12), 1884–1890, designed by H. H. Richardson and finished by Shepley, Rutan and Coolidge, is the largest building of his career. The courthouse is a vast rectangular building connected with the jail to the rear by an overstreet stone-enclosed bridge. The whole is dominated by a tall tower rising from the front of the courthouse. Built entirely of rough coursed granite, it is a masterpiece of masonry crafts-manship. It is a magnificent building, and though threatened with demolition a few years ago, has survived and has now been thoroughly renovated.

This building was the model for many public buildings of the next decade. Among these are the old *Post Office, Washington, D.C.,* 1899, by W. Edbrooke, and the *City Hall, Minneapolis, Minnesota,* 1887, by Long and Kees of that city. Architects throughout the country adopted the style, and until 1900 many public buildings, churches, and even resi-dences were built in Richardsonian Romanesque style.

*MARSHALL FIELD WHOLESALE STORE AND WAREHOUSE, Chicago, 1885–1887, by H. H. Richardson, was destroyed in the early 1920s for the necessary construction of a two-level boulevard and street widening at the edge of the Chicago River. It is included here because of its influence at the time. It was another rugged masonry composition of red granite. One of the finest landmarks of the city, it was a huge rectangle of eight stories with a subtle composition of arches. Cast iron columns and steel beams were used for the framing of the interior.

FIRST METHODIST CHURCH, Baltimore, Maryland, 1880–1882, by McKim, Mead and White, is an outstanding example of Richardson Romanesque in brownstone. This masterpiece shows the power and taste of its designer, Stanford White, who was an apprentice of Richardson

Figure 3.12 Allegheny County Court House, Pittsburgh, Pennsylvania, 1884–1890; H. H. Richardson, Architect; Romanesque Revival style. Photograph by Division of Photography, Allegheny County.

prior to the formation of his firm of later fame. One of many churches by various architects that were done in this decade, this one has a heavy multistoried tower topped by a simple shingle conelike spire. The oval nave, approximately 70 by 80 feet, is more like an auditorium than the traditional navelike church. It has individual seats instead of pews and a slanting floor. It is one of the first of the auditorium-type sanctuaries that became so very popular with Protestant churches, particularly Methodists, in the next three decades.

*GLESSNER RESIDENCE, South Prairie Avenue, Chicago, Illinois, 1885–1887, by H. H. Richardson, is a one-storied masonry house. Occupying half a block on 18th Street, from the outside it appears as impregnable as a prison. On the interior, however, it has a flowing plan opening onto two sides of an interior court and carriage yard. It is very charming and in line with a free style of residence planning that was beginning at this time. It is interesting to compare this plan with those of houses by Philip Webb in England at this period, the Babson Residence, River Forest, Illinois, 1907, by Louis Sullivan; and the Avery Coonley House, also in River Forest, 1908, by Frank Lloyd Wright. The question immediately arises whether Richardson influenced these architects, particularly in house planning for contemporary living, or whether these designs grew out of new needs in planning. Certainly Webb in England was not influenced by Richardson, though Sullivan and Wright might have been.

The Shingle Style, 1880–1890

Richardsonian styling in wood shingles instead of brownstone, became popular and is recognized as a style in its own right.

STOUGHTON HOUSE, Brattle Street, Cambridge Massachusetts, 1882, by H. H. Richardson, was one of the first of this style, although the firm of McKim, Mead and White of New York, an offshoot of Richardson's office, was already developing and building houses in this mode.

*H. VICTOR NEWTON HOUSE, Elberson, New Jersey, 1880–1881, by McKim, Mead and White, an excellent example of this style, is particularly noted for its spacious living room with beamed ceiling and wood paneling. It is also noted for its free planning, which allows easy flow through the rooms.

Other examples of the style by McKim, Mead and White are the *Isaac Bell, Jr., House, Newport, Rhode Island,* 1881–1882; the *Cyrus McCormack House, Richfield Springs, New York*; and the **W. G. Low House, Bristol, Rhode Island,* 1887. The last mentioned might be considered the masterpiece of the group. Although there were others from coast to coast by many architects, the style, with its free flow both in exterior design and in functional planning, was short-lived and was eclipsed, even by McKim, Mead and White, its innovators, by Beaux Arts influence and classical eclectic styling. Classical axial planning took precedence from about 1890 onward, even where eclectic Gothic was being used.

The Mid-Victorian Gothic Style, 1860–1890

Gothic was one of the popular styles throughout this period, but it can be divided into *Mid-Victorian Gothic* (1860–1890) and *Gothic Eclecticism* (1890–1930). Mid-Victorian Gothic followed the Gothic Revival of the period before 1860; there was no appreciable difference except that Gothic Revival before 1860 was purer in style, and that Mid-Victorian Gothic used mixed materials such as a predominance of red brick or brown sandstone for the body of the building, often trimmed with white or light gray stone and having a patterned roof of different-colored slate. Both were motivated by the same Romantic philosophy, and both had details based on Augustus Welby Pugin books. Most of the Victorian Gothic had its roots in England, where G. G. Scott, William Sutterfield, G. E. Street, and William Burgess were among the leaders of the style. However there was much copying of detail and designs from neighboring churches, and although the detail might or might not be quite correct, the overall designs were often thin and lacking in eclectic correctness. In fact, some Romantic Gothic is so unsophisticated that it can be better classified under Industrialized Romantic, also known as the Jigsaw, or Gingerbread, style. Books by Andrew J. Downing, an American, popularized the style for small houses and even showed plans and elevation drawings.

*WATER TOWER, Chicago, Illinois (Figure 3.13), 1869, designed by W. W. Boyington, architect, stands on North Michigan Avenue and is

Figure 3.13 Chicago Water Tower, Chicago, Illinois, 1869; W. W. Boyington, Architect; Mid-Victorian Gothic style. Photograph taken in 1891; furnished by Chicago Historical Society.

now somewhat dwarfed by nearby skyscrapers. Nevertheless it is one of the best-known landmarks in Chicago. It is about 50 feet square at the base, and the central tower encloses a standpipe. It houses the engines and pumps of Chicago's early water system north of the river and served well during the great Chicago Fire of 1871. It has been ridiculed for its lack of Gothic purity and smallness in scale; however it attracts thousands of sightseers every year.

UNITY CHURCH, Springfield, Massachusetts, 1866–1868, by H. H. Richardson, was his first major project after his return to America from the École des Beaux Arts in Paris. It is distinctly Victorian Gothic, though it has a robust character through the use of random rock-faced brownstone. The carved detail, however, is Puginesque.

*GRACE EPISCOPAL CHURCH, Medford, Massachusetts, 1867–1868, by H. H. Richardson, is very massive in character and has a beautiful asymmetrical composition. It is quite original in the design of the steeple tower, which was done in heavy rock-faced granite. Although this church is distinctly Gothic in spirit, the character of Richardson had begun to assert itself when this church was designed. It shows how easy it was for Richardson to adapt to the heavy Romanesque style and also how easy it was for the public to accept it.

*ST. ANDREW'S EPISCOPAL CHURCH, Ann Arbor, Michigan, (Figure 3.14), 1867–1868, was designed by Gordon W. Lloyd, who was originally from England but later had offices in Detroit. The church has an English-like tower that was added in 1880 and several interior renovations of later dates. It is an excellent example of an English parish church in Early English style with Victorial clichés here and there. The roof has zigzag patterns of variegated slate. The building is of native, rough dressed fieldstone with gray sandstone trim. The nave interior is particularly charming although the narthex is drab and inadequate in size.

*LUTHER PLACE MEMORIAL CHURCH, Thomas Circle, Washington, D.C., 1868–1870, was designed by Judson York as a memorial of thanksgiving for the end of the Civil War and the preservation of the

Figure 3.14 St. Andrew's Episcopal Church, Ann Arbor, Michigan, 1867–1868; Gordon W. Lloyd, Architect; Mid-Victorian Gothic style. Photograph by Eck Stanger. Ann Arbor.

Union. It stands at the apex of two streets and has a statute of Martin Luther in front. The church, which is German Gothic in character was built by the Lutherans of the United States as their national shrine. It is in red sandstone and has a large, high octagonal spire at the front.

MT. VERNON PLACE METHODIST CHURCH, Baltimore, Maryland, 1870–1872, by Thomas Dixon, is a typical example of Victorian Gothic in its attempt to use stone of various colors. The building is of a yellowish stone quarried nearby and trimmed with dark reddish sandstone. The color is quite unusual, and the composition has been studied for its asymmetrical and romantic effect. It is quite attractive.

Most cities throughout the country have one or two of these Mid-Victorian Gothic churches in or near their old downtown districts. Most were designed by local architect-builders using handbooks. They were usually of brownstone, rock-faced granite, or brick trimmed with carved light gray sandstone. Sometimes these churches were of wood. They often had cast iron crestings; the interiors were usually drab and had wooden trusses so thin that it was evident that they were nonfunctional appendages. They all had pointed windows, most of which were filled with leaded stained glass ranging from Gothic-like abstract designs to Renaissance-like paintings of saccharine-sweet passion. These churches are all interesting when looked upon in the light of the lives of the parishioners who built them.

*MEMORIAL HALL, Harvard University, Cambridge, Massachusetts, was designed 1865–1867 and built 1870–1878. The architects were William R. Ware and Henry Van Brunt. This is a memorial to the many Harvard men, from both North and South, who lost their lives in the Civil War. Whether this building should be classified as Victorian Gothic or Industrialized Romanticism is a question that can be argued; however it appears quite Gothic. It is designed like a large church, and what would be the nave portion was originally used as a dining hall. The transepts became the lobby, and the great apse was and still is a concert and assembly hall. The exterior is bright red brick trimmed in light gray stone. Its chief exterior feature is the great central clock tower trimmed with gray stone and cast iron finials and crestings. This tower was partially destroyed by fire a few years ago, and the original roof of the tower has been removed. The roof of the nave and the apse have geometric patterns of multicolored slate and are crested with highly filagreed cast iron. The building is large and bulky; fortunately it is placed in an island formed by streets and is separated from Harvard Yard with its intimate colonial scale.

The interior of the nave is roofed by great hammer-beam trusses of questionable structural stability; however since they are now entering their second century, there is little cause for worry.

It is interesting that the chief architect of this building, William R. Ware, was the founder and first professor of architecture at the first school of architecture in America, at Massachusetts Institute of Technology in 1865. His partner, Henry Van Brunt, became an early disciple of H. H. Richardson and embraced the Romanesque style. Ware, at MIT, immediately became an exponent of the Beaux-Arts tradition of Paris. Perhaps after doing "Old Mem Hall," as it is affectionately called by older Harvard alumni, both Ware and Van Brunt thought it better to abandon the Victorian Gothic style.

TRINITY COLLEGE, Hartford, Connecticut, 1873–1880, was designed by William Burgess, an eminent Gothicist of England. Only part of the Burgess quadrangle was constructed, but there is no doubt that this design had a great deal to do with the adoption of Eclectic Gothic for college architecture in the later three decades of the period. It was imitative of Oxford and Cambridge.

*POTTER PALMER CASTLE, Chicago, Illinois, 1882. This castle, now destroyed, was a veritable stage setting for the Potter Palmers, who were the leaders of Midwest society during the last two decades of the nineteenth century. Built of dark brownstone, it had all of the exterior details and appearances of a medieval castle. During that period the Potter Palmers and the Cyrus McCormicks led the socially ambitious of Chicago.

Needless to say, many Victorian Gothic houses followed the Gothic Revival mode. Many of these were more Romantic than Gothic and have been dealt with under Industrialized Romanticism. Most of these houses were built in the 1880s, within walking distance of the centers of the cities.

The Eclectic Gothic Style, 1890–1930

This was a period of studied eclecticism, a return to the type of styling that was done before 1860 in such churches as St. Patrick's Cathedral, New York City; Trinity Church, New York City; and others. Particular attention must be given to Ralph Adams Cram of the architectural firm of Cram, Goodhue and Ferguson of Boston, Massachusetts. He and his firm did many churches, colleges following the Tudor styles of Oxford and Cambridge, and many grand residences in the style of English manor houses built on country estates near the large cities.

Cram's influence lasted from 1895 until his death in 1942. He was assisted and abetted by his partner, Bertram Grosvenor Goodhue, a clever designer and artist, until the firm was dissolved in 1914 and each went his separate way. Cram was the dedicated Gothicist, the sincere evangelist of the style. Like Pugin a half century before him, he both practiced and wrote about the style. In his books *Church Architecture*, 1901; *The Gothic Quest*, 1907; and *Substance of Gothic*, 1916, he persuasively argued that Gothic is "the perfect union of art, philosophy, and religion." Reading Cram is almost enough to convince one that all classic, Renaissance, and Baroque designs are pagan and that only buildings in the Gothic style are fit for Christian worship.

The following are among the many beautiful Gothic churches by the firm of Cram, Goodhue and Ferguson: *All Saints Church, Brookline, Massachusetts*, 1895; *St. Stephen's, Cohasset, Massachusetts*, 1900; *West Point Military Academy* and **West Point Chapel, West Point on the Hudson, New York*, 1904–1910; *St. Thomas Episcopal Church, New York City*, 1906; *Calvary Church*, 1907; *First Baptist Church, Pittsburgh, Pennsylvania*, 1909; *Euclid Avenue Presbyterian Church, Cleveland, Ohio*, 1911; *Fourth Presbyterian Church, Chicago, Illinois*, 1912; and *Hope Presbyterian Church, Summit Avenue, St. Paul, Minnesota*, 1912. These and others are masterpieces that are quite characteristic of the Gothic severity of Cram combined with the artistic excellence of Goodhue.

World War I intervened after the firm of Cram, Goodhue and Ferguson was dissolved in 1914 to become Cram and Ferguson of Boston, and Bertram Grosvenor Goodhue of New York. Wars are almost always hiatus periods, and World War I was no exception. Cram spent most of his later years designing and redesigning the great Episcopal Cathedral Church of St. John the Divine in New York City.

**CATHEDRAL CHURCH OF ST. JOHN THE DIVINE (Episcopal), Morningside Heights, New York City (Figures 3.15 and 3.16), 1892–

Figure 3.15 Cathedral Church of St. John the Divine (Episcopal), New York City, 1892–Present; C. Grant LaFarge, original designer, Byzantine–Romanesque; Ralph Adams Cram, Eclectic Gothic style. Photograph courtesy of the Cathedral Church of St. John the Divine.

present, though still unfinished, was originally designed by C. Grant LaFarge of the firm of Heins and LaFarge. It was to be in twelfth century Romanesque style, after the plan of the great Church of Cluny in France. Work started and the great central dome was built. It was more Byzantine than Romanesque in style, and the detail in the great apse was French Gothic combined with Byzantine Romanesque. This was all prior to 1914. LaFarge was a very clever and good designer, and the several styles were very subtly blended together. However the building was severely criticized by the pseudosophisticated eclecticists—some say subtly led by Cram—until finally Heins and LaFarge were dismissed and Ralph Adams Cram was hired to restudy and redesign the building.

Now the structure which is three-quarters finished, is an enormous five-aisled Gothic cathedral, 601 feet long, 146 feet wide, and having nave vaults 85 feet high. In area of ground covered it is next to St. Peter's in Rome, and is the largest Gothic Cathedral in the world.[2] It is reported

[2] This claim is challenged by the Cathedral of Seville, Spain.

Figure 3.16 Interior view toward the altar, Cathedral Church of St. John the Divine, New York City, 1892–Present; C. Grant LaFarge, original designer, Byzantine–Romanesque style; Ralph Adams Cram, Eclectic Gothic style. Photograph by A. Hansen, Photography, New York; courtesy of the Cathedral Church of St. John the Divine.

to seat 40,000 people; however only some of them can hear the service except by loud speakers, and more than half cannot possibly see the altar.

The church is English Gothic in general concept although the west front is French in composition. It has a great rose window and two western towers that are projected to be 265 feet high. There is also to be a great central tower, 420 feet high. However all three towers have remained unfinished since all work was stopped in 1941.

St. Vincent Ferrier, New York City, 1914–1916; the ***Rockefeller Memorial Chapel, University of Chicago,* 1916–1928; and *Christ Church, Cranbrook, Bloomfield Hills (Detroit), Michigan,* 1920, all by Goodhue, are examples of Eclectic Gothic done after his break with Cram in 1914. After Goodhue died in 1924, his work was carried on for several years by former assistants.

**CATHEDRAL CHURCH OF ST. PETER AND ST. PAUL (Washington Cathedral—Episcopal), Wisconsin and Massachusetts Avenues, N.W., Washington, D.C., which was started in 1907 and is still unfinished, is in English Decorated style. It was originally designed by Henry Vaughn of Boston in association with George Bodley of London, and they remained the architects in charge until 1917. Since then Frohman, Robb and Little of Boston, Massachusetts, have been in charge of the work. The apse, transepts, central tower, and two bays of the nave are finished, and construction is continuing while the finished parts are used for worship. When completed it will compare to St. John the Divine in size and will be more uniform in design. It is being built according to medieval structural principles, although it will have radiant heating in the stone floors and, of course, modern plumbing. Woodrow Wilson and Admiral Dewey, hero of the Spanish-American War, are buried within this building.

THE METHODIST TEMPLE, Clark and Washington Streets, the Loop, Chicago, Illinois, 1921–1923, designed by Holabird and Roche, is primarily an 18-storied office building topped by a carillon tower and spire. A large church plant occupies several of the lower stories.

*RIVERSIDE CHURCH, West 122nd Street and Riverside Drive, New York City, 1927–1930, by Collens and Pelton, is said to have been inspired by Chartres Cathedral. It is especially noted for its 28-storied tower, which contains offices and church rooms and is topped by the

Laura S. Rockefeller carillon of 72 bells. This church was long famous for its associations with its director, the Reverend Harry Emerson Fosdick, famous Christian leader and social reformer.

Collegiate Gothic (Tudor Eclectic) Style, 1890–1930

Since Academic Eclecticism was fostered by the architectural schools being established in the universities throughout the country, eclectic styling became popular for college buildings. The Tudor Gothic of Oxford and Cambridge in England among the favored styles.

**ROCKEFELLER MEMORIAL CHAPEL (Figure 3.17), 1916–1928, also by Goodhue, is part of the *University of Chicago*, 1910–1916. This university was designed originally by Henry Ives Cobb, and later by

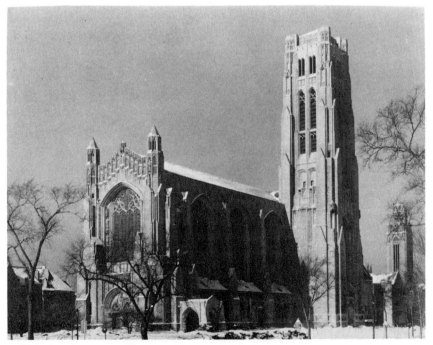

Figure 3.17 Rockefeller Memorial Chapel, University of Chicago, Chicago, Illinois, 1916–1928; Bertram Grosvenor Goodhue, Architect; Eclectic Gothic style. Photograph by Office of Public Information, Chicago University.

Shepley, Rutan and Coolidge. Other important college buildings include the *Graduate School, Princeton, Princeton, New Jersey,* 1910–1913, by Cram and Ferguson, with later buildings by Day and Klauder; the *Harkness Tower and Quadrangle, Yale University,* by James Gamble Rogers; *Duke University, Durham, North Carolina,* 1924–1930, by York and Sawyer; and the Law Quadrangle, University of Michigan, also by York and Sawyer. All of these buildings are beautiful in composition and color, and are a great joy to their respective alumni. They are very photogenic and serve as backgrounds for many reunion pictures. This list includes only the most noted of the style and is by no means complete. Other outstanding examples exist.

The Eclectic Tudor Gothic Style, 1890–1930

English-styled houses of the manor-house type, and even small half-timbered romantic cottages, were common during this period. Some were done in stone, some with fake half-timbering, and many in brick trimmed with stone. Architects became very adept at using new technologies to get Gothic effects. Nevertheless the styling was straight from the Middle Ages.

*FAIRLANE, Henry Ford's Residence, Dearborn, Michigan, 1920, was designed by Ernest Wilby of Albert Kahn, Inc., Architects, of Detroit, is now part of the Dearborn campus of the University of Michigan. A beautiful and typical example of the style, it is situated in a large natural estate, set far back and hidden from the highway. It has comfortable rooms and was once noted for its fine rose garden, greatly prized and tended by Mrs. Ford. A few other grand manor houses were the *Stuart Duncan Residence, Newport, Rhode Island,* by John Russell Pope; the *estate of J. E. Aldred, Glen Cove, Long Island, New York,* by Bertram Goodhue, and the *estate of L. F. Sherman, Lakeville, New York,* by James W. O'Conner. Other splendid ones are scattered throughout the United States near Pittsburgh, Cleveland, Detroit, Chicago, Milwaukee, and points south and west.

Classic Eclecticism, 1890–1930

This fashion began with the Columbian Exposition in Chicago (1893) and led by McKim, Mead and White, Daniel Burnham, Richard M.

Hunt, and others. During this period classical styling of all types was used. The wealthy wished to live like the nobility of Europe and built in the imperial style of ancient Rome; or of the Renaissance of Italy, like the Medicis, Borgias, and Farneses; or of France at the time of its grand monarchs of the Baroque period, Louis XIV, Louis XV, and Louis XVI. The less wealthy but no less sophisticated might satisfy themselves with Georgian Colonial; Spanish or French Colonial if in the Southern States or California; or Swiss or Bavarian in the mountain states or in Maine. Leading the Classic Eclecticism movement were architects who had been schooled in the borrowed traditions of École des Beaux Arts of Paris. There they had been taught the history of architecture as documents of form, proportion, and taste to be memorized for use in their own eclectic architecture. The philosophy of the people who had originally produced these forms and the technology of their times were rarely stressed. In fact, more often than not, the architectural historian himself did not understand these technologies. It was all a matter of outward appearance, of putting a classic facade on a building that was not classic in structure.

This group of architect eclecticists was concentrated in New York, which had become the cultural center of the United States although most of its culture was imported from Europe, not indigenous. Most architectural students did not consider their training complete until they had traveled in Europe and worked in one of the large offices in New York City, preferably McKim, Mead and White. Other offices included Carrère and Hastings, Warren and Wetmore, George B. Post and Sons, Guy Lowell, John Russell Pope, Charles A. Platt, and Cass Gilbert. In Chicago, Graham, Anderson, Probst, and White followed Burnham and Root and the Chicago Fair tradition; in Philadelphia there were Horace Trumbauer, Borie and Zantzinger, and Paul Cret, Professor of Architecture at the University of Pennsylvania. On the West Coast, in San Francisco, were Bakewell and Brown. By the turn of the century every sizable city had architectural practitioners, and all possessed *A History of Architecture on the Comparative Method* by Sir Banister Fletcher, and monographs of the work of McKim, Mead and White. All yearned to show their talents as eclecticists in one or more of the grand styles, including Gothic if they were commissioned to design a church or college building.

This was a very affluent period, one of startling growth in population, wealth, and building construction. It is not possible to list all of the very fine buildings of the time; therefore only the most typical and most renowned are given below, and these are grouped according to type.

Government Buildings

Buildings in the National Capital returned to the classic styles after a brief period of experimentation with Gothic and Romanesque. However only intermittent construction had taken place between 1860 and 1890 because of the Civil War and Reconstruction. Even during that short time a great many bad innovations had taken place. A railroad had been allowed to place its tracks and switchyards in the mall, and rough temporary buildings for freight and military uses had been built there and allowed to remain. By 1895 it was apparent that L'Enfant's plan was being destroyed. The American Institute of Architects stepped in, largely through the efforts of Glenn Brown, its Secretary, and in 1900 the A.I.A. met in convention in Washington. It proposed a planning committee and named D. H. Burnham, Frederick L. Olmstead, Charles F. McKim, and Augustus St. Gaudens to prepare plans and report their recommendations. Senator James McMillan, chairman of the Senate District of Columbia Committee, became greatly interested. The planning committee, whose members were the prime planners of the Chicago Columbian Exposition, made their report in 1902, and McMillan had it adopted by the Congress. It is known as the McMillan plan and has been in effect since that time. This plan reverts to the original L'Enfant plan except for minor revisions, and Classic became the Washington style, remaining in use even as late as 1950.

*LIBRARY OF CONGRESS, First and Independence Avenues, S.E., Washington, D.C. (Figure 3.18), 1887–1897, by Smithmeyer, Pelz, and E. P. Casey, is a classical building having a high basement and a colonnaded pavilion in the center. The building, dominated by a low dome that covers the main reading room, is quite Baroque in character. It is the only building of note to be built in Washington during the late nineteenth century. The interior has grand staircases and hallways, and its public spaces are lined with marble in different colors and elaborate paintings. It houses the largest collection of books in the world, rivaling the Bibliothèque Nationale in Paris and the Library of the British Museum, both of which also claim to be largest.

Other Classic Eclectic buildings in Washington, most of them in white marble and boasting literally miles of classic columns, either freestanding or attached, are the *Pan American Building,* 1900, by Albert Kelsey and Paul Cret, which now houses the Organization of American States; the *Old House of Representatives Building,* 1908, by Carrère and Hastings;

Figure 3.18   Library of Congress, Washington, D.C., 1887–1897; Smithmeyer, Pelz, and E. P. Casey, Architects; Classic Eclectic style. Photograph by Library of Congress.

the *Department of Agriculture,* 1908, by Rankin, Kellog and Crane; *Constitution Hall,* 1930, by John Russell Pope; the *Internal Revenue Building,* 1930, by Louis Simon; the *Department of Commerce,* 1932, by York and Sawyer; the *Department of Justice,* 1934, by Delano and Aldrich; the *Supreme Court Building,* 1936, by Cass Gilbert; the *Department of Labor,* 1935, by Arthur Brown, Jr.; the *Federal Trade Commission,* 1937, by Bennett, Parsons and Frost; and the *National Art Gallery,* 1941, by John Russell Pope. All are beautiful and prodigal buildings that only a rich country like the United States could afford.

STATE CAPITOL BUILDING, Providence, Rhode Island, 1898–1901, by McKim, Mead and White, is in the Early Republican style of the National Capitol building. The entire building, including the dome, is white Georgian marble.

**MINNESOTA STATE CAPITOL, St. Paul, Minnesota (Figure 3.19), 1890–1905, was designed by Cass Gilbert, a native son of Minnesota, though later he moved to New York City. This building also owes a debt to the National Capitol and has better proportions and detail than the Rhode Island state capitol. The exterior is all in white marble, and the general character is French Renaissance; the dome is a distinct copy of St. Peter's in Rome although much smaller in scale. The interiors, done in marble of different colors, are very lavish, and the rotunda and grand stairways are real thrillers. For many years in the 30s and 40s the grand public spaces were used for the annual junior prom of the University of Minnesota. The setting was magnificent, and no building could provide a better backdrop for the formal dress of the young people. The governor and members of the state legislature were always honored guests.

*WISCONSIN STATE CAPITOL, Madison, Wisconsin, 1906–1917, by George B. Post and Sons, is in the Italian Renaissance style. The plan is

Figure 3.19 Minnesota State Capitol, St. Paul, Minnesota, 1890–1905; Cass Gilbert, Architect; Classic Eclectic style. Photograph from collection of Minnesota Historical Society.

very ingenious, having four equal wings radiating from a central rotunda. The entire building is of gray granite and is the only all-granite dome in America. Each wing is fronted by a six-columned Roman temple form using the Corinthian order.

CITY HALL, San Francisco, California, 1915, by Bakewell and Brown, who won a competition for its design, is the largest city hall in America designed in the classic idiom and having a dome. It is another example of the influence of the Capitol in Washington, D.C. Although the exterior is classic in the Federal style, the interior has Baroque detail that is quite ornate.

Since the city hall was built, the city has built a handsome Civic Center that covers several square blocks. The buildings, all in the classic style to complement the city hall, include the *Public Library,* 1907, by George Kelham; the *State Building* and *Civic Auditorium,* 1926, by Arthur Brown, Jr.; the *War Memorial Building,* 1932; and the *Civic Opera House,* 1932, also by Arthur Brown, Jr. The San Francisco Opera, including the building, is the only municipally owned and operated opera in the United States. Although it usually uses local talent, it is very professional.

NEW YORK COUNTY COURT HOUSE, Foley Square, New York City, 1918–1920, by Guy Russell Lowell, is a large, hexagonal, ten-storied building having a grand decastyle Corinthian temple front. This very monumental and stately building has a clever plan all parts radiate from a central rotunda. This can be confusing to the casual visitor, however, as the circumference of the rotunda looks the same in each direction.

WASHINGTON STATE CAPITOL BUILDINGS, Olympia, Washington, 1921–1923, by Wilder and White, consists of a group of buildings surrounding a domical legislative building. Though these buildings are classic, they also possess a contemporary tone. The arrangement is beautifully placed on an acropolislike hill overlooking a lake.

It was at this time that city governments were becoming big businesses, and many municipal buildings were designed more as office buildings than as monuments for public receptions and legislative councils. However the idea of classic monumental building remained strong in peoples' minds, and the designs of some municipal buildings were attempts to combine classic monumentality with business efficiency. Outstanding is the *Municipal Building, New York City,* 1906–1908, by McKim, Mead and White, which has 25 stories topped by a central cupola of 9 stories. This building forms part of the New York City Hall group, which is made up of the old City Hall, the Hall of Records, and this building, all in close proximity.

CITY HALL, Oakland, California, ca. 1915, by Palmer, Hornbostel and Jones, is 16 stories high. The building is pseudoclassic in style but is topped by a Baroque cupola having a crest 366 feet above the sidewalk. It is the tallest building in Oakland.

Religious Buildings

Of the many churches built at this time, most were built in Gothic as the most appropriate style; however the classic styles were also popular, and auditorium styles were also adapted to church usage, particularly for Protestant churches. Of the classic styles, Roman Classic, Baroque, and Georgian with Wren-like spires were popular; Byzantine was modified for Jewish synagogues; and Spanish Renaissance was used in California and the Southern states.

THIRD CHURCH OF CHRIST, Scientist, 585 Park Avenue, New York City, 1920–1923, by Delano and Aldrich, is an example of Roman Classic adaptation, the exterior quite definitely resembles a Roman temple. It is one of the first churches built as an attempt by the Christ Scientists to adopt a style that would differentiate their buildings from the more orthodox churches.

**ST. PAUL'S CATHOLIC CATHEDRAL, St. Paul, Minnesota, 1906–1920, and **Pro-Cathedral,* Minneapolis, Minnesota, 1910–1924, were both designed by E. L. Masqueray, who was brought over from France by the St. Louis Exposition Committee to be in charge of the World's Exposition held in that city in 1904. Both of these edifices are in Baroque style and possess great masonry domes that dominate their neighborhoods. Their interiors also are magnificent in Italian Baroque styling.

ALL SOULS' UNITARIAN CHURCH, 16th Street and Harvard Square, N.W., Washington, D.C., 1924, by Coolidge and Shattuck, is an example of the Georgian style, spire and all, as copied from James Gibbs.

NATIONAL CITY CHRISTIAN CHURCH, 14th Street and Massachusetts Avenue, N.W., Washington, D.C., 1930, by John Russell Pope, is another example of the Georgian style.

CENTRAL UNION CHURCH, Honolulu, Hawaii, 1918, by Cram and Ferguson, is also in a very eclectic Georgian style.

ISAIAH TEMPLE, Lake Shore Drive, Chicago, Illinois, 1922, by Alfred S. Alschuler, is a pleasing example of Near Eastern Byzantine style adapted to a Jewish synagogue.

*ST. VINCENT DE PAUL, Catholic Church, West Adams Boulevard, Los Angeles, California, 1925, by Albert C. Martin, is a good example of Spanish Baroque eclecticism and has a lofty tower and dome. This style was used quite extensively in the West and Southwest because these states were discovered by the Spanish, who built a line of missions stretching from the territory bordering on Mexico northward along the coast of California. Great impetus was given to the style by Bertram G. Goodhue's very successful use of it in the San Diego Exposition of 1915.

Memorials

MEMORIAL ARCH, Washington Square Park, New York City, 1889–1892, was designed by Stanford White of McKim, Mead and White, in commemoration of the adoption of the Constitution of the United States in 1789 and the inauguration of George Washington as first President, which took place in New York City. The arch is a single-arch type in Roman style and resembles the ancient imperial triumphal arches. It stands in Washington Square Park at the lower end of Fifth Avenue. Of white marble, it has sculptured panels pertaining to the life of Washington and a spread eagle on top.

*GRANT'S TOMB, 122nd Street and Riverside Drive, New York City, 1897, by J. H. Duncan, is an ambitious granite and marble monument in Greek detail. It has a high basement about 35 feet square with Doric columns in antis on each side. On top of this is a tholoslike colonnade and a circular pyramidal top. The interior, which is treated much like Napoleon's tomb, is very impressive and contains the sarcophagi of President and Mrs. Ulysses S. Grant.

**LINCOLN MEMORIAL, Washington, D.C. (Figure 3.20), 1920–1922, by Henry Bacon, is placed at the western end of the Mall and counterbalances the Capitol at the eastern end, on the other side of the Washington Monument. Built entirely of white marble, it is Greek in style and has 36 Doric columns around the outside. These columns represent the states of the Union in Lincoln's time. Although a peripteral temple in plan, the monument does not have the usual Greek temple roof but has instead a recessed attic story that shows above the entablature of the colonnade. The building is placed broadside to the Mall so as to effec-

Figure 3.20 Lincoln Memorial, Washington, D.C., 1920–1922; Henry Bacon, Architect; Classic Eclectic, Greek style. Photograph from collection of Ralph W. Hammett.

tively block the view at this point, and is enhanced by an elongated reflecting pool between it and the Washington Monument.

Situated in the center of the interior, facing up the Mall is a seated figure of Lincoln by Daniel Chester French. It is beautifully lighted so that the solemn figure is most effective; even the most callous tourist is awed in the presence of this statue. Interior murals by Jules Guerin highlight significant events in the life of Lincoln.

Surely there is not a more beautiful or fitting Memorial to any man than this noble structure and its sculptured figure. It is appropriate that it is Greek, as this was the favored style during most of Lincoln's lifetime; however it is not a dead eclectic copy. Its nobility transcends its style.

THOMAS JEFFERSON MEMORIAL, Tidal Basin, Washington, D.C., 1943, by John Russell Pope, is a white marble building having a low, rounded dome and a templelike front—sort of a miniature Pantheon. It is beautifully set on the east side of the Tidal Basin, which is surrounded by Japanese flowering cherry trees. Inside, on a pedestal, is a figure of Jefferson. However, although this building is beautifully proportioned and correct in all detail, it seems small in scale and does not in any way possess the grandeur that it should. It does not really do justice to the great statesman and third President of the United States.

Art Galleries

Since this was a period of great affluence and America was of age culturally, there was a rash of art purchases in Europe, and every city of importance built an art gallery and established a school of art. Lectures and musicals were held in these galleries, and traveling exhibits were displayed from coast to coast.

*METROPOLITAN MUSEUM OF ART, New York City (Figure 3.21), was built in 1880 but has several later additions. The original center section was designed by Calvert Vaux and J. Wrey Mould; then it was enlarged by Richard M. Hunt and finally by McKim, Mead and White. The main building, entirely of white marble, is in the classic Italian Renaissance style and is very monumental. It is the largest museum in America, and with its growing acquisitions will probably continue to expand.

Figure 3.21   Metropolitan Museum of Art, entrance to central section, New York City, 1880; Richard M. Hunt, Architect of entrance section; Eclectic, Italian Renaissance style.

THE ART INSTITUTE, Michigan Avenue, Chicago, Illinois, 1890–1892, was originally designed by Shepley, Rutan and Coolidge, but large additions have been added later. The building, originally the Parliament of Religions during the Columbian Exposition, is in Italian Renaissance style. Although the building itself is not too distinguished, it houses the second largest art collection in the United States. It is especially famous for its collection of French Impressionist paintings.

*FIELD MUSEUM OF NATURAL HISTORY, Grant Park, Chicago, Illinois (Figure 3.22), 1894–1900, by Daniel Burnham, is a monumental building with a great Ionic colonnade facing northward over Lake Shore Drive and the Park. It houses a fine collection on the Indians of the Americas and the progress of man from the Stone Age through Egypt, the Middle East, Africa, Asia.

Figure 3.22   Field Museum of Natural History, Grant Park, Chicago, Illinois, 1895–1900; Daniel Burnham, Architect; Eclectic Roman Classic style (Ionic) portal. Photograph from Chicago Historical Society.

*MUSEUM OF FINE ARTS, Huntington Avenue, Boston, Massachusetts, 1895–1900, by Guy Russell Lowell, is an extensive building of white marble. It has a high base on which are composed monumental Hellenistic Greek temple fronts and other Greek details. Its art collection is the third largest in the United States and probably the best balanced of all types and periods of art in the Western World.

Other museums of note in classic style are the *Museum of Art, Toledo, Ohio,* 1901; the *Albright Art Gallery, Buffalo, New York,* 1905, by Green and Wicks; the *Museum of Fine Arts, Minneapolis, Minnesota,* 1909–1912, by McKim, Mead and White; *Brooklyn Museum,* 1897–1924, McKim, Mead and White, with later revisions by Philip Youtz; *Museum of Art, Cleveland, Ohio,* 1916, by Hubbell and Benes; and the *Philadelphia Museum,* 1920–1928, by Trumbauer, Borie and Zantzinger. The last named is a very distinguished building of light yellow limestone in Greek style with polychrome, Greek-like sculpture in the pediments.

Other museums in this style include the *Museum of Art, Detroit, Michigan*, 1923–1927, by Paul Cret with Zantzinger, Borie and Medary.

**THE NATIONAL GALLERY, 6th Street and Constitution Avenue, N.W., Washington, D.C. (Figure 3.23), 1939–1941, by John Russell Pope. This building is of white marble and has a temple front and dome in Roman style. Located on the Mall, it is a handsome building even though by the time of its construction the style had become hackneyed and *de trop*. It contains a magnificent collection of art that was begun with a European collection by Andrew Mellon and is being added to every year. It is now one of the leading collections of art in the world and may soon surpass the Metropolitan collection, if it has not already done so. A large addition in the form of a second building and a sculpture garden is now being completed to the east of the original building (see Chapter 10).

There are also other, smaller museums in the classic style, many of which were private collections, such as the *Frick Collection, New York City*, 1914, by Carrère and Hastings. Built in Louis XVI style, this was

Figure 3.23   The National Gallery, Washington, D.C., 1939–1941; John Russell Pope, Architect; Eclectic, Roman style. Photograph courtesy of the National Gallery of Art.

originally the palatial residence of a steel industrialist. Then there is the *Isabella Gardner Museum, Boston*, 1902, by Edwin H. Sears, which is in Italian Renaissance style and contains a complete facade of a fourteenth century Venetian palace in a glass-covered courtyard. This facade was transported stone by stone from Venice. The *Huntington Library and Art Gallery, in San Marino, a suburb of Pasadena, California*, occupies two white marble buildings in Italian Renaissance style, set in a beautiful botanical garden. The *Fine Arts Gallery*, San Diego, California 1915, by William T. Johnson, is in Spanish Churrigueresque style and was built as part of the San Diego Exposition, which was all in this style. The *Palace of the Legion of Honor, San Francisco, California*, 1920, is a copy of the palace of the same name in Paris. Though a memorial to California's dead in World War I, it is primarily an art gallery and contains a fine collection. Noteworthy also is the *John and Mable Ringling Museum, Sarasota, Florida*, 1929–1930, designed as a Baroque Italian villa around a large courtyard. This was built by John Ringling of Ringling Brothers' Circus fame and given to the city of Sarasota.

Libraries

A great surge of library construction occurred at this time, greatly aided by generous gifts to small and medium-sized cities by the steel magnate Andrew Carnegie, founder of the U. S. Steel Corporation. Most of these Carnegie libraries were small, classic buildings, more often than not poorly designed for function but looked upon lovingly by the hinterland citizenry as its hometown claim to culture. Often they housed a small art collection in addition to books.

Large cities, of course, set the pattern by building large classic buildings that follow the Library of Congress in ostentation.

*BOSTON PUBLIC LIBRARY, Copley Square, Boston, Massachusetts, 1888–1892, by McKim, Mead and White, is in a neoclassic style quite reminiscent of the exterior of the Bibliothèque de St. Geneviève in Paris by Henri Labrouste. It is a very fine building, more reserved than the Library of Congress, but also more monumental than necessary for its purpose. The building is noted for its murals in the Main Reading Room depicting "The Quest of the Holy Grail," by Edwin Abbey, and for those on the stairways by John Singer Sargent, "The Triumph of Religion."

COLUMBIA UNIVERSITY, Low Memorial Library, New York City, 1893–1897, by McKim, Mead and White, carries monumentality to the limit. It is a great classic domical structure, obviously inspired by the Pantheon in Rome, as had been the library of the University of Virginia a century before. It is fronted by a decastyle Ionic colonnade and a grand flight of steps full width, plus a terrace that can accommodate the ingress and egress of thousands of people. The interior of the rotunda, originally intended as a reading room, is now a large lobby used occasionally as a lecture hall on special occasions. Book stacks have been expanded underground to the sides and rear, so that the building continues to function quite well.

**NEW YORK PUBLIC LIBRARY, Fifth Avenue between 40th and 42nd Streets, New York City (Figure 3.24), 1897–1911, was designed by Carrère and Hastings. It is a huge square building that is fronted by a great three-arched portico framed by double Corinthian columns. Both exterior and interior are very monumental. The building possesses grandstair cases and a huge reading room that dominates the second floor. It is one of the great buildings of the era, and in this case no less a library in spite of its monumentality.

Other large libraries of the period are the *San Francisco Library,* 1907, by George Kelham (mentioned under Government Buildings above); the *Widener Memorial Library, Harvard University,* 1915, by Horace Trumbauer, which is too monumental in scale when compared with other buildings on the Yard; the *Detroit Public Library,* 1920–1922, by Cass Gilbert; and the **St. Paul Public Library, St. Paul, Minnesota,* 1918–1920, by Eclectus D. Litchfield. The last mentioned is no doubt the most aesthetically satisfying of the four just mentioned.
There are a few private libraries in the country that are famous for their architectural impact as well as their specialized collections. The more important ones are described here.

**MORGAN LIBRARY, 36th Street between Madison and Park Avenues, New York City, 1903–1906, by McKim, Mead and White. It was built for J. Pierpont Morgan, Sr., whose mansion on 37th and Madison adjoined the library, and houses one of the best private collections of manuscripts, books, prints, and small art objects. The building is of white marble and is in a very refined Italian Renaissance style. It is said

Figure 3.24 New York Public Library, New York City, 1897–1911; Carrère and Hastings, Architects; Eclectic, Italian High Renaissance style. Photograph by Irving Underhill, 1916; courtesy of the Bettmann Archive, New York.

to have been inspired by the Orangerie of the Villa Farness at Caparola, Italy, and of this there is little doubt. An addition to the library was built in 1928.

CLEMENTS LIBRARY, University of Michigan, Ann Arbor, Michigan (Figure 3.25), 1923, was designed by Ernest Wilby, designer for Albert Kahn. It too is in very refined Italian Renaissance style and is very similar in size and concept to the Morgan Library in New York City. It was given to the University by W. L. Clements, a wealthy lumberman, and houses one of the finest collections of Americana—early books, letters, and manuscripts up to 1860—in the United States.

Figure 3.25 Clements Library, University of Michigan, Ann Arbor, Michigan, 1923; Albert Kahn, Architect; Ernest Wilby, Designer; Eclectic, Italian Renaissance style. Photograph by Daniel Bartush; courtesy of Albert Kahn Associates.

Railway Stations

*PENNSYLVANIA TERMINAL, New York City (Figure 3.26), 1906–1910, by McKim, Mead and White, was considered the epitome of classic grandeur at the time it was built and for several decades thereafter. The superstructure was demolished in 1966–1967 to make way for a new sports arena and a huge office building; the passenger station still operates at the basement and subbasement levels. But it was the upper structure that was of note. The exterior was a series of classic colonnades, and it was the interior, the grand concourse, that was so magnificent. It was a replica of the tepidarium of the Baths of Caracalla in Rome, as restored by archaeologists. However it was not too well adapted to railway station usage, as anyone who ever tried to meet an incoming passenger might have found. There were so many entrances and exits at several levels that it was very easy to get lost. The grand concourse, a good city block in length, was cut in the middle by an ever-flowing mass of people.

Figure 3.26 Pennsylvania Terminal (interior), New York City, 1906–1910; McKim, Meade and White, Architects; Classic Eclectic style. Photograph by Bettmann Archive.

**GRAND CENTRAL STATION, 42nd Street at Park Avenue, New York City, 1903–1913, was designed by Reed and Stem, an architectural firm of St. Paul, Minnesota, which won a national competition held by the New York Central Railway Company. Warren and Wetmore later got the commission and tried to take credit for the design; however Reed and Stem entered suit against them, and after 30 years in court were awarded damages. It is a better design in plan and circulation than the Pennsylvania Station although not as imposing. Nevertheless it is very grand and handles the daily crowds with a minimum of confusion.

UNION STATION, Chicago, Illinois, 1922–1926, by Graham, Anderson, Probst and White, is suggestive of the Pennsylvania Station, New York City. It has similar grand colonnades on the exterior and a grand waiting room in the character of a large Roman basilica. The concourse to the train gates is of steel and glass.

Other railway stations of the period in classic design were the *Union Station, Washington, D.C.,* 1904–1908, by Daniel H. Burnham; the *Union Station, Kansas City, Missouri,* 1914, third largest in the country; and the *Union Station, Richmond, Virginia,* 1924–1926, by John Russell Pope. The *Union Station, Los Angeles, California,* 1930–1936, by Donald B. Parkinson, is in Spanish Renaissance style, as were many in California, Arizona, New Mexico, and Texas.

Commercial and Semipublic Buildings

In this group are included lodge buildings, clubs, hotels, hospitals, and commercial buildings. During this prosperous period almost everyone belonged to one or more clubs or lodges. Masons, Knights of Columbus, and other secret orders built meeting places throughout the country, and these varied in style from Egyptian to Greek and Gothic according to the dictates of the architects and building committees. Other buildings as well were dressed up in eclectic styles, particularly classic, as this was the popular mode of the time.

*TEMPLE OF THE SCOTTISH RITE, 16th and S Streets, N.W., Washington, D.C. (Figure 3.27), 1908–1910, by John Russell Pope, is a very beautiful building. It is a reproduction of the ancient Greek tomb of Mausolus at Halicarnassus, as interpreted by M. Bernier, a French archaeologist, in 1892. The large ritual room on the second floor is most impressive and gives an idea of what the bouleterian of the Mysteries of Eleusis must have been like in Greek times. At the time of its construction this temple was heralded as a masterpiece and acclaimed as the most beautiful building in America.

Figure 3.27 Temple of the Scottish Rite, Washington, D.C., 1908–1910; John Russell Pope, Architect; Classic Eclectic, Greek style. Photograph by Ralph W. Hammett.

UNIVERSITY CLUB, 1 W. 54th Street, New York City, 1899, by McKim, Mead and White, was designed to look like an Italian Renaissance palace.

CHICAGO CLUB, Michigan Avenue, Chicago, is on Michigan Avenue opposite the Art Institute and overlooks the huge Grant Park parking lot and Lake Michigan beyond. The building is in the style of a fourteenth century Venetian palace.

Country clubs were made to look like oversized eighteenth century colonial farmhouses, or English Tudor manor houses.

Hotels grew to enormous sizes in the large cities and were decorated in Louis XIV style, Spanish, or other eclectic styles.

PONCE DE LEON HOTEL, St. Augustine, Florida, 1888–1890, by Carrère and Hastings, was a magnificent pile in Spanish Renaissance style in deference to the Spanish founders of the oldest city in the United States. Sadly, this once-fine hotel was demolished in 1972, because of wear and obsolescence.

BILTMORE HOTEL, Los Angeles, California, ca. 1920, by Schultze and Weaver, is a multistoried building with Baroque detail and an interior lobby that looks like an elegant Spanish churrigueresque hall.

FRANCISCAN HOTEL, Albuquerque, New Mexico, 1920, by Trost and Trost, is a six-storied building that is cube shaped and quite devoid of decorative detail. An adaptation of Pueblo Indian styling, it has heavy block walls and deeply revealed windows.

SHELTON TOWERS HOTEL, Lexington Avenue at 48th Street, New York City, 1924–1926, by Arthur Loomis Harmon. It is a 32-story building with setbacks as required by New York's 1916 zoning law. Designed to give the appearance of a brick masonry building, it is treated with Lombard Romanesque detail. The design is very subtle, and the entire building has entasis from the third story upward. It is primarily a residential hotel.

THE STATLER-HILTON (originally the Pennsylvania Hotel), Eighth Avenue across from Pennsylvania Station, New York City, 1922–1924, was designed by George B. Post and Sons in the Italian Renaissance style. This hotel has over 1000 guest rooms and was the largest hotel in the world at the time it was built. It has beautiful public rooms and caters to many large conventions.

THE HILTON STEVENS HOTEL, Michigan Avenue at South Eighth Street, Chicago, 1925–1927, by Holabird and Root, is also in the Italian

Renaissance style, which has been cleverly adapted here to a large steel-framed building. It boasts of being the largest hotel in the world. It has over 1300 rooms—if a person stayed in this hotel continuously, but in a different room each night, it would take almost three and a half years to complete the process. It has beautiful public rooms for conventions and other public purposes.

Hospitals, which became large, multistoried institutions, were often designed to look like hotels. Sanitariums were given the appearance of country clubs.

Skyscrapers

Commercial buildings, particularly the large multistoried skyscrapers, were more difficult to design. These buildings utilized the many technical innovations that had been brought about by industrialism—steel construction, central heating, plumbing, vertical circulation by high-speed elevators, communication by telephone, and lighting by means of gas, which was followed almost immediately by electricity. The new techniques were wonderful, but the eclecticists were puzzled about the style. They insisted that these steel structures should look like masonry—indeed they did have to be fireproofed—and they tried to apply the old historical styles to them. This was particularly true of New York practitioners led by McKim, Mead and White. They argued that in theory a skyscraper could be treated like a classic order having a plinth and base, plain shaft, and then cap, entablature, and cornice. As commercial buildings increased in height, they continued to be built with details in Renaissance, Baroque, Gothic, and sometimes Greek. One or two buildings in New York and Chicago have a Greek temple form perched on the very top, and several have Halicarnassus-like pyramids. These have the central-heating stacks emitting smoke and vapor from large urns at the apexes.

This may seem silly enough now, but it was treated in all seriousness from about 1920 and until the Great Depression, which started in 1930. Some politicians, led by architects of the time, tried to limit the height of commercial buildings, and Boston passed a zoning law (since repealed) limiting the height of buildings to 125 feet. But it was all futile—the soaring skyscraper won, and New York City continued to build higher and higher commercial office buildings in the idiom of Classic Renaissance.

WESTERN UNION BUILDING, New York City, 1873–1875, by George B. Post, was a nine-storied building dressed in French Second Empire style, which was the fashion of the time. This building, now demolished, was wall bearing and showed no great technical advancement except that it did have passenger elevators.

WORLD BUILDING, later known as the Pulitzer Building, New York City, 1889–1890, by George B. Post, has 26 stories and was at the time the tallest building in the world. It was not built entirely of steel but was a mixture of wall-bearing and steel construction.

McKim, Mead and White, as well as Bruce Price, designed a number of large office buildings, even as far west as Omaha and Kansas City, that employed a classic approach, quite inappropriate to skyscraper form.

It is an interesting note that at one of the A.I.A. national conventions, ca. 1890, a paper was read to the membership condemning steel construction and claiming that in time, owning to earth and other vibrations, steel members would crystallize, become brittle, and fail. One could almost feel the deadly crash of these steel buildings as they splintered and disintegrated into piles of worthless debris. A motion was made to condemn steel construction, but it was tabled for further study and was not brought up later.

*SINGER TOWER, New York City (Figure 3.28), 1907, by Ernest Flagg, was a 41-storied tower (612 ft.) that was the highest office building in the world at the time of its construction. It used a cleverly articulated Baroque styling and had a bulbous mansard-roofed topping. For years it was the headquarters of the world-renowned Singer Sewing Machine Company. It was a very distinguished building, and pictures of it were used by that company in their international advertising. It was demolished in 1967.

METROPOLITAN TOWER, Madison Square, New York City, 1909, by Napoleon LeBrun and Sons, is an oversized 700 foot high campanile tower. It was a sophisticated design, but by that time New York City was dotted with office buildings of classic design. Recently many have been demolished to make way for Miesian steel and glass cages, which are much more functional but distinctly dull.

Figure 3.28 Singer Tower, New York City, 1907; Ernest Flagg, Architect; Eclectic Baroque style. Photograph courtesy of the Bettmann Archive, New York.

**WOOLWORTH TOWER, 233 Broadway, New York City (Figure 3.29), 1911–1913, by Cass Gilbert, architect, was for many years the most distinguished of all skyscraper office buildings. Although it is sometimes criticized by purists because its outer terra-cotta dress is detailed in Gothic style, the building was so cleverly conceived as a steel tower of 55 stories (792 feet), and the Gothic detail was so well scaled and articulated as part of the fabric, that its eclecticism cannot be too strongly condemned.

Figure 3.29 Woolworth Tower, New York City, 1911–1913; Cass Gilbert, Architect; Eclectic Gothic style. Photograph by Ralph W. Hammett.

It marked a milestone in skyscraper design, the end of the experimental period. Here is fireproofed steel framing with such services as high-speed electric elevators, electric lighting, thermostatically-controlled central heating, adequate plumbing, and complete telephone service along with a tower of consummate beauty in mass and detail.

In the first decade after World War I a new philosophy of architecture began to develop around the world. At first it was not clear precisely what this new philosophy would be but change was in the air. In Europe the new philosophy was led by Walter Gropius and Mies van der Rohe, and by their Bauhaus School in Germany. This school emphasized industrialized art and architecture. Other leaders of the new philosophy were Auguste Perret and Le Corbusier in France; J. J. P. Oud in Holland; E. G. Asplund in Sweden and Alvar Aalto in Finland; Berthold Lubetkin and his group, known as *Tecton,* in England; Juan O'Gorman and the Garcias in Mexico; and Lucio Costa and Oscar Niemeyer in Brazil. The United States had the industrial work of Albert Kahn in Detroit and that of William Lescaze in Philadelphia, also the work of R. M. Schindler and Richard Neutra in Los Angeles. These last three were Europeans who had taken up residence in the United States: Lescaze from Switzerland, Schindler and Neutra from Austria. There were others, of course, but this list comprises most of the architectural leaders in the 1920 decade. However more about them in a later chapter.

Not all was advancement during the post-World War I decade. There was an attempt to go back and resume where history had stopped at the start of the war. In the United States particularly the slogan was "Back to normalcy," meaning a return to the philosophy of 1910–1915, days of dollar diplomacy, isolationism, freedom to amass wealth without taxes, and freedom to build any type of building on any lot—in architecture this meant idolization of pompous historical styles and rugged individualism. Indicative of this short period was the American Institute of Architects' refusal to participate in the *Exposition des Arts Decoratif,* held in Paris in 1925, which called for a showing of new architecture and art. The United States reply was in essence that it had nothing new to show.

In 1923 the Chicago Tribune advertised and conducted an international competition for the design of a skyscraper to serve as the headquarters for the "World's Greatest Newspaper." Colonel McCormick, chief owner of the paper dominated the competition, which was held under the auspices of the American Institute of Architects and which offered a first prize of $20,000. The competition program stated that the Tribune was seeking the most beautiful office building in the world, a tower that would rank among the world's most beautiful towers such as the famous Tour de Buerre of Rouen, France. The result was that a very beautiful tower was built in a very eclectic Gothic design remindful of the Tour de Buerre of Rouen. However this tower more or less marked the end of eclectic historical styling applied to skyscrapers.

*TRIBUNE TOWER, Chicago, Illinois (Figure 3.30), 1924–1925, by John Meade Howells and Raymond Hood, was an adaptation of the famous Tour de Beurre of Rouen. This design won the first prize and is very beautiful although it is a steel structure clothed in stone of Gothic detail. It even has flying buttresses supporting a crown at the top.

Second prize went to Eliel Saarinen, who came to the United States from Finland to do this competition and stayed on. Many judged Saarinen's design better than the first prize; at least it was a fresher approach. It was not radical, and though it was Gothic in feeling, it was not in detail, which struck a new note at the time.

There were several hundred entries to this competition; most of those by Americans were eclectic: Gothic, Spanish, Louis XIV, Baroque, or other historical style. There were a few entries from Europe, one by Max Taut and one by Gropius, that were notable for their direct approach. Gropius particularly seemed to pick up the philosophy of the old Chicago School and to carry on where it had left off 20 years before. His design was somewhat marred however by the addition of several unrelated bands of balconies and sunshades which might better have been omitted or at least reduced in number. Nevertheless, though this and similar entries from abroad had a profound effect on skyscraper design 25 years later, they did not receive immediate attention by American designers.

Residences

Some of the most important domestic architecture in the Classic Eclectic style was produced under the direction of members of the New York social register. Most of these mansions are in the Italian Renaissance style, and many are indirect copies of Florentine or Roman palaces.

Figure 3.30 Tribune Tower, Chicago, Illinois, 1924–1925; John Meade Howells and Raymond Hood, Architects; Eclectic, Gothic style. Photograph courtesy of the Chicago Tribune.

Many have been demolished, but a substantial number are still standing and in use as consulates, clubs, prestigious offices, or residences of foreign delegations to the United Nations.

*THE BREAKERS, Newport, Rhode Island (Figures 3.31 and 3.32), 1890–1892, by Richard M. Hunt, was the seaside summer home of Cornelius Vanderbilt II. In Italian Baroque style, it is the epitome of palatial elegance and is said to have cost $3,000,000. The mansion is entirely of marble and has large paved and balustrated terraces overlooking the sea. The interiors are lavish with marble columns, gold-leafed ornament, bronze metalwork, and marble floors and stairways. As a seaside residence it seems almost ridiculous now, but in that ostentatious period, known as the "Gilt Age," it was most expressive. It is now owned by the New-

Figure 3.31 Exterior: The Breakers (summer home of Cornelius Vanderbilt, II), Newport, Rhode Island, 1890–1892; Richard M. Hunt, Architect; Eclectic, Baroque style. Photograph by John Hopf, Newport; courtesy of the Preservation Society of Newport.

Figure 3.32 Interior: grand hall, The Breakers (summer home of Cornelius Vanderbilt, II), Newport, Rhode Island, 1890–1892; Richard M. Hunt, Architect; Eclectic, Baroque style. Photograph by John Hopf, Newport; courtesy of the Preservation Society of Newport.

port Preservation Society and is kept as a historic curiosity, open to the public for a fee. Not too far away is another luxurious estate, Marble House, also by R. M. Hunt, and there are many more in Newport.

**BILTMORE, Asheville, North Carolina (Figures 3.33 and 3.34), 1892–1896, by Richard M. Hunt, is truly a chateau in the Francis 1st Style. It is beautifully situated in an eastern mountain estate of several hundred acres and was the country home of George W. Vanderbilt. Its principal exterior feature is a copy of the famous tower stairway of the Chateau of Blois. The interiors are gorgeous, especially the grand banquet hall, which has a pipe organ in the minstrel's gallery and a double row of noble heraldic flags hanging from the ceiling. All rooms are palatial and exquisitely furnished in French style. The gardens in the immediate

Figure 3.33 Exterior: Biltmore (summer home of George W. Vanderbilt), Asheville, North Carolina, 1892–1896; Richard M. Hunt, Architect; Eclectic, Francois Premier style. Photograph courtesy of the Biltmore Estate.

Figure 3.34   Interior: Biltmore (summer home of George W. Vanderbilt), Asheville, North Carolina, 1892–1896; Richard M. Hunt, Architect; Eclectic, Francois Premier style. Photograph courtesy of the Biltmore Estate.

vicinity of the palace vary from formal rose terraces to English-type landscaping. The estate is now supported by a large dairy farm and tourist fees.

*VILLARD RESIDENCES, Madison Avenue between 50th and 51st Streets, New York City, 1881–1884, by McKim, Mead and White, are now used for offices of the Roman Catholic Archdiocese and other organizations. Located directly behind St. Patrick's Cathedral, they resemble a marble palace and bear a strong resemblance to Bramante's Palazzo Cancelleria in Rome. Henry Villard, the original owner, was the principal stockholder and builder of the Union Pacific Railroad.

VISCAYA, VILLA OF JAMES DEERING, Miami, Florida, 1918–1922, by F. B. Hoffman and Paul Chalfin, is an Italian Baroque villa that would make Vignola drool could he see it. It was built by James Deering, a farm-machinery tycoon from Iowa.

R. M. BISSELL HOUSE, Farmington, Connecticut, 1918, by Aymar Embury, is an adaptation of Georgian Colonial in a small city that has many old houses in the original style. It shows careful attention to detail and is a beautiful example of Georgian eclecticism.

E. T. STOTESBURY ESTATE, Chestnut Hill, Pennsylvania, 1920, by Horace Trumbauer, is a lavish Borghese-like palace in white marble and has formal gardens.

FRICK GALLERY, formerly the Henry Clay Frick Residence, 1 East 70th Street, New York City, 1914, by Carrère and Hastings was completely renovated by John Russell Pope in 1935 and turned into a public museum for the Frick Collection. The residence is entered through a glass-covered courtyard, which is a restful transition from the traffic of Fifth Avenue to the quiet interiors.

CONVENT OF THE SACRED HEART, formerly the Otto Kahn House, 1 East 91st Street, New York City, 1918, by C. P. H. Gilbert and J. Armstrong Stenhouse, is a large palacelike building remindful of the Palazzo Cancelleria in Rome.

COUNCIL ON FOREIGN RELATIONS, formerly the Harold I. Pratt Residence, 58 East 68th Street, off Park Avenue, New York City, 1920, by Delano and Aldrich, is an Italian High Renaissance adaptation after the style of Raphael.

ALGER RESIDENCE, Grosse Pointe, Michigan, 1920, by Charles Platt, is an exquisite villalike residence in Italian Renaissance style. It stands on the shore of Lake St. Clair along with a whole row of palacelike structures.

Florida, Texas, the Southwestern states, and California have many adaptations of the Spanish style; that it, Spanish Renaissance. Some outstanding examples are given here.

HERBERT CAPPELL RESIDENCE, Pasadena, California, 1918, by Bertram G. Goodhue, is an adaptation of the Spanish Renaissance. The general formula for this style is plain stucco walls to simulate adobe construction, red tile roofs, and an elaborate doorway of carved stone in Spanish Baroque detail. The motion-picture colony that settled in Hollywood and Beverly Hills, California, in the second and third decades of the twentieth century built lavish homes, and many of these are pseudo-Spanish in style.

*SAN SIMEON CASTLE, California, 1920–1930, was by no one architect. It is located in the coastal mountains of the state about midway between San Francisco and Los Angeles. This was the country estate and private playground developed by William Randolph Hearst, the great nineteenth and twentieth century newspaper tycoon. It resembles an alcazar of Spain and dominates its own village of dependencies. It is a Spanish-style extravaganza where Mr. Hearst reigned supreme. The castle contains an assimilation of parts of several Medieval and Renaissance Spanish castles and palaces. Whole rooms and ceilings were often purchased, dismantled, and moved here; Mr. Hearst also collected many objects of art including paintings from all over the world. Although Mr. Hearst hired several architects, he did most of the supervision himself and assembled the parts with an architect who happened to be available at the time. Most of his architects were young men, just out of architecture school who were given housing on the site or sent abroad to find works of art and parts of palaces, most of them owned by bankrupt noblemen.

The estate had fabulous gardens with fountains and pools, its own flying field, and a sizable zoo. It is a part of land holdings estimated at 270,000 acres.

PHASE 3. FUNCTIONAL ARCHITECTURE, 1860–1920

During the first years of the period from 1860 to 1890, when the pioneer spirit was strong and technology was advancing, it might seem odd that functional design in architecture did not advance more rapidly. However in the so-called cultural centers of Boston, New York, Philadelphia, Charleston, Atlanta, and New Orleans, society and its architects were so busy copying Europe that they turned their backs on, in fact were almost ashamed of, anything native or new. To be accepted, architectural design had to be imported: French Second Empire, Romanesque (H. H. Richardson), or classic. Most new designs, although technically fresh, were permiated by Industrial Romanticists. They were done for newly rich and unsophisticated clients, who loved ornament; as a result most designs were clumsy and overly romantic. Structural design was considered to be separate from architecture, and the wonderful bridges of Eads and Roebling were thought of not as architecture, but as engineering.

Bridges

*EADS BRIDGE, St. Louis, Missouri, 1859–1870, designed by J. B. Eads, a prominent engineer of that day, was designed before the Civil War although it was not built until after that conflagration. One of the great engineering feats of the age, it was one of the first structures to use steel throughout. It linked the eastern half of the United States with the West, so that for the first time railroads were able to cross the Mississippi River in midcontinent. The bridge is a double-decked structure set high enough for large river boats to pass under it. On the lower deck are double railway tracks, and on the top a wide wagon and pedestrian roadway. It is still in use, though there are now other bridges that divert some of the traffic.

*BROOKLYN BRIDGE, New York City, 1868–1883, was designed by John A. Robeling and his son, Washington A. Roebling, who took over completely in 1869 after his father was accidentally killed on the bridge during construction. The principle of wire-cable suspension bridges, which was known and tested as early as 1824, was greatly facilitated by the development of steel and drawn steel wire. The Brooklyn Bridge has a center span of 1595 feet, and the cables are held by two great masonry towers 296 feet high.

John A. Roebling had already designed and built a suspension bridge at Wheeling, West Virginia, 1838–1844; the Monongahela River Bridge, Pittsburgh, Pennsylvania, 1844–1848; a suspension bridge at Cincinnati, Ohio, 1847–1851; and a very dramatic railway bridge at Niagara Falls,

New York, 1851–1855. The Wheeling and Cincinnati bridges as well as the Brooklyn Bridge are still in use. The Niagara Bridge, however, crossed the river just below the falls and obscured the view; it was removed and a new bridge was built further downriver 30 years later.

Commercial Buildings

During this time urban centers were growing rapidly, modern business methods were introduced, and the skyscraper office building was developed. Downtown districts were becoming increasingly crowded. The only direction in which to expand was up. Technology had kept pace with the development of materials and devices necessary for the skyscraper: such as terra-cotta, and later ferroconcrete; the passenger elevator, central heating, and plumbing. The centrifugal pump was the most important factor in the solution of supplying water to high places. Other developments included the pneumatic tube, a quick means of communication soon displaced by the telephone; gas-lighting, and soon afterward electric lighting. In a short period of time a generation of architects trained in the tradition of historical styles in masonry had to deal with these changes. As pointed out previously, the New York Beaux Arts group found it increasingly difficult to use classic or Renaissance forms in the designing of skyscraper office buildings. The cast iron commercial buildings of the 1850s through the 1880s could superimpose classic orders on 4 or 5-storied buildings with some degree of success, but using the orders for 10 stories, as George B. Post did on one of his projects, bordered on the ridiculous.[3] In 1875 Richard M. Hunt used the Industrial Romantic style in designing the Tribune Building, New York City, but this also was not very successful aesthetically; however its height was added to in 1890, and the building continued in use until it was demolished in 1967.

Chicago was one place where the problem was met head on—by Major William LeBaron Jenny, the firm of Holabird and Roche, Burnham and Root, and Adler and Sullivan. This group became known as the *Chicago School.* It was not a school, except in the sense that William Jenney was the senior member of the group, and several of the others, John W. Root, Louis H. Sullivan and William Holabird, had worked for and been influenced by him. In this way it might be said that William

[3] Post and Telegraph Building (since demolished), by George B. Post, was ten stories in stone, and had superimposed classic columns and entablatures rising one per story.

LeBaron Jenney was to the Chicago group as Otto Wagner was to Austria, Peter Behrens to Germany, and Henrick Berlage to Holland.

No doubt a thesis could be written showing how the Chicago steel and glass commercial buildings developed out of the earlier Bogardus cast iron buildings. However both the need for and acceptance of these new high-rise office buildings came quickly during the 1880s decade. Very little time could be given to research of past accomplishments, and actually there were no past accomplishments in similar buildings. Here new demands were calling for a new technology. Here were new materials—steel, plate glass, terra-cotta, concrete, and a great deal of new and necessary mechanical and electrical equipment. The architects of Chicago were forced to use this new technology as functionally and as quickly as possible. Design followed technology: form followed function.

FIRST LEITER BUILDING, 208 West Monroe Street, Chicago, 1879, by William LeBaron Jenney, is a seven-storied loft building. Widely spaced brick piers serve as the outer supports, with cast iron columns on the interior. Between these brick piers are triple windows of plate glass separated by cast-iron mullions which support cast-iron spandrels. This triple window grouping became a Chicago cliché. This building, though not a skyscraper, has the elements of the glass and steel buildings that soon followed.

*HOME INSURANCE BUILDING, Chicago, 1884–1886, by William LeBaron Jenney, was an 11-storied structure having cast iron columns and steel, hollow-tile, and cement floor construction. This fireproof building, often given credit for being the first modern skyscraper, has been torn down. The facades were of the triple window type, and the main structural piers of cast iron were encased in brick.

*TACOMA BUILDING, Chicago, 1887–1889, by Holabird and Roche, was a 12-storied building of skeleton construction that used cast iron columns, like the Home Insurance Building, and the triple window cliché, like Jenney's building. Both the Home Insurance and Tacoma buildings were landmarks in the Chicago Loop until torn down in 1925 and 1927, respectively; both have been given credit for being the first iron-framed skyscrapers.

*ROOKERY BUILDING, Chicago, 1885–1886, designed by Burnham and Root, is a 10-storied block in the heart of the financial district on Jackson Avenue. The exterior elevations fronting on the streets are rather mixed up adaptations of Richardsonian Romanesque thinned out to suit this multistoried project. The building is a hollow square, and the facades facing the interior court are remarkable for their clarity, wide openings between iron-supported brick piers, and spandrels. The vestibule to the lobby under the light court was redesigned by Frank Lloyd Wright in 1910 and is interesting as an example of his early work. However the most interesting interior features are the decorative iron and glass roof over the lobby, and the iron stairway that rises grandly up to and through it. Above this glass roof the stair continues as a circular spiral to the topmost story. This old building is still a prestige address in Chicago and is occupied by many brokers well known in the financial world.

*MONADNOCK BUILDING, Dearborn and Jackson Streets, Chicago (Figure 3.35), 1889–1891, was designed by Burnham and Root. A 16-storied building, this was the last tall building to be built with brick masonry-bearing walls. In design the building has ultraplain brick walls and is devoid of superfluous ornament. It is most successful aesthetically, although its walls at the ground level are 6 to 8 feet thick to support the great weight of the masonry. It proved without argument that steel construction was advisable for this type of building; masonry alone is not practical for skyscrapers.

SEARS ROEBUCK STORE (Second Leiter Building), Van Buren and State Streets, Chicago, 1889–1890, by William LeBaron Jenney, architect, was designed by William Bryce Mundie, who was hired by Jenney "to give better aesthetic quality." Although the fenestration is wide and open, the building is a huge rectangular block nine stories high. Mundie tried to treat this as a classic composition having a high base on which rested six-storied classic pilasters and a simplified entablature a full attic story in height. The result was a compromise, and the concealed steel framing is quite evident in the proportions. Aesthetically the result is pleasing and not slavishly eclectic.

**RELIANCE BUILDING, State and Randolph Streets, Chicago (Figure 3.36), 1890–1895, by Burnham and Root, is a 15-storied steel, con-

Figure 3.35 Monadnock Building, Chicago, Illinois, 1889–1891; Burnham and Root, Architects; Functional design. Photograph by Chicago Historical Society.

Figure 3.36 Reliance Building, Chicago, Illinois, 1890–1895; Burnham and Root, Architects; Functional design. Photograph by Chicago Historical Society.

crete, and glass building. The vertical exterior steel is protected by a thin covering of white terra-cotta. This building, designed by John Root, who died suddenly in 1891, is the high spot of the Chicago School and brought together all of the clichés of the style: the protruding bay windows of plate glass, frank expression of the structure, and an unadorned sheer rise to a projecting flat cap. This cap was later removed because the overhang was dangerous; however aesthetically it was not essential, and its removal has not marred the design. Although the terra-cotta covering of the structural steel is lightly ornamented, it does not hide the structural quality; this ornamentation was necessary to prevent the terra-cotta from warping during the firing process. The Reliance Building is a masterpiece of steel skyscraper design, a true expression of steel and glass that has been balanced and proportioned to give an excellent aesthetic expression.

Buildings of Louis Sullivan

John Root's untimely death was a great loss to the Chicago group and marked the end of functional design for the Burnham and Root office. The firm was carried on by Daniel Burnham, the senior member of the firm, who was the salesman and administrator. In 1890 he was appointed chief architect of the Chicago Columbian Exposition of 1892, which was later postponed until 1893. Under the influence of McKim of the New York firm of McKim, Mead and White, and others of the Eastern group, Burnham soon swung over to the Classical Eclectic school. The tobacco-chewing Midwesterner quickly became a cane-carrying, cigar-smoking, sophisticated gentleman. He was introduced to New York's Upper 400 and began hobnobbing with the elite of the eastern seaboard. He carried it off in grand style, but functional architecture was all but forgotten.

The only one to carry the ball from this time onward was a young red-haired Irish-American by the name of Louis Sullivan, a brilliant designer who carried on where John Root left off. However it became more and more of an uphill fight. The forces of Classic Eclecticism became ever stronger, and though Sullivan had several triumphs toward the end of the 1890s decade, it became a losing battle. In final frustration Sullivan took to drink and died in 1924, a broken man.

However during most of his life Sullivan was a fighter and a convincing writer who inspired many young architects in the early decades of the twentieth century. His dictum *Form follows Function* became the rallying cry of young American architects even as late as 1950. By then it had become the creed of Walter Gropius and Mies van der Rohe, who had come to the United States in 1936 and 1940, respectively. They were already of the structural-functional group and were readily accepted for the masters that they were.

Chief among the students of Sullivan in the 1890s decade was Frank Lloyd Wright, the greatest architectural genius of this century. However Wright was not a follower of anyone, and his philosophy and designs ranged far and wide, from Functional to Craft to Structural Romanticism. His aesthetic forms were often undertaken for the sake of aesthetic kick. Frank Lloyd Wright is discussed in Chapter 5.

*THE CHICAGO AUDITORIUM, 1887–1889, and the AUDITORIUM HOTEL, Congress Street, Chicago, 1889–1891, by Adler and Sullivan, formed a remarkable complex combining opera house, office building, and hotel. The hotel portion has now been converted to a downtown college complex, Roosevelt University, and the Auditorium, at one time the most famous theater in America, was abandoned in 1928. It has now been restored and was reopened in 1967.

The bottom two stories of this complex, of rough stone masonry, show Richardsonian influence and detail, but the upper stories are of dressed limestone. The 10-storied building is well composed aesthetically and has a 16-storied tower on Congress Street that once housed Sullivan's architectural offices on its top floor. The interiors of the hotel were famous for their beauty and luxury. In the second floor of the hotel portion (now university) is a parlor that has been restored (1967) with original furnishings and decorations. Otherwise the old hotel has lost most of its former grandeur since it has been converted to academic uses.

Although the exterior walls of the auditorium are of masonry, the interior structure is of steel, and the auditorium and stage are masterpieces of planning and structure. The auditorium, which seats 3000 people, was designed with one continuous stadiumlike floor, not like a horseshoe, as were the European and most other opera houses, which have a tier of boxes surrounding the main floor. It has perfect sight lines and acoustics, and the stage has every convenience. It is a marvelous opera house, and the most famous opera stars from all over the world have appeared here. However it has one cardinal fault, location. As the city grew and the Loop all but strangled itself, the auditorium entrances, one on Congress Street and the other on Wabash Avenue, became almost inaccessible. In later years (1920 to 1930) on opera nights traffic would be stalled for blocks, and automobile drivers, after discharging their ladies and parking their cars in Grant Park, several blocks away, were often not able to get to their seats until after the second act or during intermission. A new opera house was therefore built on the west side of the Loop, where traffic is much freer. However the new opera house is not as good a theater, and now the old Auditorium has been restored and reopened. Nevertheless the ultimate question remains: even though Chicago has restored its perfect auditorium, how is the public to get to it?

*WAINWRIGHT BUILDING, St. Louis, Missouri, 1890–1891, was designed by Adler and Sullivan. Although this is only a 10-storied building, Sullivan studied verticality in design and used the steel structure quite objectively. The lower two stories, treated as a base, were faced with smoothly dressed cut stone, and the piers above were cased in a hard-finished brick that matched the stone in color. The window spandrels are of highly ornamented terra-cotta. Sullivan partially followed the steel skeleton in his design, and the resulting form was pleasing, but only every other exterior pier contained steel. The wide glass openings at street level indicate the actual steel structure. Nevertheless this building was a far step forward in skyscraper design, and the concept was consummated in the Prudential Building in Buffalo, New York, three years later.

**TRANSPORTATION BUILDING, World's Columbian Exposition, Chicago (Figure 3.37), 1893, was by the firm of Adler and Sullivan, though Adler gave Sullivan full credit for the design and its execution. Demolished long ago, it was the most outstanding building of the fair, partially because of its color and its noneclectic design, which was in radical contrast to the predominating classic buildings. It was awarded a gold medal of merit by the French Government as the best building of the exposition, much to the dismay of Burnham, McKim, and the other architects of the fair, who had relegated this building to a secondary site. The long rectangular building was basilican in sectional form and had wide side aisles flanking a central rectangular core with clerestory windows. The framing of light steel was covered on the exterior by a plain stucco wall punctured by repetitive large-scale arches at the ground level and a series of small arched windows encircling the clerestory. In the center of one of the long facades was a grand entrance motive consisting of a large, square block of richly detailed terra-cotta that framed a large, low centered, and deeply recessed arched doorway. The whole exterior

Figure 3.37 Transportation Building, World's Columbian Exposition, Chicago, Illinois, 1893; Adler and Sullivan, Architects; Louis Sullivan, Designer; Functional design. Photograph by Chicago Historical Society.

was elegant, with rich painted designs in reds, yellows, greens, and browns—autumn colors with accents of gold. The central doorway was even more gorgeous because of the addition of more gold and autumn-colored ornament in terra-cotta. This doorway was named "The Golden Doorway."

The eclecticists and public who saw this doorway by Sullivan, with its ornament that only Sullivan could do, tried to find a name. Some called it *Art Nouveau,* and indeed the new Art Nouveau style was developing in Europe at this time. Others said it was Persian-Mohammedan inspired because of two small Mohammedan-like kiosk pavilions that flanked the golden doorway. However this doorway and its ornament cannot be said to belong to any historical or other style. If it can be said to have any stylistic forebear, it evolved from the Romanesque-inspired ornament of H. H. Richardson, and its development can be clearly seen in the Auditorium Building in downtown Chicago. This ornament was too individual to be named anything other than Sullivanesque.

**PRUDENTIAL BUILDING (also called the Guaranty Trust Building), Buffalo, New York (Figure 3.38), 1894–1895, was designed by Louis Sullivan just before he dissolved his partnership with Dankmar Adler.

Figure 3.38 Prudential Building, Buffalo, New York, 1894–1895; Louis Sullivan, Architect; Functional design. Photograph by Buffalo and Erie County Historical Society.

Here Sullivan conceived a beautiful 16-storied building that has direct reference to his earlier Wainwright Building in St. Louis but better proportions and refinements of detail. He used an ornamented low-textured terra-cotta over the entire exterior; this texturing was necessary at that time to prevent the surface of the terra cotta from warping during the firing. Sullivan loved ornament but always kept it subjective. In 1974 this building suffered fire damage and soon after went bankrupt. It is now threatened with forced sale. However, the Landmarks Society of the Niagara Frontier has recently called for help, and a survey is being made to determine the feasibility of renovation and restoration. It is hoped that they will be successful.

**GETTY TOMB, Graceland Cemetery, Chicago, 1890, by Sullivan, is a family mausoleum. A most sublime monument, it is of tooled gray granite with an arched doorway containing beautiful decorative bronze doors which open onto a set of even more beautiful bronze gates. Both gates and doors are composed with Sullivanesque ornament.

CHARNLEY HOUSE, 1892, and, in the same year, his own residence, the **SULLIVAN HOUSE,** were built on the near North Side of Chicago. The latter house was later sold to his brother and is often known as the Albert W. Sullivan House. The Sullivan residence was destroyed in 1970, and the Charnley House may soon follow. The location suffers from urban decay and is rapidly deteriorating.

Sullivan's loss of Dankmar Adler as a partner in 1895 proved to be a great loss for both men. Adler dissolved the partnership to become consulting architect and sales manager for the Crane Elevator Company. However this only lasted for six months, and Adler wanted to restore the partnership. Sullivan refused. Adler was the practical businessman and structural engineer. There is no doubt that Adler's structural solutions for the fabric and foundations of the Auditorium and other buildings were as important as Sullivan's aesthetic contributions. Adler's solutions of the foundation problems of high buildings on Chicago's mud, and his final development of caisson footings on top of driven piles, give him an important place in architectural history. He belongs among the great engineers of the nineteenth century, with Eiffel, Roebling, and Eads. Adler was also a salesman and diplomat who knew how to deal with people, which Sullivan did not. Sullivan was a design genius, but he was uncompromising and tempetuous, as well as impetuous, traits that most clients neither understand nor tolerate.

In spite of the loss of Adler's talents, the first few years of Sullivan's office after the breakup were successful, and during this time Sullivan did some of his best work.

*CONDICT BUILDING (later called the Bayard Building), 65 Bleecker Street, New York City, 1897–1898, by Sullivan, is a glass and steel building with the steel encased in terra-cotta. Narrow piers rise to an ornamental cornice and accent the vertical; however the top seems overly rich as the ornament is excessively bold and all but defeats its purpose.

**GAGE BUILDING, 18 South Michigan Avenue, Chicago (Figure 3.39), 1898–1899, by Sullivan, is one of three buildings for the same owner. Numbers 24 and 30 South Michigan, 1897–1898, were by Holabird and Roche, and these buildings set the theme for the completed block. However Sullivan's building, originally 8 stories but increased to 12 in 1902, has a refinement and pattern not evident in the other two. His terra-cotta covered steel and glass building truly bears out the dictum *Form follows Function* and has aesthetic beauty as an additional factor (see Condit, *The Rise of the Skyscraper*).

**CARSON, PIRIE AND SCOTT DEPARTMENT STORE, State Street, Chicago (Figure 3.40), 1899–1904, by Louis Sullivan, was originally the Schlesinger & Meyer Department Store but was later sold and reorganized under the present name. Here Sullivan used the steel frame quite directly to develop the design theme; in addition he designed a strong circular and vertical corner entrance motive at State and Madison Streets. This is flanked by a simple pattern of 10 upper stories of horizontal rectangular Chicago windows. Two later additions, of 1903–1904 and 1906, repeat the same design. The base consists of two stories of display windows encased in Sullivanesque ornament in painted cast iron. This ironwork is strikingly beautiful, particularly at the semicircular State and Madison entrance, where the floral detail is richest. The building originally had a simple, projecting terra-cotta slab which formed the crowning cornice feature and provided a handsome cap to the building. However because of the hazard of such overhanging terra-cotta cornices

Figure 3.39 Gage Building, 18, 24, and 30 South Michigan Avenue, Chicago, Illinois, 1898–1899; Nos. 24 and 30 by Holabird and Roche, No. 18 by Louis Sullivan; Functional design. Photograph by Chicago Historical Society, taken prior to additions to Nos. 24 and 30.

deteriorating and falling, this was ordered removed in 1948. A simple parapet was substituted, which is quite satisfactory, although from a design point of view the original was better.

There is a small feature on the Wabash Avenue side of the building that should be mentioned. This is a covered footbridge from the elevated railroad platform to the second floor of the store. It is a gem of Sullivanesque design in metal and glass.

After 1900 Sullivan's practice declined because of the growing popularity of Classic Eclecticism, and he had to be content with small projects. However, though small, some of these are masterpieces of beauty and innovative in design.

Figure 3.40   Carson, Pirie and Scott Department Store, Chicago, Illinois, 1891–1904; Louis Sullivan, Architect; Functional design. Photograph by Chicago Historical Society.

*NATIONAL FARMERS' BANK, Owatonna, Minnesota, 1907–1908, by Sullivan, is one of a series of small banks by that architect in Minnesota, Wisconsin, and Iowa. This bank is of russet-brown, rough-cut brick on both the exterior and interior, with terra-cotta trim of Sullivanesque detail. This tradition was carried on by two of his assistants, William G. Purcell and George C. Elmslie, who later formed their own firm under the name of Purcell and Elmslie (1910–1913) in Chicago. Their work can easily be mistaken as late work of Sullivan, particularly the *Merchant's National Bank, Winona, Minnesota*, 1914, and the *First National Bank, Mankato, Minnesota*, 1912. Both of these are gems. All three of these banks have had excellent care, and have recently been cleaned and renovated.

*HENRY BABSON RESIDENCE, Riverside, Illinois, 1907, by Louis Sullivan, was an excellent example of open planning and most beautiful in the way the exterior terraces and landscaping flowed out from the interior of the house. It also shows how close Louis Sullivan and Frank Lloyd Wright were in their philosophy of residential architecture at this time. (Note the Avery Coonley House in Riverside, Illinois, 1908–1909, by Frank Lloyd Wright.) Sad to state, the Babson House was demolished a few years ago, and the estate grounds were bulldozed to make way for a government housing project; also the Coonley house and grounds have been allowed to deteriorate over the last few years.

Later Buildings

Louis Sullivan died in 1924, in near obscurity and poverty. Adler had died in 1900. Purcell and Elmslie had looked after Sullivan in his last years. His final project was the *Kraus Music Store, 4611 North Lincoln Avenue, Chicago,* 1922, a small two-storied building on an interior lot. It is a distinctive little building in terra-cotta and carries a strong central motive of decoration, but is as nothing compared with his masterly work of former years.

Mention should be made of S. S. Beman, who did a steel multistoried building thinly covered in terra-cotta. This was the Studebaker Building, which ranked with Sullivan's Gage Building as a clear expression of glass and structure. S. S. Beman was also architect for the old Grand Central Station, Chicago, 1889–1894, terminal for the Baltimore and Ohio railroad at Harrison and Wells Streets. This station was famous for its great train shed, which at that time was the second largest span in America. Only the Grand Central Station in New York (1871) was larger.

Since the advent of Amtrac (1970), the government-operated system of railway passenger lines, this station is no longer in use and no doubt may soon be destroyed. The main building is a Norman Romanesque adaptation, noted for its high clock tower, which was a landmark in Chicago at the turn of the century.

*STUDEBAKER BUILDING (now known as the Brunswick Building), 629 South Wabash Street, Chicago, 1895, by S. S. Beman, is a 10-storied building with thin terra-cotta piers running full height and spanned between by large Chicago windows. These windows, which are flat and slightly behind the face of the vertical piers, are separated at the floor lines by decorative iron spandrels. The detail of the terra-cotta is Gothic,

and though a bit arbitrary in its treatment of the original central doorway and the castellated parapet, the facade presented a composition of
vertical piers and glass that was quite ahead of its time.

Sadly, this building has been badly mutilated in late years: the parapet
has been removed and replaced by a brick wall entirely out of keeping
with the original design, and the lower two floors have been masked by a
plain wall-like obstruction that bears no relation to the original piers
and glass.

From 1900 onward a second generation of architects tried to carry on
the traditions of the Chicago School. Clinton J. Warren made a reputa-
tion in efficiently planned hotel buildings; William B. Mundie and his
firm of Mundie, Jensen and McLurg inherited the office of William
LeBaron Jenney. Richard B. Schmidt started practice in 1887, but entered the big field after he established a partnership with Garden and
Martin in 1906. Both Schmidt and Garden were influenced in design by
Louis Sullivan. Dwight Perkins, Max Dunning, and George Maher,
among a few others, were the second generation inheritors of the functional tradition. However the public demanded classic design, and the
new architectural schools all over the country taught the French Beaux
Arts design.

Graham, Anderson, Probst, and White grew out of the office of
Daniel H. Burnham and Company, but succumbed completely to the
Classic Eclectic mode. They did large works all over the country, but
these had little distinction.

There is an interesting anecdote regarding the steel-framed building.
In 1888 Leroy S. Buffington, architect of Minneapolis, Minnesota,
secured a patent on steel-framed construction and soon after sued several
architects in Chicago for infringement on his patent. However William
LeBaron Jenney had already built the Home Insurance Building, Chicago, and the Tacoma Building, by Holabird and Roche, was then under
construction. Thus Buffington was late with his patent, and the court
passed over his claims.

FISHER BUILDING, 343 South Dearborn Street, Chicago, 1897, by
D. H. Burnham Company, like Beman's Studebaker Building (Brunswick Building), used Gothic detail in its terra-cotta covering. It is 18
stories high and a clever composition of projecting Chicago window bays
which contrast with flat three-part windows and rise from the third floor

through the sixteenth story. It is a distinguished building, though overly ornate in its detail.

RAILWAY EXCHANGE BUILDING, Jackson and Michigan Boulevard, Chicago, 1904, was "one of the last good designs that came from the office of D. H. Burnham and Company." (see Condit, *The Rise of the Skyscraper,* Chicago Press, 1952). A large 18-storied building of white terra-cotta, the building has a masonry rather than a skeletal steel appearance. Although it has large horizontal windows alternated with projecting bays, there is neither a horizontal nor a vertical accent. The attic story is accented by large bull's-eye windows that are distinctive but of no great aesthetic value. This building is not unpleasant; it is rather good in proportion, and large and imposing.

FLATIRON BUILDING (formerly the Fuller Building), Fifth Avenue and Broadway, New York City, 1902, by D. H. Burnham and Company, was heralded as an innovation in office building design although it did not introduce anything new. It is an 18-storied, fireproof, steel-framed building that is individual for its shape. It takes advantage of its triangular site, which gave it its name. Nevertheless the exterior is completely faced with heavy stone masonry of Florentine palace detail to give the appearance of a wall-bearing building. Its great overhanging classic cornice is entirely inappropriate to steel construction.

*MONTGOMERY WARD WAREHOUSE, on the Chicago River, 1906–1908, by Schmidt, Garden and Martin, is a huge building covering two city blocks in length and rising nine stories throughout most of its length. It has a reinforced concrete frame and was hailed as the first large and high building with heavy floor loads to use a concrete frame. This concrete frame is directly reflected in the exterior design. There is no attempt here to accent the vertical; on the contrary, accent is on the horizontal. The regularly spaced horizontal windows are further accented by projecting bands at top and bottom that run the length of the building. The entire aesthetic effect is dependent on the proportions of the windows in relation to the plain surfaces and the horizontal spandrels.

*CARL SCHURZ HIGH SCHOOL, Milwaukee Avenue and Addison Street, Chicago, Illinois (Figure 3.41), 1910, by Dwight Perkins, is a large

Figure 3.41 Carl Schurz High School, Chicago, Illinois, 1910; Dwight Perkins, Architect; Functional design. Photograph by Kaufman and Fabry, courtesy of the Chicago Historical Society.

city high school almost a city block in length. Of reddish brown brick with buff stone trim, it is topped by green tile roofs that cap different masses.

The design is somewhat whimsical in the way the masses are broken up into vertical components. Nevertheless it is a very pleasant and distinguished design and a relief from most educational buildings of the era, which were either classic or Collegiate Gothic. A great deal of Frank Lloyd Wright influence can be seen in this building, and except for the great roofs the design might mistakenly be attributed to Wright's work of the period.

Other than the multistoried steel-framed office buildings and large city hotels of the Chicago group, a few banks and a residence here and there by Louis Sullivan and Frank Lloyd Wright, there were very few other types of buildings of this era that can be classified as representative of the functional approach. An exception was the work of Irving Gill of Los Angeles, California, who did a number of residences that apparently developed out of the Spanish Mission style, as some of his early work followed that mode. The resulting houses of white cement plaster depended on form only: voids to solids for aesthetic effect. His work was surprisingly like that of Adolf Loos of Austria, and though the two were contemporary, their design arose from different roots and there is no evidence that the two men were ever in communication.

*WALTER DODGE HOUSE, 950 North Kings Road, Los Angeles, California, 1915–1916, by Irving Gill, was of masonry covered by cement plaster. This house, which was set in a city square block and beautifully landscaped, had large window openings in plain white walls. The mass and proportions were excellent. Recently this house was destroyed, and the landscaped grounds have been taken over for a complex of apartment buildings.

THE ART CENTER (formerly the Scripps House), La Jolla, California, 1917, by Irving Gill, is also of masonry covered with cement plaster. Its aesthetic effect is dependent on window openings that contrast with plain walls.

Albert Kahn of Detroit, Michigan, accomplished more in the field of warehouse and factory design than any other architect. He worked with the early automobile manufacturers (1900–1920) such as Henry Ford, the Dodge brothers, and others to plan and fabricate their factories along functional lines both in structure and layout. The assembly line introduced about 1910–1912 into the new Highland Park Ford factories was as much Albert Kahn's idea in planning as Henry Ford's. The two worked together at diagramming the inflow of raw materials, storage and stockpiling of materials, outflow of finished products, circulation of workers, and supply of human amenities, as well as supervision and administration. Kahn proved the importance of complete functional planning, the presence of light and air, economical construction with minimum upkeep, and easy control and service.

At the height of Albert Kahn, Inc., in the 1920–1930 decade, this firm was doing industrial work all over the world. In 1928 the Russian government commissioned Kahn to lay out a program for over $2 billion worth of industrial buildings. Forty of these factories were designed in Detroit; the remainder were done in Moscow, where Kahn set up an office with 1500 draftsmen. In other parts of the world, including the United States, his firm did over a million dollars worth of work per week in a variety of buildings: airplane factories, auto assembly plants, steel mills, warehouses, docks, textile mills, distilleries, and even a cosmetic plant.

Prior to World War I and during the 1920–1930 decade, it might be said that Albert Kahn ran two offices: one in collaboration with Professor Ernest Wilby, the designer who turned out Classic, Gothic, and other eclectic buildings, all of very high quality; and one that did factories and other buildings in which the functional idea was paramount. Kahn worked with light steel and was greatly preoccupied with the idea of letting in as much daylight as possible. Some of his designs at this time, which were contemporary with those of Peter Behrens of Germany, are quite similar to the work of that master. Like Behrens he used great areas of steel factory sash and, unable to get this sash in the United States, he was forced to import it from England, sometimes at great delay. To satisfy the growing need, he designed and patented the Trus-Con window.

Kahn's office was departmentalized and became the most efficient architectural office in the country. Although he started as an office boy at the age of 11 and became a sensitive designer and critic, he was also a twentieth century organization man. He is credited with saying, "Architecture is 90% business and 10% art."

PACKARD AUTO FACTORY, Detroit, 1903, by Albert Kahn, was a three-storied reinforced concrete building that was added to a number of times. It was designed for the Packard Motor Car Company, whose product was coming up fast as the foremost car in America. Henry B. Joy, a wealthy Detroiter, was president of the company. The building, strictly functional, was not inspiring but is noted as the first of many showing a long development in factory design.

OLD FORD FACTORY COMPLEX, Highland Park, Detroit, 1910–1918, by Albert Kahn, is a large group of multistoried buildings, all of reinforced concrete with brick-veneered facades over tile and with maximum windows of steel sash. Although the buildings were electrically lighted, incandescent lighting at that time was quite inefficient. Maximum daylight was the ideal. These buildings were laid out for assembly line production and were heralded at the time as the ultimate in production efficiency, as well as workers' welfare. In contrast to the greasy and dark machine shops of the nineteenth century, this factory was kept immaculately clean. In constant attendance on the floors were sweepers who wore white uniforms. Average mechanics were paid $5 per day, an extraordinarily high wage at that time. These buildings, now obsolete and in the process of being abandoned and torn down, were given international advertising, and Henry Ford profited as the great innovator. This was the home of the Model T Ford (retail price $500), built to fulfill Henry Ford's boast that he would put a Ford in every backyard in America.

About this time, just prior to World War I, Albert Kahn introduced the concept of one-storied factories of light steel construction covering large areas of ground and daylighted by monitored-type roofs containing glass. He soon turned the monitored sash toward the north and secured even distribution of daylight throughout the floor area. *Continental Motor Company, Detroit,* 1912, and *Paige-Detroit Motor Car Company,* 1914, were examples of these daylighted factories that have since been destroyed.

From 1941 to 1942, during World War II, to comply with blackout regulations and to take advantage of the then new fluorescent electric lighting, his firm designed factories that were without exterior windows and completely air conditioned; these were lighted to daylight brightness by fluorescent tubes. *The Ford Bomber Plant (now General Motors Hydramatic Division) at Willow Run, near Ypsilanti, Michigan,* 1943, is an example of his latest perfected factory type.

*COLLEGE OF NATURAL SCIENCE, University of Michigan, Ann Arbor, Michigan (Figure 3.42), 1917, by Albert Kahn, is a large three-storied building on a high basement. It is a reinforced concrete structure with an exterior in decorative brick pattern and maximum-sized classroom windows of plate glass in large, triple-divided frames that are similar to the Chicago window. At the time it was built the building was criticized as being too much like a factory, though it was admitted to be excellently laid out and beautifully daylighted. Nevertheless the next building than Kahn did for the university was in Greek styling to satisfy the aesthetic taste of the academic community. This was *Angell Hall,* a large classroom building for the College of Literature, Science and the Arts. It has a grand frontal colonnade of Doric columns that supports a huge parapet wall, which completely hides an attic story of classrooms and offices. Angell Hall is a beautiful academic building.

Figure 3.42 College of Natural Science, University of Michigan, Ann Arbor, Michigan, 1914; Albert Kahn, Architect; Functional design. Photograph by Forster Studio; courtesy of Albert Kahn Associates.

*U.S. ARMY SUPPLY BASE, 58th Street, South Brooklyn, New York City, 1916–1917, by Cass Gilbert, is another building that represents functional design. This huge building of eight stories, built entirely of reinforced concrete, covers more than 10 acres of ground. The mass is beautifully broken up and is an honest expression of utility and structure. It is of great credit to Cass Gilbert and his designer, T. R. Johnson, who usually did Classic Eclectic buildings such as the Minnesota State Capitol and several government buildings in Washington, as well as the pseudo-Gothic Woolsworth Tower.

*OHIO STEEL FOUNDARY COMPANY, ROLL AND HEAVY MACHINE SHOP, Lima, Ohio, 1938, is an almost exact replica of the **Chrysler Half Ton Truck Division Export Building, Detroit,* 1938.

Both are by Albert Kahn, Inc. These seem to be examples of almost exact requirements bringing almost exact design results. No doubt Mr. Kahn's research in daylighting and light steel construction influenced these factory buildings and helped bring about these results. The end views of both buildings are beautifully proportioned, and the Lima, Ohio, building is enhanced further by a reflecting pool. Interior working conditions are quite ideal in both cases.

PHASE 4. ART NOUVEAU, 1890–1910

During the time of Industrial Romanticism, Eclecticism, and the Functional styling of the Chicago group in the United States, a group of avant-garde architects in Europe, beginning about 1885, were trying to introduce a new style principally in opposition to the Eclecticists. Their stated aim was to create a new art, *Art Nouveau*. Two names stand out as the innovators of the style: Antonio Gaudi of Barcelona, Spain, and Victor Horta of Brussels, Belgium.* Other names could be added, for example, Raimondo d'Aronco, who was architect for a great exposition in Turin, Italy, in 1902; but although this exposition was superb in its newness and clever articulation, it followed what Horta and others were doing and had done elsewhere. It did not pioneer a new style. Another devotee of the style was Otto Wagner of Austria.

However Art Nouveau had little effect architecturally in the United States. The style was an attempt to be novel and new, and it glorified the willowy curve above all. It was based on nature, particularly flowers, which were imitated in wrought iron, colored glass, stucco, plaster, paint, and enamel. The innovators argued that since Gothic piers and ribbed vaults suggested the sturdy trunks and spreading branches of trees, why not design piers and ribbed vaults in conventionalized tree forms? Gaudi in Spain did this. Designers often used grapevine forms in plaster for decorative friezes, and long-stemmed lotus flowers in wrought iron for stair and balcony railings. Rooms were planned in oval and other curved forms. Some of these undulating forms for both plans and elevations were somewhat remindful of Baroque and Rococo forms; however whereas eighteenth century Rococo retained overtones of classic design, these Art Nouveau designers studiously avoided historical forms of any

---

* It is definitely known that though these two men were contemporary and worked for similar goals, they were absolutely separate, one from the other.

kind. Curves were carefully balanced and often geometrical in final result; still it was the willowy line that predominated.

Although Art Nouveau fashions in metal and glass art objects, as well as in ladies fashions, were popular for a brief period in the United States and Canada, as an architectural style it never took hold here. A few examples had been imported to the St. Louis Exposition, 1904, from Austria and Germany, but they did not receive popular acclaim. Art Nouveau was bypassed in that extravaganza of Beaux-Arts–Baroque eclecticism. In New York City the *New Amsterdam Theater* on 42nd Street, just off Broadway, was built with very clever Art Nouveau detailing on the proscenium arch, and boxes at each side of the stage that look like hollowed-out tree tops. However it was accepted only as a theatrical *tour de force* at the time, not something to be taken seriously.

The studios of Louis C. Tiffany in New York became famous for their stained glass productions, Favrile Glass; however these were mostly limited to domelike dining room electric fixtures, table lamps, and vases of grape and flower designs which were soon extensively imitated. The highly stylized and curvilinear poster drawings of Aubrey Beardsley were popular in America as well as in Europe, as were Charles Dana Gibson's drawings of what were known as Gibson Girls in America and Flora-Dora Girls in Europe.

PALACIO DEL BELLES ARTES, Mexico City, 1906–1930, designed by Adam Boari and Federico Mariscal, is the outstanding example of Art Nouveau architecture in the Western Hemisphere. It was ordered to be the finest and most gorgeous opera house in the Western Hemisphere. Because there were long periods of inactivity during the Mexican Revolution of 1911 and the following long periods of political chaos, this building was not finished until 1930. Also in 1911, when the huge bulk was being roofed in, the building was found to be sinking. The spongy subsoil of Mexico City could not sustain its huge weight. Foreign and local engineers were called in, and immense amounts of concrete were pumped in and around the foundations. The sinking process was slowed but not stopped, just as with the great Cathedral of Mexico, the National Library, and many other buildings in the central city.

The Belles Artes has now lowered itself over 6 feet so that the lobby floor, originally a podium with monumental steps, is now almost level with the street. Fortunately the building has settled evenly and has not cracked, even though it has been shaken by earthquakes several times. The interior has gorgeous lobbies of Mexican onyx, colored marble, and gold leaf. There are fine exhibition halls, galleries, and a splendid auditorium with complete stage. One of the features of the building is the great Tiffany glass stage curtain, which weighs several tons. It depicts a beautiful Art Nouveau landscape showing the two great mountain peaks of Popocatepetl and Ixtaccihuatl and features electric lighting effects which change the coloring from sunrise to sunset. The curtain alone cost $50 thousand and could not be reproduced today for over $1 million.

Thus, although the Art Nouveau style of Europe had some influence, in America as an art form, it had little effect in America architecturally. Even in Europe it was a decorative style more than anything else and was not concerned with function or structure. Its sole aim was to be new and different, clever and fashionable at all costs. It claimed to be based on nature—flowers, vines, and sinuous forms—but its roots were not too deep. Though some of its European works were original and attractive, the fashion was somewhat popular only from 1895 to 1905, then grew tired and passed out of style about 1910.

PHASE 5. THE CRAFT MOVEMENT, 1890–1920

The fifth group of architects of the Age of Steel and Steam (1860–1930) had still another philosophy of design. This was known as the *Craft Movement,* and its main promoter was William Morris (1834–1896) of England. Morris started as an architect in the office of George Edmund Street, a London Gothicist, but he was a young man of some wealth and quit this office in 1856 to become a painter. He had some talent and soon became linked with the Pre-Raphaelite group of artists in England, and with Burne-Jones in particular. With him Morris did a number of mural decorations and stained glass windows. In America the north transept window (1877) of Trinity Church, Boston, by H. H. Richardson, was a collaboration of Burne-Jones and Morris.

Morris loved his craft but soon realized that he was in competition with machine art. He began to write articles opposed to the machine and its dangers to handcrafted art. These writings had great influence on younger architects, and during the 1880s and 1890s a group formed to take up the cause of handcrafted art. An Arts and Crafts Exhibition Society, formed in England in 1888, exerted great influence. They decried the bad taste often displayed by the Industrial Romanticists and were out of sympathy with the Functionalists who embraced the machine. They also disparaged the Art Nouveau group as merely decorators, although many of the crafters borrowed Art Nouveau designs. Their style antedated those of the *de stijl* group of Holland and the Cubists, though some of their work might be aligned with these later stylists. They talked of getting back to fundamentals, which to them meant handcrafted art.

In 1861 William Morris organized the firm of Morris and Company to promote and execute handcrafted woodworking and carving, metal work, textiles, and wall paper design, in fact all of the decorative arts. The painter Burne-Jones, architect Philip Webb, and others were associated. However making things by hand is expensive, and the group soon found themselves working only on luxuries for the rich. Mechanical production could supply the wants of the middle and lower classes much more cheaply. Morris and Company eventually dissolved, but William Morris continued to preach and to write. He became fearful of the machine and the dire effects that he feared it could have, not only on art but on society as well. Eventually he became a radical socialist. Nevertheless some of his theories were good. He proposed that craft training should accompany academic training and sought the introduction of manual arts courses in English elementary schools. Soon the movement spread to Scandinavia and America.

Mention should be made of the influence of William Morris on domestic furniture. He recognized that most of the machine-made furniture of the time was not only aesthetically atrocious but also quite uncomfortable. The Eastlake furniture of the Industrial Romanticists had become overly scrolled, filagreed, and balled, and the 1890 attempts of Grand Rapids manufacturers to reproduce English and American colonial styles were often gaudy and stiff. American Art Nouveau designs were generally no better since they were often thin and unsteady.

The way was open for something better when Morris designed his Morris chair, a spacious lounge chair with an adjustable back that allowed a person to sit up straight, lean back, or recline. Low-slung with two mattresslike cushions, one for the seat and one for the back, it was the first of the modern comfortable lounge chairs. The overstuffed upholstered sofa also made its appearance at this time. Now, 80 years later, the squarish mattresslike cushions of our lounge chairs are of foam rubber, and much of today's styling derives from Scandinavian machine-made models; however the Morris chair can plainly be seen as the prototype.

In the Scandinavian countries, where craftsmanship was already prized over the machine, the handcraft movement was embraced with open arms. Although it had some adherents in Holland, Belgium, and Germany, it was in Sweden that the movement was most influential. There it dealt with structure as well as with handcrafted detail, and though it did not turn its back on the machine as an aid, the handcrafted look was paramount. Whereas in Britain and America the movement had to do mostly with domestic architecture and artifacts, in Scandinavia it dealt with such large buildings as churches, town halls, and railway stations. Among their architects the most outstanding were Ragnar Östberg of Sweden, architect for the Stockholm City Hall, and Eliel Saarinen of Finland, architect for the Helsinki Railway Station.

Eliel Saarinen came to the United States in 1923 to enter the Chicago Tribune Tower competition, for which he won second prize. After that he spent a year as Professor of Architecture in the Department of Architecture, University of Michigan. However George Booth of Scripps–Booth newspaper fame then persuaded him to take charge of Cranbrook School for Boys (Figure 3.43), and Kingswood School for Girls, both college preparatory schools that stressed handcrafts along with academic training. Booth, a very sympathetic patron of the arts, also commissioned Saarinen to design the buildings and arrange the vast grounds of the Booth estate. Mrs. Saarinen, also an artist, was an advisor in the schools and taught weaving and other manual arts. Later Booth established the Cranbrook Academy of advanced study in architecture, city planning, painting, and sculpture. Students from art and architectural schools throughout the hemisphere could go there for advanced study in architecture, city planning, painting, and sculpture. Saarinen surrounded himself with famous figures in the art world, among them Carl Milles, a sculptor from Sweden, and Zoltan Sepeshy, a painter from Hungary.

Earlier, around 1890, Elbert Hubbard of Buffalo, New York, started a craft school known as "Roycroft" outside of Buffalo, and though this school ended only as a fashionable dilettante group, it had considerable influence. It was based on William Morris's teachings in England and dealt in woodwork, pounded brass and copper, tooled leather, tile and pottery, weaving and hand blocking of cloth and wallpaper.

Another group, working on the Pacific coast and moving eastward, introduced a type of handcrafted furniture known as "Mission." This was essentially handcrafted furniture, primarily of oak, although it was soon imitated by the machine. It was stained and waxed, or fumed—given a natural finish gained by penetrating the wood with a burned-oil smoke that gave a rich brown color quite impervious to water or scratches. This furniture was square and blocky in design, often had pegged joints, and if upholstered as were the couches and Morris chairs,

Figure 3.43 Cranbrook School for Boys, Bloomfield Hills, north of Detroit, Michigan, 1926–1941; Eliel Saarinen, Architect; Handcraft style. Photograph donated by Cranbrook School.

were done in brown leather, corduroy, or even burlap. The furniture got its name from the California missions, but the designs were purely manual-training craft type.

In architecture the leading exponents of the movement were the Greene brothers, Charles and Henry, of Pasadena, California. They developed a style of residential wooden buildings based entirely on crafts-

manship. They trained their workmen—most of them Japanese craftsmen—to mortice and dowel the frames of their buildings. These frames
are somewhat remindful of Japanese wood joinery as used in Oriental
temples and houses. However, these men were clever designers, and their
houses can in no way be said to be copies of Oriental buildings.

The Greenes exploited the use of California redwood in its natural
color. They fabricated much of the hardware in wrought iron or
pounded brass or copper; designed and leaded their own Art Nouveau-
like windows; made decorative tile; and designed and fabricated their
own furniture, both movable and built-in. Their houses were notable
for their wide overhanging eaves with open joists and decorated rafter
ends and for wide and open verandas having terrace walls of rough stone
or colorful textured brick. Fireplace fronts were also of rough stone or
colorful textured brick. All elements blended with the rich dark brown
color of the redwood, which on the interiors was combined with
mahogany, teak, or ebony all hand rubbed to a satin finish.

These houses were given the name of *bungalow* from the Polynesian
hut called "Bangaloo," and from them the so-called California bungalow
style swept the West and Midwest. Greene and Greene's Houses were
handcrafted and were thus expensive residences; however with simplifi-
cation the bungalow became a style that was used largely for working-
men's small homes.

Some architects who adopted the style saw similarities to the Swiss
chalet, and indeed there were interesting parallels. In the East the style
was rarely used in cities and suburbs, though it was often employed on
the coast of Maine or in the eastern mountains, where it was used for
rustic summer habitation.

In the West and Midwest, however, the one-storied all-on-one-floor,
two- or even three-bedroom house became very popular. It had a porch
across the front, wide eaves with exposed rafter ends, and huge supporting piers of wood, rough stone, or brick. Inside there was often a fireplace of boulders, a beamed ceiling in the living room, and other features borrowed from Greene and Greene. Lumberyards provided plans
and ready-cut lumber so that owners could put these houses together
themselves. A lumber mill in Bay City, Michigan, provided several
models and sold them under the name of "The Aladdin House." Houses
that were partially prefabricated but needed craftsmanship in masonry
and carpentry to be put together were merchandized through lumberyards and Sears Roebuck. In 1910 and for several years thereafter a large
part of Highland Park, a suburb of Detroit, was built with these bunga-
lows for Ford factory workers. These very livable houses were easy to
live in and were the forerunners of the California Bay style and the

present ranch-type houses so popular with real estate developers catering to young families.

*R. R. BLACKER HOUSE, 645 Prospect Crescent, Pasadena, California, 1907, by Greene and Greene, was for many years considered their masterpiece. The property was large, and the whole project was landscaped and designed by the architects. It included a small artificial lake, or pond, with a waterfall, a gardener's cottage, and a garage. Most of the house appeared two storied, although it was three on the downhill side. A masterpiece of wood joinery, the house had exterior walls of redwood shakes, and there were porches, balconies, and large overhanging roofs. All were detailed in redwood and stained to blend with the landscaping. The interiors were mostly of wood—walls, floors, and ceilings—all beautifully detailed, doweled, and pegged. All were hand rubbed. The furniture, designed by Greene and Greene, was beautifully fabricated and very original. In harmony with the wood, it was very functional and straight-lined. The lighting fixtures also were original works of art in wood and stained glass. The entire project had Japanese overtones.

It is sad that this house, though still standing, has now been stripped of its furnishings and badly remodeled. The gardens have been destroyed and the property subdivided.

**DAVID H. GAMBLE HOUSE, 4 Westmoreland Street, Pasadena, California, 1908–1909, by Greene and Greene, is the best of their houses that still stand. The heirs of the original owners sold it in 1964 to a group of Pasadena citizens for local museum purposes. Although the grounds were never as extensive as the Blacker estate, they also are beautifully landscaped to take advantage of a magnificent distant view. The house is on a par with the Blacker residence though not as large. It is elegant, nevertheless, and the interiors are a synchronism of fine woods, decorative stained glass, handwrought hardware, and other handcrafted details.

WILLIAM H. THORSEN HOUSE, Berkeley, California, 1908, by Greene and Greene, is now a fraternity house, and though it has had extremely hard usage, it is still a good example of the Greene brothers' work and style. All of the original furnishings have long since disappeared, but the building itself retains a great deal of charm.

CHRISTIAN SCIENCE CHURCH, Berkeley, California, 1910, was designed by Bernard Maybeck, a prominent architect of the San Francisco Bay area. It is a bungalowtype church with a large Gothic window in the front. The low-pitched roofs have wide overhanging eaves, and the base story has a screen of pergolalike grillage across the front. The mixture of Gothic window detail and bungalow styling is rather odd to say the least, but the interiors are interesting and in the handcrafted tradition.

Bernard Maybeck is often compared with the Greene brothers as a member of the prominent handcraft group, and so he was in his early years. Although a gifted designer, he was trained in the École des Beaux Arts of Paris and seems to have had no strong predilection for any one design philosophy. In 1915 he did the Palace of Fine Arts for the Panama-Pacific Exposition, a classic composition that was one of the most beautiful of that fair. It shows that by that time (1915) he had given up his enthusiasm for the bungalow-handcraft style, and had become one of the sophisticated classic eclecticists.

Before World War I, the influence of Greene and Greene on the residential Bungalow style was widely felt by builders and the younger members of the architectural profession. One of these was Jud Yoho of Los Angeles, whose outstanding work included tile and stucco structures that had low-pitched roofs with wide overhanging eaves. John Galen Howard, Dean and Professor of Architecture at the University of California, denigrated the sytle, as did all of the other schools in the United States. The bungalow-handcraft style began to lose favor immediately before World War I, and Greene and Greene closed their offices in 1914 because of lack of work.

4

GREAT WORLD EXPOSITIONS,

1860–1974

Expositions have had great influence on architecture. They are one of the best means for large numbers of people to see and learn about new developments in construction and architecture, as well as in manufactured items.

Several fairs were held in the 1850s after London's 1851 Golden Jubilee with its Crystal Palace. The daring construction of the *Palais de l'Industrie* of the Paris Exposition of 1855 surpassed that of the Crystal Palace. The main span of its glass and iron vaulting was 160 feet, over twice the 73 feet of the Crystal Palace. This great Parisian palace took the form of a huge rectangle surrounding a central court of approximately 10 acres; the building itself covered an area of more than 22 acres. There was also a hall devoted exclusively to machines, a large train shed–like pavilion, the *Galerie des Machines,* which was over 4000 feet long, approximately four fifths of a mile.

These first great exposition halls in France had exteriors with masonry, and one of the features of the design of the main hall of 1855 was a great triumphal arch. This *Palais de l'Industrie* stood in the Champs Elysées until 1897 and was used for local exhibitions of various kinds until it was torn down to make way for the Exposition of 1900 and the two more elegant permanent halls now known as the *Grand Palais* and the *Petit Palais.*

In 1867 France under Napoleon III put on a second great exposition in Paris. There another attempt was made to contain a great show all under one roof, and a huge elliptical building was projected. This building, which consisted of seven concentric rings of steel and glass around a central court, had a long axis measuring 1608 feet and a short axis of 1265 feet. The central court was a palm garden with flowers and statuary, surrounded by a colonnade of decorative cast iron columns. The exhibition galleries increased in width as the distance from the center increased. The largest gallery, the outermost, was the *Galerie des Machines,* which was 115 feet wide by 85 feet high. The circumference of this gallery measured almost a mile.

Nine years later, in 1876, Philadelphia staged the United States Centennial Exposition. New York had had a crystal palace in 1855, but the Philadelphia Centennial was the first great international trade fair to be held in the United States. This great exposition included several buildings of glass and steel construction, similar to the pavilions in Paris. A Hall of Machines housed the latest achievements in mechanization, and there also were great Halls of Agriculture and Horticulture. The presence of an art museum exposed people to the art and culture of the world. Paintings and sculpture from famous European galleries were on display, and many puritanical Americans were shocked at the nudity displayed in some of the art.

The big question however was what to do with the exteriors of these steel and glass pavilions. The Paris Exposition of 1867 treated the exteriors with simplicity. There was no attempt to cover the steel and glass although, like a circus tent, the ensemble was made gay with flags and tricolored bunting. The Philadelphia buildings had thin eclectic forms, most of which were not understood by their architects.

The Fine Arts Building was a domed stone-faced Italian Renaissance design and was to be a permanent building. The Agricultural Hall was a series of glass and steel sheds having exteriors treated in Romantic English Gothic. The architectural result, quite thin and unconvincing, was no doubt inspired by the Smithsonian Institution of Washington, D.C. Machinery Hall was made up of huge train shed–like steel and glass structures having decorative exterior details of pseudo-Spanish derivation. The result here was also rather thin. Horticultural Hall, which stood until a few years ago, was a mammoth greenhouse that had Moorish-like detail pressed out of sheet steel. The interior, with exotic tropical plants and flowers, was gay and very pleasing. Minor pavilions ranged from a Stick style Eastlake type representing Michigan and its lumber industry (see p. 91) to a pseudo-Spanish building for California. Philadelphia's exposition was certainly representative of the Industrial Romantic movement, which was popular at that particular time.

Soon after the Philadelphia show, in 1878 France put on its third International Exposition to prove to the world that France had recovered from her German defeat and the Commune uprising of 1870 and to show that France was still one of the world leaders in commerce and industry. This fair was the first one in which France decentralized its various displays into separate pavilions as Philadelphia had done two years before. A number of structural engineering advances were made. De Dion, who designed the *Palais des Machines* for this fair, used precise mathematical calculations in figuring the weights and stresses of the steel; Eiffel also added a great deal to the experimental calculations. Except for the Trocadera (now destroyed), which was designed as a permanent concert hall and auditorium, most of the buildings were temporary steel and glass pavilions that had been sheathed with pressed sheet steel which allowed the structures to show through. The steel and glass domes were gay in form, and with its beautiful landscaping, sculpture, and many flags, this fair was appealing and gay. Great technical advancement in all fields was shown.

The exposition of 1889 in Paris went even further in this direction, culminating in the superb *Palais des Machines* by the engineer and builder, Cottacin, and architect, Dutert. The central feature of the fair was the Eiffel Tower, which remains to this day an awe-inspring *tour de force*. This fair showed the world the latest steel structures, planning, and landscaping.

Four years later came the world's Columbian Exposition of 1893 in Chicago (Figures 4.1–4.3). Structurally there were no innovations; steel

Figure 4.1 Panoramic view of World's Columbian Exposition, Chicago, Illinois, 1893; Committee of architects headed by Daniel H. Burnham; Classic Eclectic style. Photograph by Chicago Historical Society.

engineering had by then become an exact science. The only apparent
way to awe the public was by a great exterior display. The same large
steel and glass train shed–like pavilions were built as in former expositions, with miles of marvelous exhibits inside. The exteriors were done
by a committee of architects headed by Daniel H. Burnham of Chicago,
and they leaned heavily on the advice of the New York group, particularly Charles F. McKim of the architectural firm of McKim, Mead and
White. A great extravagant "White City" was the result. The exposition
was classically planned around a central lagoon, and the various super-

Figure 4.2 Administrative Building, World's Columbian Exposition, Chicago,
Illinois, 1893; Richard M. Hunt, Architect. Photograph from collection of Chicago
Historical Society.

Figure 4.3   Palace of Fine Arts, Columbian Exposition, Chicago, Illinois, 1893; rebuilt in 1928, now Rosenwald Museum of Science and Industry; Charles Atwood, Architect. Photograph by Chicago Historical Society.

sized steel and glass pavilions were fronted by Renaissance and Baroque of white plaster that looked like white marble. The American public may have dreamed it, but they had never before seen such magnificence. Here they saw fountains and sculpture, marble balustraded terraces, magnificent classic arches and Corinthian colonnades.

The fair was extremely dramatic, and though much of it was merely a show in a fake setting, it had great influence on the architecture of the next 30 to 40 years. The nearest thing to functional architecture was Louis Sullivan's Transportation Building, and looking back now it can be seen that even that had merely changed one dress for another. Throughout the world the public became sold on Classic Eclecticism, and most subsequent expositions up to 1925 were done in variants of this style. Functionalism was forgotten, or if planned for, was covered with historical classic styling of one period or another. Public buildings even residences, followed. If it could be afforded, the material would be marble or limestone, or failing that, brick or stucco; even pressed sheet metal would be painted to look like marble. Since the next three decades, until the Great Depression, were very prosperous, buildings and styling were very extravagant.

The Paris Exposition of 1900 was a great Beaux-Arts extravaganza in painted plaster over shells of steel and glass. It was beautiful of course, but not as truthful as the fair of 1889.

The Chicago Exposition was followed by a succession of smaller fairs sponsored by Chambers of Commerce and industry throughout the United States in such places as New Orleans, Omaha, and Buffalo.

Then followed in 1904 the Louisiana Purchase Exposition in St. Louis (Figure 4.4). E. L. Masqueray, a talented Beaux-Arts designer, came from France to supervise and design this great show; New York City architects supplied the drawings for most of the pavilions. There seemed no limit to size, as for example the Palace of Agriculture by Carrère and Hastings, which measured 1600 by 500 feet. The Transportation Building was 1300 feet long; Machinery Hall 1000 feet, and the Palace of Industry 1200; the Palace of Manufacturers also was of similar length. These are only half of the great pavilions, and the others were comparable. One permanent building, the Palace of Fine Arts—now the St. Louis Museum—was designed by Cass Gilbert. The buildings were all Baroque under criticism of Masqueray, as interpreted by the École des Beaux Arts in Paris. Thereupon American schools of architecture and the profession in general capitulated completely to this type of design. Chicago introduced the grand classic style to America in 1893; St. Louis clinched it in 1904.

Other smaller fairs followed in Portland, Oregon; Norfolk, Virginia; Seattle, Washington; Turin, Milan, Vienna, Munich, Dresden, Cologne, and other places. Most of these were in pseudoclassic dress, except the Turin Exposition of 1901, which was in Art Nouveau style. Cologne's Deutsche Werkbund Exposition in 1914 by Walter Gropius, Van der Velde, and others was a successful and early attempt at Structural Functionalism.

In 1915 San Francisco staged another International Fair, the Panama–Pacific Exposition (Figure 4.5). This great and extravagant show in Classic Eclectic style used color beautifully, and the floral landscaping was magnificent. The introduction of floodlighting added greatly to the night effects. Louis Sullivan and Frank Lloyd Wright ridiculed it for its lack of originality, and it is true that taken separately each part had been done many times before. There were Roman triumphal arches and Roman Columns of Trajan which had Trajan supplanted by a youthful archer pointing his bow and arrow to the rising or the setting sun. Nevertheless it was a magnificent show, done on a grand scale and with color, flowers, and lighting that could not be surpassed.

The same year that San Francisco held its great Panama–Pacific Exposition, San Diego, California, put on a rival fair, the Panama–Cali-

Figure 4.4 Louisiana Purchase Exposition, St. Louis, Missouri, 1904; E. L. Masqueray, Architect in charge; Baroque style. Photograph from collection of Missouri Historical Society.

194

Figure 4.5 Palace of Fine Arts, Panama–Pacific Exposition, San Francisco, California, 1915; Bernard Maybeck, Architect; Classic Eclectic style. Photograph from California Historical Society, San Francisco.

fornia Exposition. Bertram G. Goodhue, in charge of design for this show, decided on the Spanish Baroque style (churrigueresque) as the theme because of the historical significance of the missions of California. He did a masterful job, and though the ensemble was small compared to the San Francisco Fair, it was more intimate and had a freshness that San Francisco lacked. In a sense this fair was not an industrial trade exposition, but a show dealing with the history of California and the Old West. Goodhue's architecture however had great influence on California and the entire southern half of the United States, where the style was used and copied until 1930. In fact, architects attempting to do Spanish Eclectic architecture often referred to Goodhue's brochure of the fair rather than to original sources.

World War I began in 1914, just before the California fairs opened, and attendance was low at both of these expositions. Great social, political, and philosophical changes took place during and immediately following the war. In the decade immediately following the war, there was an attempt to return architecture to its prewar status. Eclecticism continued, and skyscrapers were built in Gothic or Classic Renaissance styles. Steel-framed buildings were made to look like masonry.

However students began to talk about the Bauhaus of Germany, under Walter Gropius, and to listen to Frank Lloyd Wright, who lectured occasionally in schools of architecture around the country. The students were temporarily inspired, but this soon wore off and they returned to their libraries for academic design inspiration.

In 1925 Paris held an Exposition of Decorative Arts, and all countries were invited to show their new art and architecture. To this the American Institute of Architects responded, through the State Department, that the United States had nothing to show. The Exposition of Decorative Arts was more concerned with ornament than with structural forms, and the fair actually accomplished very little. Most of the buildings were made to look like masonry. Only one, by Le Corbusier (Charles Edouard Jeanneret), showed the skeletal form that portended the future.

But the search for new forms and a new philosophy continued in Europe, though not in the United States. The new spirit of architecture had begun with the 1914 Werkbund Exposition Buildings in Cologne, by Walter Gropius. In 1922 Auguste Perret and his brother, Gustave, designed the church of Notre Dame at Raincy, a suburb of Paris. Built entirely of reinforced concrete, it is a skeletal type with stained glass panels between supports. All of the concrete structure is exposed and has a Gothic effect, even as the structural stone of European Gothic is exposed. In 1926, Karl Moser, architect, introduced this type of Perret design in St. Antonius Catholic Church in Basel, Switzerland.

Between 1920 and 1925 Le Corbusier collaborated in the publication of an art magazine in Paris known as *Le Esprit Nouveau,* which was soon translated into English and German. In 1922 he published drawings of "The Radiant City," a hypothetical project for a city of 3 million people. Here he proposed a central business district of cruciform skyscrapers resting on great piers that allowed free pedestrian traffic at ground level. Around this core were blocks of apartment buildings of moderate height, also resting on supports spaced to allow a parklike terrain including space for automobile parking. Elevated superhighways threaded traffic through and around the city, and pedestrian walkways ran over, under, and through the central business district.

This Radiant City was never accepted as more than a fanciful idea; yet it haunted those who studied it. It solved many of the problems of cities of the day, including the growing traffic problems. It would have concentrated the growing population into great city complexes without destroying too much of the terrain or the surrounding rural land for agricultural purposes. Actually the more it was studied, the more rational it appeared.

Then in 1925 Le Corbusier published his famous book on city planning, *Urbanisme,* which is still quoted as a great source book on the subject. He became a great force in the architectural world, and though much of his writing took place in the 1920s, his acceptance and influence was greatest 25 years later.

In 1927 an experimental housing project for low-income families, known as the "Werkbund Housing," was built at Weisenhof, just outside of Stuttgart, Germany. Ludwig Mies van der Rohe, Walter Gropius, Le Corbusier, J. J. P. Oud, and other architects, with Mies in charge, each presented his individual solution. They attempted to show different improved types of walk-up apartments, row housing, and single-family dwellings. It was a brilliant experiment in arrangement of living spaces and economical use of materials. The results were interesting, particularly because solutions by the different architects were so similar. Here Le Corbusier's famous statement that the house should be a "machine for living" was really made to apply.

The German Pavilion at the Barcelona Exposition in Spain, 1929, by Mies van der Rohe, was a beautiful and original bright spot in an otherwise very mediocre fair done mostly in Spanish Renaissance. It was a one-storied space with curtain walls of polished marble and a thin reinforced concrete roof slab supported by sensitively spaced polished steel columns. Some partitions were merely screens of rich materials. There was also a reflecting pool that set off a lone piece of sculpture. The effect was one of exquisite beauty.

And in 1930 Stockholm staged an Arts and Crafts Exhibition in charge of Erick Gunnar Asplund, architect. This exposition, a beautiful ensemble of steel and glass, was light and elegant, and expressed gaiety through form. It had strong influence on all buildings in Scandinavia, as well as the rest of Europe, from that time onward.

Other buildings were designed in this new spirit in Europe which might be called the *International Functional* style. A few of the more important ones include the *Bauhaus, Dessau,* Germany, 1925–1926 by Walter Gropius; *Columbia Haus, Berlin,* 1929–1930, by Erick Mendelsohn; the *Van Nelle Factory in Rotterdam,* 1928–1930, by J. A. Brinkman and L. C. vander Blugt; and the *Dormitory for Swiss Students, University of Paris,* 1930, by Le Corbusier.

In the United States, however, the eclectic styles held sway. Until the stock market crash in the fall of 1929, it was a very prosperous period, and monumental buildings of all kinds were popular. Kansas City, for example, built a great war memorial: a stone shaft that had an eternal fire on top and two mastabalike buildings at the base. Indianapolis constructed a grand mall and placed a huge mausoleumlike building on axis, another replica of the Mausoleum at Halicarnassus. Other grandiose schemes were contemplated, not all of which materialized. Many universities built great football stadiums which they dedicated to their war dead, and the City of Chicago built its beautiful and monumental Soldiers' Field, a stadium for football and other athletic events.

Then in 1933 came the Century of Progress Exposition in Chicago (Figure 4.6). This fair was dedicated to scientific progress, and though it was put on in the depth of the depression, and its buildings and designs were not allowed to be too ostentatious or costly, it was a great show and drew great crowds. Charles Dawes, banker and financial wizard of Chicago, was in charge, and many of Chicago's architects participated. An architectural office was set up on the grounds, and Louis Skidmore, then a young architect just out of M.I.T., was put in charge of the work. All architectural drawings went through his office, and many were revised to fit the overall concept. However there was variety in the individual buildings, as well as continuity, which was largely given by a color scheme that was masterfully applied with fluorescent paint and combined with wonderful night lighting effects. Some of the buildings attempted to be monumental in a cardboard sort of way, but none were historical copies. Some were skeletal in appearance—steel and glass—and two of the best were the Chrysler Pavilion (Figure 4.7), by Holabird and Root; and a house, "Design for Living" (Figure 4.8), by John C. Brown-Moore, who lived in New Canaan, Connecticut, and had offices in New York City. This house, of skeletal concrete frame and plate glass, was planned for efficient and comfortable living. These two buildings and a few others introduced the United States to the International Functional style.

After the Chicago fair of 1933, which was carried over through the summer of 1934, San Francisco held a fair in 1939 on Treasure Island, which had been artificially dredged up in San Francisco Bay. This exposition was well organized and, though much smaller than the exposition of 1915, was very worthwhile. Both New York City and Paris, France put on fairs in 1939–1940. Although both of these later fairs were large, there were no innovations of note except for the General Motors Pavilion in the New York world's fair. This housed a display, called "Futurama," which stole the show.

Figure 4.6 View of the Century of Progress Exposition, Chicago, Illinois; 1933; Committee of Architects under Louis Skidmore; Charles Dawes, Chicago banker, Chairman of Fair; Noneclectic in style (Cardboard Monumental). Photograph by Chicago Aerial Survey Co., from collection of the Chicago Historical Society.

Figure 4.7 Chrysler Pavilion, Century of Progress Exposition, Chicago, Illinois; 1933; Holabird and Root, Architects; International Structural style. Photograph from collection of Chicago Historical Society.

NEW YORK WORLD'S FAIR, New York City, 1939–1940, was not distinguished for its architecture. Except for "Futurama," New York's fair retrogressed architecturally: a replica of Independence Hall was the central feature. Several of the foreign pavilions, namely, the *Swedish Pavilion,* by Sven Markelius; the *Finnish Pavilion,* by Alvar Aalto; and the *Brazilian Pavilion,* by Lucio Costa and Oscar Niemeyer stood out as innovative.

*GENERAL MOTORS PAVILION, known as "Futurama," New York World's Fair, 1939–1940, by Albert Kahn, Inc., was a massive, extremely plain structure of cement plaster over metal lath. This balloonlike building encased a panoramic model of the future of the United States designed by the great industrial designer, Norman Bel Geddes. From a moving platform of seats, a continuous line of spectators saw great superhighways spread out over the continent, highways elevated in and around cities, new cities like Le Corbusier's Radiant City, automated

Figure 4.8 A residence, "Design for Living," Century of Progress Exposition, Chicago, Illinois; 1933; John C. Brown-Moore, Architect; International Structural style. Photograph from collection of Chicago Historical Collection.

factories and farms, and airlines traversing the continent. It was hailed as wonderful, but few people realized how true this prediction was: within 20 years, even including World War II, many of these national superhighways came to pass, cities underwent great changes, and factories became fully automated.

This technique of display by models and moving platforms, although first used in 1939, has been used at several of the great fairs since World War II.

In 1958, a great exposition dedicated to the Atomic Age was held in Brussels, Belgium. Most of the buildings in this successful fair were in the International Functional style. However the U. S. Pavilion, by Edward Durell Stone of New York, was the highlight of the show.

Five years later Seattle, Washington, opened an exposition which featured science and transportation. A monorail was built to transport people from downtown Seattle to the fairgrounds in a matter of minutes, a distance of about a mile up a very steep hill. A feature of the fair was a several hundred foot tower with revolving top where patrons could enjoy food and a panoramic view of the city and surrounding environs including Puget Sound. Of particular interest was the Science Group, by Minoru Yamasaki.

In 1967 Montreal, Canada, held a World's Fair known as "Expo '67." A great show with many innovations, it was dedicated to man's progress and used cinema, models, and other devices to tell the story. Almost every country was represented, and it was a great and extravagant display. Buildings ranged from tentlike structures suspended from piers to the United States pavilion, a geodesic sphere of magnificent size.

The following year, 1968, San Antonio, Texas, presented its "Hemisfair," a smaller show dedicated to the culture of the Western Hemisphere. This was a well-organized exposition contiguous to downtown San Antonio, and it did a great deal for slum clearance and extension of San Antonio's beautiful river. The fair also featured a shaftlike tower with a revolving top that offered a panoramic view of the city and a restaurant featuring good food. This tower is now a permanent tourist attraction; San Antonio also gained a civic theater and an exhibition hall for conventions and large shows.

In 1974 Spokane, Washington, staged an exposition located on two islands in the river that flows past the back of the downtown business district. This accomplished a great deal for urban renewal and Spokane, a medium-sized city, was revitalized. Whether the effect will be permanent, time will tell; however some effects are certain to be lasting, as with San Antonio.

It is regrettable that there was no bicentennial exposition during 1976. Possibly the age of great expositions has past, that the effort and expense overshadows the results. Only time will tell whether it is over.

5

FRANK LLOYD WRIGHT, 1869–1959

The foregoing chapters have attempted to classify and explain the different phases and fashions of architecture of the 1860–1930 period. The architecture of one man, Frank Lloyd Wright, spanned several periods, from 1893 to 1959. Neither this man nor his architecture can be classified as belonging to any one group. Wright, the architectural genius of this century; cannot be typed too closely, and his philosophy was too profound to be completely understood and accepted during his lifetime. Some of his early training took place under Louis Sullivan and in later life he referred to Sullivan as "the Master." Though some of his early work shows the Sullivan influence, he was by no means a follower. He always seemed to be 30 to 50 years in advance of the age in which he lived. Eero Saarinen speaking to a symposium on Modern Architecture shortly before his untimely death, said that as yet Frank Lloyd Wright had not been understood by the profession, and that it might be many years before he would be fully appreciated.[1]

Although Wright agreed with the Sullivan thesis that *Form follows Function,* at heart he was a Romanticist, and his work seems to follow the idea that form follows aesthetic appeal as much as pure function. He was in sympathy with the Handcraft group, and some of his early residences (1900–1910) appear similar to some of those of Greene and Greene. However Wright embraced the machine and only used handcrafts when they suited his purpose aesthetically. In his architecture he was a poet, a musician, and above all a philosopher. To him architecture should be a living thing, an organism. He deplored the Eclectic group and condemned architectural history as it was then used by architects. In fact, he advocated doing away with architectural libraries in which so many students and practitioners copied the work of others. In his own

---

[1] "Conversations Regarding the Future of Architecture," collected and edited by John Peter, a phonograph record published by Reynolds Metal Company, 1956.

203

work every project was a fresh challenge. He had certain theories on open planning and flow, but throughout his lifetime he pursued and preached his doctrine that architecture should be organic. Many listened, but few if any understood.

What he meant by *organic* is that a work of architecture should be a complete aesthetic and functional experience—it should have life and spirit. It should fulfill its function, certainly, but more than that it should have character, be beautiful, and create a vibrant environment. If a project was located in a natural setting—mountains, prairie, or desert—it should conform to that setting and enhance it. If however, said project were in an urban location, he might ignore the surroundings and create an environment in itself. This he did with the Larkin Company Office Building (1904) and 40 years later with the Guggenheim Museum in New York City. Long before the Kerner Report on American cities during Lyndon B. Johnson's administration, Mr. Wright said that most of our cities were a mess and should be torn down because of their ugly appearance and inefficiency.

For him every project was a search for better arrangement and shape of space. He studied the fabric of the design and how it might be made expressive and living. Each project was created as a special environment, whether it was a residence, church, factory, outdoor beer garden, hotel, museum, or office building. This might be expensive and exceed the original budget—in his personal life he was often on the verge of bankruptcy—but all of his designs were beautiful.

Frank Lloyd Wright was always an iconoclast, a nonconformist. He had a deep philosophy of life and made a religion of truth and beauty. He hated sham and he did not live a double life. His first love was architecture, and the women in his life had to live as he lived in an atmosphere of change, constantly searching for beauty and, above all, truth. A naturalist and a Romanticist, he loved music, poetry, and the dance; the earth, sun, moon, and stars. All of these to him were backgrounds for architecture. He was a dreamer, but he worked excessively hard and expected others to do the same.

Wright liked young people and until he died, was surrounded by young architectural followers. He demanded of these young people hard work and, above all, individuality. From 1932 onward he ran a workshop-type of school housed at his family estate at Spring Green, Wisconsin. He called this estate *Taliesin*, a Welsh name meaning "shining brow," because he had built his house and studio as part of a brow of a hill that commanded a view of the entire estate. His workshop school he named

"The Taliesin Fellowship." Here the students did farm work part of the time, as well as talking and studying construction and architecture.

Later in 1938 he designed, and his students, built another Taliesin in the Arizona desert. From that time his school was held in Taliesin West in the winter and Taliesin East in the summer.

Frank Lloyd Wright's work may be divided into three broad periods: (1) work done before World War I; (2) work done between the World Wars; and (3) work done after World War II.

PHASE 1. THE EARLY YEARS, 1893–1910

His most important work done before World War I was his "Prairie Architecture," 1900–1910. During the first years of practice (1893–1899) Wright did a number of houses of which the *W. H. Winslow House, River Forest, Illinois,* 1893, was one of the most successful. However none of these houses was very distinctive, and though it is interesting to see the progress that was made, the first project that emerged as a pacesetter was the *River Forest Golf Club,* 1898–1901.

During the next decade (1899–1909) he designed many residences, all of which can be grouped under the heading "Prairie Houses," a name given by Wright to this group. These houses all accent the horizontal line; all have overhanging, wide-eaved roofs and use rows of casement windows much like those Voysey was using during the same period in England, though there was no connection between the two men. These prairie houses have plans that flow from one living area to another. All were articulated for efficient and beautiful living. Construction varied from stud walls covered with rough stucco, to board and batten exteriors, to very wide rough-sawn siding. Wright liked to open his houses onto terraces and porches that gave extension to the houses by means of wide swinging French doors. He tied the indoors to the outdoors, and all seemed to hug the ground and to become organic with it.

The many Prairie Houses that he did include the *Warren Hickox House, Kankakee, Illinois,* 1900; the *W. W. Willitts House, 715 South Sheridan Road, Highland Park, Illinois,* 1902; the *C. S. Ross House, Lake Delevan, Wisconsin,* 1902; and the *Arthur Heurtley House, 318 Forest Avenue, Oak Park, Illinois,* also in 1902. In 1904 he did the *Darwin Martin House, Buffalo, New York,* followed by the *Glasner*

House, Glencoe, Illinois, 1905; the *Adams House, Highland Park, Illinois,* 1905; then the *W. R. Heath House, Buffalo, New York,* 1906; and a little later the charming *Isabel Roberts House, River Forest, Illinois,* 1908. This is not a complete list, but it includes most of the houses still in use; it can be said that by these dates, 1900–1909, he had arrived at complete mastery of his art.

**LARKIN COMPANY OFFICE BUILDING, Buffalo, New York, (Figure 5.1), 1904 (destroyed in 1938), was one of Wright's triumphs in architecture. Here he introduced many ideas and proved his ingenuity and thoroughness. This building was located in an industrial area and surrounded by railroad sidings and factory buildings. Therefore he turned the building inside out and built an interior skylighted court five stories high. The office spaces were balconies opening off of this court. These balconies had planting boxes to give a garden atmosphere, and on the ground floor was a pipe organ, on which one of the employees put on half-hour concerts each workday morning and afternoon. The interior

Figure 5.1 Larkin Company Office Building, Buffalo, New York, 1904 (destroyed 1938); Frank Lloyd Wright, Architect. Photograph by Buffalo and Erie County Historical Society.

Figure 5.1 (*continued*)

was evenly daylighted throughout and sealed from the noise and dirt of the traffic and trains outside. It was one of the first air-cleaned and air-circulated buildings in America. *Wright called it "The Grandma of The*

The top floor had a dining room, kitchen, and also a brick-paved roof *Profe* garden where employees could sun themselves. The building was entirely fire proof and had enclosed stair towers at each end that were treated as huge pilons on the exterior. The outside appearance was that of recti-linear brick monolith.

Another innovation was fireproof pressed steel and magnesite office furniture, including metal vertical letter files—the first to be designed and used anyplace. It is said that the manufacturer who made these files from Wright's drawings and under his supervision later patented them, but that no advantage was gained by Wright for his original idea.

The building was a great success economically as well as aesthetically, and the Larkin Company used pictures of it in their advertising for many years. The company prospered until the Great Depression; then business declined and the company was sold. The building was demol-ished in 1938. However in the history of architecture this building was one of the outstanding pacesetters for commercial buildings. When com-pared with Peter Behren's Turbine Factory in Berlin and Walter Gropius Werkbund Buildings at the Cologne Exposition, it was a leader.

UNITY CHURCH, Lake Street, Oak Park, Illinois (Figure 5.2), 1906, was another triumph. This was built for a Unitarian congregation that wanted a church seating 400 people in the sanctuary, along with a fel-lowship hall and Sunday school to be known as Unity Hall, for a budget of $45,000. The building was designed as two cubes connected by an entrance hall. These cubes were set tandem on the lot with the larger cube, the church, jutting out toward Lake Street, which had very noisy traffic. For this reason the front was sealed, and the entrances from each side were set halfway back on the lot.

Massive Geometry

Since cost was a limiting factor, Wright used reinforced concrete that was poured into the forms of the building in place. The exterior surfaces were brushed and cleaned with acid after the forms had been removed, thus exposing the gravel aggregate to produce a textured surface. The interior was painted cement plaster. Even the overhanging flat roofs were poured concrete supported by sturdy walls and window piers. The total effect was of a group of cubes juxtopositioned around a central cube. It appeared very simple and direct, which it was, but how subtle! The final cost exceeded the budget by only a few thousand dollars.

Figure 5.2 Unity Church, Oak Park, Illinois, 1906; Frank Lloyd Wright, Architect. Photograph by Balthazar Korab.

After serving the congregation for over 50 years of continuous use, the church was renovated and restored a few years ago; however even then it was only necessary to clean and paint the weathered and dirty surfaces. It was not necessary to repair or reconstruct any major portions.

**AVERY COONLEY HOUSE, 300 Scottswood Road, River Forest, Illinois, 1908–1909, was one of Wright's finest houses. Here he had a large plot to work with, and the home was quite like the nearby Babson House (now destroyed), 1907, by Louis Sullivan. These two houses showed how similar were the design philosophies of both of these men at this time. The Coonley house has a central living room opening onto a sidewall terrace with a pool in front. At one end of the living room is the dining room with nearby kitchen, service quarters, and yard. At the other end is the bedroom wing. This was domestic zoning as explained by Wright: that is, living zone, eating and service zone, and bedroom zone, with easy flow from one part to another. Here were openness and vistas, yet with utmost privacy where necessary. Here were house and landscape, structural materials with earth color harmony, all coordinated into an organic whole.

✳✳ROBIE HOUSE, 5757 Woodlawn Avenue, Chicago, Illinois (Figure 5.3), 1909, was built for a wealthy Chicagoan on the South Side of the city near the University of Chicago. A masterpiece of special design that overcame the limitations of a very small and crowded lot, it was designed as Wright said a building should be, "from the inside out." The ground floor area was almost entirely taken up with service yard and quarters plus a garage, which was a new element in house design at that time. The principal living rooms were one flight up, and the large living room and dining room were built around a huge central fireplace. Family bedrooms were on the next floor above. The entire house, of Roman brick with stone trim, was designed with strong horizontal lines. The house has recently been restored at a cost of over $200,000; the original contracts were for approximately $40,000 which was considered an extravagant sum at the time.

PHASE 2. THE MATURE YEARS, 1910–1945

By 1909 Frank Lloyd Wright was 40 years old and had been in practice on his own for 17 years, for most of that time in his studio attached to his Oak Park home. Later he opened a downtown office in the Schiller Building on Randolph Street, Chicago. He had now developed a definite philosophy of organic architecture, and his taste had fully matured. In his Larkin Building, Unity Church, and the Robie and Coonley residences, he had produced four masterpieces. They were individual entities, beautiful and alive.

His life now entered a tragic period. He abandoned his home, wife, and family of six teenage children to spend a year of reflection in Italy. He craved freedom.

Newspaper publicity and gossip almost ruined him, and on his return to America in 1910, he went to Spring Green, Wisconsin, his ancestral home, where he had inherited his grandfather's farm. There in 1911 he built a studio and home as part of the crest of a beautiful hill and named it *Taliesin*.

Figure 5.3 Robie House, Chicago, Illinois, 1909; Frank Lloyd Wright, Architect. Photograph by Balthazar Korab, Troy, Michigan.

TALIESIN I, Spring Green, Wisconsin (Figure 5.4), 1911, was built of native ledge stone, roughly laid almost as it had appeared in the quarry. This was combined with stained lumber to form a home that was sculptured onto as well as into a Wisconsin hilltop. It was a place he could live and dream and escape to. He reestablished his offices in Chicago and spent most of his time there for the next 15 years, commuting to Taliesin on weekends. However in 1913 a terrible tragedy took place. Frank Lloyd Wright was in Chicago, spending most of his time on Midway Gardens. Word was received that a hitherto trusted servant had run amuck, brutally murdering Wright's wife, her two children, and four of the workmen on the property. He had then set fire to Taliesin, totally destroying the house. Wright was crushed. He designed a plain box coffin for his loved one and had her buried under the flowers in her garden. To his last days this garden was a sacred spot to him. Later, in 1915, he built *Taliesin II,* which was bigger and better, on the old foundations.

**MIDWAY GARDENS, Chicago (Figure 5.5), 1913–1914, was another masterpiece, and though long since demolished, it must be mentioned as one of his outstanding works built just prior to World War I. An out-

Figure 5.4 Taliesin I, Spring Green, Wisconsin, 1911; Frank Lloyd Wright, Architect. Photograph by Balthazar Korab, Troy, Michigan.

door terraced garden with promenades and loggias, it was a place where people could dine and listen to symphony music, or dance to popular music later in the evening. There was also a large indoor space with bar and terraced winter garden. It was in a sense an indoor and outdoor beer garden, but of the highest order. Many of its patrons dressed formally.

After Wright had received the commission and had started to build, he found that the promoters did not have enough money to complete it, and both he and the contractor, Paul Mueller, became part of the cor-

Figure 5.5 Midway Gardens, South Side of Chicago on site of the Midway of the Columbian Exposition, 1913–1914; Frank Lloyd Wright, Architect. Photograph by Chicago Historical Society.

poration. However they did not stint. This gave Wright more control over the design, and he went all out to complete the dream. It became a symphony of the visual arts: architecture, sculpture, and painting, which when combined with excellent food, drink, music, and ballet was a fantasy indeed.

Midway Gardens was built mostly of concrete with limestone. The sculpture, by Alonzo Ianelli and several helpers, was part of the fabric. It was cubistic and abstract, yet had living quality. Color was similarly used as ornament, in abstract murals that were 40 years ahead of their time. This work was carried out by several painters from the Chicago Art Institute, but retrained by Wright.

Midway Gardens prospered briefly, then went bankrupt. It was taken over by Eidelweiss Brewery, which operated it as a rowdy beer garden for a year before closing it. Its total life was less than three years. World War I had cast gloom over the country, and Prohibition caused the closing. The building was finally destroyed in 1923.

*IMPERIAL HOTEL, Tokyo, Japan, 1916–1922, has now been destroyed (1968) to make way for a larger and much less beautiful edifice. Nevertheless it had a long life and for 30 years was the center of Western entertaining in Tokyo, much of it on an ambassadorial level. It was originally built by the Japanese government at the request of the Imperial Family. During the Allied occupation following World War II it was General MacArthur's headquarters. Following the war, during the 1950s and 1960s, the building deteriorated badly and became obsolete in a growing metropolis soon destined to be the largest city in the world. By the time the wreckers moved in, it was beyond the point of saving.

The edifice had hundreds of points of outstanding beauty, and descriptions of the building are many. Ianelli did the sculpture and ornament. Japanese painters trained by Wright did the color work. Durr Engineering Company of Chicago did the mechanical layouts; the electric lighting was worked out by Wright himself. Though both heating and lighting were insufficient, originally all radiation was behind heavy wall grilles. All lighting was indirect and decorative; it was unobtrusive, perhaps too much so.

Because of the poor subsoil and a water table only 2 feet below the surface, foundation problems were most difficult. Wright profited from his experiences in Chicago, where the business district has similar conditions. He used floating foundations similar to those of many early Chicago buildings and tested the bearing qualities of the soil most carefully. This building rode out the great earthquake of 1923 with no appreciable damage, as did a few other buildings in Tokyo on similar foundations but engineered by German professionals. However Tokyo is subjected to many earth tremors per year, and over a period of more than 40 years the several concrete pads that supported the central portion and wings tipped and sank. Everything got out of line, and the fabric was finally beyond repair.

Although The Imperial Hotel was a great building and had hundreds of beautiful features, it lacked unity and was never a good hotel from the standpoint of management or guest comfort. Guests got lost in the narrow corridors and the narrow, almost hidden stairways. Both public and guest rooms were cold in winter. It was difficult with the original lighting to read a newspaper or write a letter anywhere. Though not completely organic as were Wright's other buildings, it was beautiful. It created a magnificent environment for a short visit, even though the Wright-designed desks and chairs were most uncomfortable. Compared with the Larkin Building of 12 to 18 years before, it did not answer its requirements half as well.

During its planning stage Frank Lloyd Wright made many trips to Japan, and during its four years of construction (1918–1922) he lived on the site.

In 1924 Wright returned to Taliesin permanently. He married Marian Noel, who had been his mistress in the Tokyo days. The marriage lasted only a few months; she then left for Los Angeles, and a legal separation was granted. Then another tragedy struck. Taliesin II burned during a raging electric storm. Wright's mother died. He was very lonely, although he immediately set about to build Taliesin III. Then he found solace with Olgivanna, a beautiful Montenegrin, who was a member of the Russian Ballet Company of Moscow. He brought her to America and to Taliesin and they were married. Together they built Taliesin III.

However there was more trouble. His by now divorced wife, Marian Noel, disclaimed the divorce, assumed the role of an adandoned and persecuted wife, and accused him of bigamy and worse. She gave her story to the Sunday supplement newspaper writers, and the scandal-loving public read the stories with relish. Wright, his wife, and their little daughter were even jailed for several days and nights without charges. In the end they were never proven guilty of any of the accusations. Nevertheless the physical and mental strains took their toll on the family. Frank Lloyd Wright was declared bankrupt. The bank that had held the mortgage on Taliesin foreclosed and sold every movable piece of personal property. For over two years he had been unable to practice since he was considered a fugitive from justice. However many of Wright's friends and former clients remained loyal; they secured excellent legal advice for him and gave money. So finally the storm subsided.

Frank Lloyd Wright, in overcoming the tragedies of his life, proved himself a very strong person. By 1927 he was again working on several fine projects and rebuilding his fortunes. One of his most important projects, started years before (1920), was a glass- and copper-sheathed skyscraper for the entrepreneur A. F. Johnson, president of the National Life Insurance Company of Chicago. It was never to be built, even though Frank Lloyd Wright worked out the details completely. This is regretable, for it was to have been a four-winged building of mosaiclike copper and glass. It was 25 years ahead of its time.

Another project was a retirement village to have been built on a mesa in the Arizona desert and known as San Marco in the Desert. Promoted by a Dr. Alexander Chandler, this seemed to be so sure of construction that Wright set up a temporary office-camp near the site and lived there for almost a year with his family and staff. He also studied and made drawings for a high-rise apartment building in New York City for a local church, St. Mark's in the Bouwerie. This building, planned as an income project for the church, would have been a handsome structure. However in October, 1929, the stock market crashed and the following seven years were marked by economic depression. All projects folded. Within a few days of the crash Dr. Chandler of San Marco in the Desert was reduced from a millionaire to poverty. At the time he owed Frank Lloyd Wright $42,000 and eventually paid $2,500. Other commissions had similar endings. Business stopped. Luckily Taliesin was not then under mortgage (that had been settled in 1927), and the farm produced plenty of food. Frank Lloyd Wright was able to pick up a little money here and there lecturing and writing. In his lifetime he wrote and published 18 books, all dealing with his philosophy of architecture.

In 1932 Wright announced his Taliesin Fellowship, and soon 40 architectural apprentices were working and studying there.

From this time until the end of his life, Wright lived happily with his wife, Olgivanna, who has outlived him. She was always his helpmate and inspiration. The Taliesin Fellowship prospered, and he was continuously surrounded by eager young architectural students.

He worked unceasingly and never grew old mentally. He was in great demand as a lecturer and spoke at every major university in the United States. He was showered with honors from France, Holland, Britain, Germany, Brazil, and Japan. Although he was greatly admired all over the world, honor in his own country came late. It was not until 1948, in his seventy-ninth year, that the American Institute of Architects conferred its Gold Medal on Wright.

During his lifetime he did over 250 commissions and produced more masterpieces than any other architect of the century, probably more than any one architect in all of history. All of his work received his personal attention; perhaps he was the last of the great studio architects. He had draftsmen and helpers, sculptors, colorists, model makers, and apprentices, of course, but he never ran a production office like those of the large architectural corporations that now do the bulk of present-day work. He lived to be 89 years old and practiced up to a few weeks of the day he died. He was the architectural genius of the age, and his practice extended over a period of 65 years.

The *California Houses,* 1920–1940, were a group of several projects in which he experimented with decorative concrete blocks. These houses were a complete departure from his prairie houses of years before, mainly because of their settings in and on top of hillsides. Some of the concrete blocks have geometrical designs cast on the faces, somewhat remindful of the Mayan designs of Mexico.

Among the buildings designed in his second period are the following:

*BARNSDALL, (HOLLYHOCK) HOUSE, Barnsdall Park, Hollywood, California, 1917–1920, is a large but closely knit complex that includes a residence, studio workshop, garage, and other buildings with garden. It is located on top of an acropolislike hill. Although Frank Lloyd Wright made the drawings and visited the site several times during construction, this was built at the time that he was occupied with the Imperial Hotel in Tokyo, and much of the work was left to his son, John, and a young Austrian apprentice, R. M. Schindler. These buildings now belong to the city of Los Angeles and are used as a museum and art school.

**MILLARD HOUSE (LA MINIATURA), Pasadena, California 1923, is often referred to as Wright's masterpiece among his California houses. It is a small house, set back from the street and fronting a sunken garden with reflecting pool. Adjacent to this pool is a ground floor terrace, and the main floor of the house, which has a band of windows opening from the living room, overhangs this terrace. The house is entered from a street to the rear, at the living room level.

*ENNIS HOUSE, 2607 Glendower Avenue, Los Angeles (Figure 5.6), 1924, is an impressive ensemble of decorative concrete block that includes a pool and garden. It is a veritable palace.

*FREEMAN HOUSE, Hollywood Hills, Los Angeles, 1924, is built out from the top of a hill and has a terrace overlooking the city. It fits into the hillside so well that it becomes a part of it. The house is entered from the top, where the living rooms are located. The bedrooms are below.

*PROFESSOR AND MRS. HANNA HOUSE, Palo Alto, California, 1930–1937, was another open-plan house. It adapted the hexagon as the module and proved that this unit allows much freer movement than the square or rectangle. In a square all movement within the plan must be parallel or at right angles; in a hexagon it can be parallel or at 30 and

Figure 5.6 Ennis House, Los Angeles, California, 1924; Frank Lloyd Wright, Architect. Photograph by Balthazar Korab, Troy, Michigan.

60 degrees to parallel. This house of brick, wood, and plaster seemed to flow very smoothly in three directions. The hexagon module used here measured 26 inches on a side. The house opens out onto terraces most gracefully and possesses a congenial intimacy that in the owner's words, "adapted itself to a few people as well as to a crowd of a hundred."[2]

[2] Professor Hanna is a professor at Stanford University.

Through the years it has gone through three phases of family living: growing family, parents and young adults, and finally parents alone. During the years the landscaping has been extended with formalized walks, steps, vistas, and plantings; several outbuildings such as a hobby shop and guest quarters, pool and water cascade have been added. This house is calm and natural; it is living and organic.

FALLING WATER, Kaufmann House, Bear Run, Pennsylvania (Figure 5.7), 1936–1937, was a mountain retreat built for a wealthy Pittsburgh family. The site was hidden in a wooded mountain area possessing a mountain stream and small waterfall. Wright made this house blend with the horizontal stone formations of the rugged area by using concrete construction and wide cantilevered terraces running the length of the house and molding into the hillside. He also used the native ledge stone, much as he had done years before in Taliesin I. The house was placed over the stream and waterfall so that it became part of the composition both in view and with the tinkling sound of the falling water. It was a very romantic retreat.

This house has been given wide publicity because of its organic beauty. It does have one fault caused by the mountain stream and the dense woods: it is subject to interior dampness and mold. However this should be a correctable condition in this day of dehumidifiers and air conditioners.

JOHNSON WAX COMPANY ADMINISTRATION BUILDING, Racine, Wisconsin, 1936–1939 was a commercial project in which Wright excelled. Here the main room, which is a large stenographic space, is without windows. This concrete structure has slender toadstool-like columns supporting the ceiling, giving an interesting 100-umbrella effect. Indirect lighting comes from above. There are growing plants inside, and the space has a light and airy appearance. The exterior walls are of light yellow-buff colored brick, and the lack of windows gives the outside a rather forbidding first impression. Here the beauty is mainly on the inside.

JOHNSON WAX COMPANY FACTORY AND LABORATORY, Racine, Wisconsin (Figure 5.8), 1946–1949, adjoins the Administration Building and is of the same brick with cut stone rim. The main feature,

Figure 5.7 Falling Water, Kaufmann House, Bear Run, Pennsylvania, 1936–1937; Frank Lloyd Wright, Architect. Photograph by Balthazar Korab, Troy, Michigan.

a squarish glass and brick tower, rises six stories above the extensive flat roof of the factory. This tower encloses an unattached circular tower that is thus free from vibration. The tower is the main portion of the laboratory devoted to special research and experimentation. The entire complex of factory, laboratory, and administration building covers a rather

Figure 5.8 Johnson Wax Company, factory and laboratory, Racine, Wisconsin, 1946–1949; Frank Lloyd Wright, Architect. Photograph by Balthazar Korab, Troy, Michigan.

extensive area, and as an ensemble is quite impressive. Quite in contrast to most manufacturing plants, it is uncluttered in design. It is said that the completed project exceeded the company budget by more than a million dollars; however S. C. Johnson, president of the company and an admirer of Wright, is quoted as saying that in efficiency of operation and advertising value it has been well worth the extra cost.

It is interesting also that Racine has a large Johnson clan, most of whose houses lie along the shore of Lake Michigan and have been designed by Frank Lloyd Wright. They are all beautiful and most livable, and no two are alike.

*FLORIDA SOUTHERN UNIVERSITY, Lakeland, Florida, 1940–1952, is a complex of several buildings. Chief among them are the Ann Pfeifer Chapel, 1940; the T. R. Roux Library, 1941; and the Administration Building, 1946–1950. It is a very interesting group of buildings, highly individual in design and all connected by covered walkways. Again Wright did the overall planning including the landscaping. The ensemble is therefore full of beautiful vistas and little surprises of beautiful detail. This university is also satisfying because it was built on a limited budget which Wright met without sacrificing beauty, function, or stability. It works, it lives, and it is organic.

TALIESIN WEST, Maricopa Mesa, Arizona (Figure 5.9), 1938–1959, was no doubt dreamed up when Wright was camped on a similar mesa from 1928 to 29 doing the San Marco in the Desert project. He subsequently bought a sizable tract of desert and in 1942 built this, one of his finest projects. Stones picked up on the site were bedded into the rough concrete surfaces of the base structure. The sand and aggregate were also indigenous. The superstructures, though only of one story and consisting mostly of rooms, are of redwood, rough sawn and stained. The main

Figure 5.9 Taliesin West, Maricopa Mesa, Arizona, 1938–1959, Frank Lloyd Wright, Architect. Photograph by Balthazar Korab, Troy, Michigan.

drafting room was originally covered with oiled canvas stretched between huge redwood beams. This let through light and could be rolled
back if need be. Later this was replaced with fiberglass, not as flexible as
canvas but more permanent. Both materials gave a tentlike impression,
particularly from the inside. Other portions of the project include his
residence, a large fellowship dining room, lounge, kitchen, and service
rooms, all with outside terraces and pool. The students lived in small
individual cabins most of which they designed and built themselves with
Wright's criticism.

The whole ensemble is lovely, completely part of the desert, and has
magnificent vistas wherever the project opens outward. Prototype of Solar design

PHASE 3.   THE LATER YEARS, 1945–1959

**GUGGENHEIM MUSEUM, Fifth Avenue (between 88th and 89th
Streets), New York City (Figure 5.10), designed in the early 1940s but not
built until 1956–1959. After World War II most of the delay in construction was caused by the New York City building department, which challenged the drawings from every angle. They said that it was not structurally sound and that it did not have the proper percentage of window
area or enough stairways and exits, even though the entire building was
a ramped escapeway opening directly through a rotunda lobby to the
outside. However every architect knows the problems of most city building departments, which have to interpret lawyer-written building codes.
These codes are always based on past building methods and designs, and
anything new is frightening to any bureaucrat or legal practitioner.
Often such innovations have to be tested in the courts before they can
be accepted.

The Guggenheim was finally built without too many changes from
Wright's original concept. It is a concrete structure of domical design
having a large spiral form as the exterior motive. This spiral is the result
of a circular ramped interior that wraps around the rotunda and has
alcove displays placed continuously along the outer perimeter. The idea
was that viewers of the collection of contemporary art would ride elevators to the top of the spiral and then walk slowly down, viewing the
pictures on the way. These works of art were to have been lighted by
indirect daylight, which was to filter in from the ceiling of the different

Figure 5.10 Guggenheim Museum, New York City, 1956–1959; Frank Lloyd Wright, Architect. Photograph by Balthazar Korab, Troy, Michigan.

levels of the spiral. However this daylighting proved inadequate, and now all pictures are electrically lighted, though most cleverly.

The basement has a large auditorium, planned for both small and large gatherings. A smaller adjacent wing houses offices. The building is beautifully and organically planned—it is a living thing. The main rotunda may be too overpowering; some visitors go there to see the building rather than the pictures. Certainly the building does not fit into the neighborhood, but it was Wright who is supposed to have said, "It is the city that is wrong, that needs to change its environment, to be torn down and redone."

*UNITARIAN CHURCH, Madison, Wisconsin, 1947, a simple building of wood, has a large gable roof covered with green copper in a wide-banded striped pattern. Both the interior and exterior are very impressive, and the design is so well integrated into the site that the whole structure seems to be pushing out of the ground.

*H. C. PRICE TOWER, Bartlesville, Oklahoma (Figure 5.11), 1953, a 16-storied high-rise building of concrete and glass, was designed as an office building with professional offices and a duplex apartment on every two floors. H. C. Price has his office and residence apartment with garden terrace in the top area. It is a very unique building, square in plan and freestanding so that light and air enter on all sides. The structural core consists of four concrete walls set at 90 degrees one to another, and these hold the cantilevered floors that flare out at each side. A glass-enclosed stairway juts out at one side, and the elevators and plumbing shaft are in the center. The exterior composition of glass panels and masonry is odd, almost one might say, exotic compared to most city buildings.

THE ILLINOIS, Mile High Office Building (a project), 1958, was to have been 5280 feet high with 528 floors. The original concept was a mile-high television tower, but this was developed into an office building to make it more attractive financially. Originally to have been underwritten by 20 Chicago businessmen, it was designed as a steel structure that soared skyward, receding in size to an arrowlike antenna. Frank Lloyd Wright presented figures to show that it was structurally rational and that it was practical from an economic viewpoint, but many engineers challenged his rationale and practically every engineering college in the country undertook to either prove or disprove his figures. One thing it did show was that at 87 years of age he still had architects and engineering guessing. However the project was abandoned when the financial backers withdrew their support.

*ANNUNCIATION GREEK ORTHODOX CHURCH, Wauwatosa, Wisconsin, 1955–1961. Although this building was designed in 1955, it

Figure 5.11 H. C. Price Tower, Bartlesville, Oklahoma, 1953; Frank Lloyd Wright, Architect. Photograph by Balthazar Korab, Troy, Michigan.

was not built until two years after Wright's death. It is interesting to note that until this time most of his designs used horizontal lines, cubes, or hexagons. He used great cantilevers and occasionally introduced an arch or dome, but these were overpowered by horizontal structural forms, even in such designs as the Guggenheim Museum. But here was something new again: a flat turtlelike dome set on four high concrete piers. Light was admitted under the rim of the dome, and the curtainlike white exterior walls were quite blank. The concept is different from anything that Wright had done before. The interior is exciting, particularly the icon screen—a very important element in a Greek church. Here Wright used several Byzantine pictures of saints in a setting of fanciful interlaced circles, all in color, over a background of an anodized aluminum grid. This screen is suggestive of a wall treatment in the old Midway Gardens which was effectively introduced in 1914.

**MARIN COUNTY CIVIC CENTER, San Rafael, California (Figure 5.12), 1958–1972, was the last important building designed by Wright

Figure 5.12 Marin County Civic Center, San Rafael, California, 1958–1972; Frank Lloyd Wright, Architect. Photograph by Balthazar Korab, Troy, Michigan.

and was finished after his death. Here, like his Greek church at Wauwatosa, Wisconsin, he used flat arches, circles, and domical forms. It is a large complex that houses county administration offices, a library, auditorium, and other civic spaces to service the community. A roadway passes under and through it via one of the low sweeping arches, and similar arches repeat themselves several times on both sides of the long rectangular building surrounding a large interior court. A flat domical structure at one end serves as an auditorium. Most of the building is three stories high, and though it seems to span between two low hills, it is very compact. Again Frank Lloyd Wright won: it is a fresh and a very beautiful organic ensemble.

6

A TRANSITIONAL PERIOD BETWEEN WORLD WARS I AND II

1920–1940

In the period between World Wars the population movement from farms to the cities accelerated. Cities, most of which had been founded and laid out in the nineteenth century, were bedeviled by passenger automobiles and trucks, traffic and parking problems. Central business districts, originally designed for pedestrians and a few horse-drawn vehicles, became overcrowded and parking of cars increased the problem. Housing was also a problem as old city buildings deteriorated and became slums. Large apartment buildings were built but most of the middle and upper classes moved to the suburbs, where there was more space and air. These people depended on their cars, buses, or trains for commuting to the centers, but individual automobiles were the most convenient means until traffic arteries became so crowded and parking in the centers so costly and impossibly jammed that it led to strangulation. Cities tried to solve the difficulties and are still trying today.

During the first years of this period, and from the Great Depression until World War II, architects seemed to be searching for a new style or expression. Eclecticism was passé, but what was to take its place? Most cities adopted building codes, and these often proved to be stumbling blocks for new ideas and structural innovations. Americans preferred monumentality, and large slabs of Indiana limestone could be used to veneer buildings almost as cheaply as terra-cotta or brick. The Nebraska State Capitol, by Bertram Goodhue in 1920, was one triumphant accomplishment, and his Los Angeles Library, 1924, was also accepted as something new and quite American. The Century of Progress Exposition, Chicago, 1933–1934, made some attempt to introduce new economical

229

styles and was successful to some extent. Much of this fair was "cardboard monumental" and not particularly convincing, but it did offer a breath of fresh air and a few buildings with structural innovations.

Building technology progressed between the wars, but the building codes lagged behind. For example, it was not until after World War II that the codes began to allow 2-inch metal curtain wall panels backed by blanket insulation or similar material, instead of heavy masonry.

Architectural education in the first two decades of this period (1920–1940) still emphasized the Eclectic tradition. Students had begun to talk about the Bauhaus School in Germany under Walter Gropius and Mies van der Rohe but then Hitler closed the Bauhaus and it was not until World War II that architectural educators began to appreciate its philosophy.

In the United States the Society of the Beaux Arts in New York City dominated architectural education. Schools imported French critics, and students accepted the jargon of the Ecole des Beaux Arts of Paris as their vocabulary. The Society of the Beaux Arts of New York City, the clearinghouse for student design projects, wrote the programs, judged the submitted projects, and handed out the prizes. However it soon became dominated by a small group of persons from three of the leading schools of architecture at that time: the University of Pennsylvania, Cornell University, and the University of Illinois. They generally passed out the prizes among themselves. Gentlemanly criticism of the system began to take place, and M.I.T., Harvard, Michigan, and Minnesota quietly refused to participate. However these schools continued the *Beaux-Arts* philosophy. Presentation—colored renderings and extravagant sheet compositions—was overly stressed irrespective of how well the project had been conceived. The programs for the projects, which it was said were written to develop the student's imagination, often went to extremes bordering on the ridiculous, for example, "A Palace and Grounds for an Eastern Potentate on an Island in the South Seas."

The American Institute of Architects tried to establish a requirement that young architecture graduates serve an apprenticeship of two or more years to be spent in technical and practical training to prepare them for the practical business world. However it proved impossible to standardize the apprenticeship. Finally state licensing laws were introduced requiring examinations in the different disciplines of the profession, and schools had to become more practical so that their graduates could pass these state board examinations. It was accepted, of course, that no school can teach practical experience, but curricula did begin to include economics, sociology, and business law as well as steel and concrete construction. The Bachelor of Architecture degree requirement was increased from four to five and then six years. As a result architectural graduates, by and large, are now much better prepared than in the period between World Wars.

Thus eclectic styling went out of fashion, and Beaux-Arts teaching for architects was finally given up. A breathing space took place during the Great Depression; because of the economic failure, buildings were designed without the expensive and extraneous detail of the past. They were blocks of masonry, simple in mass and outline, even though they remained monumental in effect and continued to simulate solid masonry. Nevertheless they were economically planned, and function became the password.

In 1936 Walter Gropius came to Harvard from Germany via England, and the architectural profession in the United States stood back to see what the effect would be. Gropius was a great personality, and though his architectural design at first seemed radical, he was so practical, and his reasoning and philosophy so clear, that he soon had the architectural profession persuaded of the validity of his arguments. Then in 1940 Mies van der Rohe came to the school of architecture at Illinois Institute of Technology in Chicago, which had formerly been named the Armour Institute of Technology. A new young president was in command, and one of Mies van der Rohe's first assignments was to lay out and design a new campus. Another was to develop an entirely new curriculum. However World War II came on, and the effects of both Gropius and van der Rohe were postponed until after the war. The new campus by Mies van der Rohe was not built until the 1950s.

OFFICE BUILDINGS

NEW YORK TELEPHONE BUILDING, 140 West Street, between Barclay and Vesey Streets, New York City, 1923–1925, by Voorhees, Gmelin and Walker, is a huge block of masonry over steel. This was one of the first skyscrapers to conform with the then-new zoning ordinance calling for setbacks in the upper stories to allow sunshine at a 60 degree angle to reach the streets below. It is a satisfactory composition that stresses the monumental.

*DAILY NEWS BUILDING, 220 East 42nd Street, between Second and Third Avenues, New York City, 1928–1929, by John Meade Howells and

Raymond Hood, is their best skyscraper. The design accents the vertical and is reduced to the utmost simplicity. The piers rise in uninterrupted sheaths from the base to the very top, without cap or overhanging cornice. The building is veneered with Indiana limestone, and although it follows the steel structure in module, the stone piers are unduly wide compared to the steel columns that support them. However this was a step in the evolution of the International Functional style.

EMPIRE STATE BUILDING, 350 Fifth Avenue, between 33rd and 34th Streets, New York City, 1930–1931, by Shreve, Lamb and Harmon, until 1970 (with the construction of the World Trade Center) the tallest building in the world. Its 86 stories rise 1250 feet. The design lacks historical detail and conforms to the New York City zoning law; however the mass is quite undistinguished. It has a dirigible mooring mast on the very top which became obsolete even while it was being erected. This building, like the Eiffel Tower in Paris, has been a favorite spot for sightseers. The view of the city and the surrounding countryside from the observation platform at the top is magnificent.

**ROCKEFELLER CENTER, West 48th to 51st Streets, Fifth to Sixth Avenues, New York City (Figure 6.1), 1931–1940, was designed by Reinhard and Hofmeister with Corbett, Harrison and MacMurray; and Hood and Fouilhoux. It is a group of tall buildings spread over several city blocks, covering an area of 17 acres. Excellently laid out, it has a cascaded, flower-planted central court and culminates in a central office tower, the RCA Building, of 65 stories. All buildings are sheathed in Indiana limestone and express a monumentality somewhat in excess of their utility.

The back of this complex, which fronts on Avenue of the Americas (Sixth Avenue), houses Radio City Music Hall, home of first-run movies and the famous chorus line known as the Rockettes.

Skyscrapers were also built in other cities throughout the United States and Canada during this era. Chief among these were the *Fisher Building, Detroit,* 1925, by Albert Kahn; and the *Telephone Building, Newark, New Jersey,* 1929, which was greatly influenced by Eliel Saarinen's Tribune Tower Competition. Several skyscrapers were built in Chicago, including the **Daily News Building, Chicago,* 1928; *333 North Michigan,*

Figure 6.1 Rockefeller Center, New York City, 1931–1940; Reinhard and Hofmeister, Architects, with Corbett, Harrison and McMurray; Hood and Fouilhoux. Photograph from Rockefeller Center, New York.

Chicago, 1929; and the *Palmolive Building* (Figure 6.2), 1930 (now re-named the Playboy Building); all three of these by Holabird and Root. Also in Chicago was the huge *Merchandise Mart,* 1929, by Graham, Anderson, Probst and White. *The Philadelphia Saving Fund Building, Philadelphia, Pennsylvania,* 1932, by George Howe and William Lescaze, made history by accenting the horizontal. It is a very sensitive design that is comparable to others of the period.

All evidence shows that leading designers of the time took extreme care to create monumentality, whether they accented the vertical or hori-zontal, and New York led the parade. Even the buildings of Holabird and Root in Chicago were like their counterparts in New York City. There was no reference to the earlier and more direct work of the Chicago School of the 1890–1900 period.

KLEINHANS MUSIC HALL, Buffalo, New York, 1938, by Eliel Saari-nen, is a building that embraced the functional philosophy in planning but should be classified as transitional. A dignified and beautiful struc-ture depending on careful integration of plan and structure for an ideal symphony hall, it has a steel frame although the structure is covered with brick to give it a solid masonry appearance. The building is cylindrical in plan and was designed with this preconceived form in mind. It is quite monumental.

MOTION-PICTURE THEATERS

This was the era (1920–1930) when magnificent motion picture houses were being built from coast to coast in almost every city of any size and in neighborhood districts of large cities. These theaters boasted seating capacities of 2000–2500 in a setting of ultramagnificence. Extravagant entertainments were presented prior to the main cinema attraction, such as concerts on great special organs which rose from pits in front of the stage. Very often there was also a 20-piece, or larger, orchestra, a stage show featuring soloists, and, perhaps, a chorus line. Some theaters also had glowing ceiling effects: stars twinkled in a domical sky while birds chattered to announce the coming sunrise, and finally the full light of day shone forth. All this took place amid gorgeous surroundings, plush seats and thick carpeting, that competed with Europe's royal opera

Figure 6.2 Palmolive Building (now the Playboy building), Chicago, Illinois, 1930; Holabird and Root, Architects. Photograph from collection of Ralph W. Hammett.

houses. The architecture ran the gamut of extravagant historical styling. Most famous were *Grauman's Egyptian Theater* and *Grauman's Chinese Theater* on Hollywood Boulevard in the Hollywood district of Los Angeles. Their exteriors were introductions to what was to be revealed inside. Although these theaters were the apex of motion picture theater design in the United States, others almost as sumptuous included the Oriental Theater in Chicago. This was the glorious age of the silent cinema and theater design had reached its peak.

*GRAUMAN'S CHINESE THEATER, Hollywood Boulevard, Los Angeles (Figure 6.3), 1928–1930, by Meyer and Haller, has been called an architectural fantasy, and surely it is. It is noted for its cement slabs in front and to the sides that have hand- and footprints of motion picture celebrities. It is also noted for its premieres of pictures featuring top stars. On these past occasions klieg lights waved great streams of light into the sky, music was played, and a crowd of curious people jammed the side-

Figure 6.3 Grauman's Chinese Theater, Hollywood Boulevard, Los Angeles, California, 1928–1930; Meyer and Haller, Architects. Photograph courtesy of Grauman's Theater.

walks hoping to get a glimpse of important personages. The latter arrived in chauffeur-driven cars, the women dressed in gorgeous gowns, diamonds, and furs; their escorts in capes and top hats. There was much ballyhoo in the press before and after these premieres, all staged by the great motion picture producers.

RESIDENCES

Domestic architecture between World Wars I and II in the United States remained quite static. Colonial and eclectic styles were popular in the East, South, and Midwest until after the Century of Progress Exposition of 1933–1934, and even after that it was difficult to get a bank loan on a house unless it was in one of the conservative styles. Several mill-work companies issued catalogs of "authentic Colonial details" which could be applied by architects and builders.

Some change was noted in the West, particularly in California from Los Angeles southward. This was the period in which Frank Lloyd Wright developed his cast concrete block houses. These were followed by the work of his son, John Lloyd Wright, whose work was much like that of his father although the two did not work together.

TAGGERT HOUSE, 5423 Black Oak Drive, Los Angeles, California, 1922–1924, by John Lloyd Wright, juts out from a hillside and takes full advantage of the view. Very severe in design, it is built of wide bands of brick contrasted with white cement.

DERBY HOUSE, Glendale, near Los Angeles, 1926, another house by John Lloyd Wright, is built of decorative concrete blocks. This house is so much like the work of his father that it is often mistaken as a work by the Senior Wright.

*SNOWDEN HOUSE, 5121 Franklin Avenue, Los Angeles, 1926, by John Lloyd Wright, has plain cement walls that flank a huge entrance feature of decorative cement blocks. This entrance has a grottolike doorway at ground level and a large window above. The decorative blocks that surround it look like a stalactite formation. The house is designed around a central courtyard, and all is very clever and unusual.

Foreign architects brought new ideas. Among those who espoused the new International style were Rudolph Michael Schindler and Richard Neutra of Los Angeles, lately from Austria; William Lescaze of Philadelphia and New York City, originally from Switzerland; and later (1936) Walter Gropius and Marcel Breuer of Cambridge, Massachusetts, originally from Germany. Ludwig Mies van der Rohe (1940) and several others arrived later. Although some of these architects practiced in the 1920s and 1930s, their work was so avant-garde that it did not receive acceptance until after World War II, when International Functionalism was recognized as an accepted style.

**WALTER GROPIUS HOUSE,[1] Lincoln, Massachusetts, 1937, was designed by Walter Gropius in partnership with Marcel Breuer. This modest wood-framed, two-storied house is set in an old apple orchard. It is flat roofed, and the exterior is of matched vertical siding painted white. Much glass is used in sliding sashes to give a maximum view of the rolling New England landscape.

The house is essentially a cube, but interesting appurtenances that jut out here and there add interest and fulfill certain functions: a welcoming canopy projecting at an angle meets a driveway approach from the west; a freestanding cast iron circular stairway gives direct access to a second-floor sleeping porch; a large wooden trellis for climbing plants projects into the garden from the east; and a large, screened living porch, that was used for outdoor dining and table tennis much of the year is located on the south side of the house.

The interior was designed for informal living and entertaining. There has been criticism because to reach the living room at the east end of the house from the entrance vestibule, a person had to pass through either the study or the dining room; however as the Gropius family lived all over the house, this is not really a valid criticism.

This house was the first in its neighborhood to be built in the so-called Modern style, but soon there were others such as Professor James Ford's house, Marcel Breuer's house, Walter Bogner's house, and others.

---

[1] To preserve and maintain this house an endowment fund is now being raised, and the property is to be turned over to the Society for the Preservation of New England Antiquities.

SCHOOLS

Architects of Educational buildings, particularly elementary and high schools, starting about 1935, turned to a functional approach for their solutions. Several architects in different parts of the United States seemed to get the idea at the same time: William Lescaze in Connecticut; Maynard Lyndon and his partner, Eberle Smith, in Detroit; Ernest Kump in San Francisco; and Richard Neutra in Los Angeles. There were already a number of examples in Europe, particularly in Switzerland, where the new philosophy of education and architecture was accepted. The adoption of this theory for school houses was actually a natural: elementary education in the modern world called for new teaching methods and new spaces to house them. Also the economic depression of this period did not allow costly historical styling. The new functional approach to planning and design ensured greater efficiency with more light and air. Albert Kahn, Inc., an architectural firm of Detroit, Michigan, was designing factory buildings that were clean and light—why not school buildings?

GRADE SCHOOL, Northville, Michigan, 1935, by Lyndon and Smith, was one of the first schools in the United States to be designed in the philosophy of the Functionalists. This two-storied building has six classrooms on each floor and an adjoining Kindergarten with separate entrance and playground. All of the class rooms have large steel-sash windows and bright interiors. Orientation to the sun was carefully studied, and all activities were considered. Although many later schools have designs that are as good or better, this was the model in this part of the country.

*BEECHER HIGH SCHOOL, Flint, Michigan (Figure 6.4), 1936, by Lyndon and Smith, was both built and opened in 1936. Because of the tightness of money and World War II, the gymnasium and auditorium were not completed until 1947. It is an excellent building. It is said that the Flint School Board wanted a school as light and healthful as the Buick automobile plant that Albert Kahn, Inc., had recently designed there. After seeing the Northville School, they employed Lyndon and Smith to fulfill their wishes.

Figure 6.4 Beecher High School, Flint, Michigan, 1936; Lyndon and Smith, Architects. Photograph donated by Eberle Smith.

HIGH SCHOOL, Ansonia, Connecticut, 1936, by William Lescaze, is a very functional, well-designed school that is surprisingly similar to the Beecher High School in Flint, Michigan. However there is no reason to believe that there was any connection between the two except the period of time. Modern education was calling for modern solutions.

CORONA SCHOOL, Bell, Los Angeles, California, 1936, by Richard Neutra, is a five-room wing to an older building. These rooms were lighted on two opposite sides and could be completely opened to the weather. Although the idea seemed quite radical at the time, it has been used many times since, particularly in southern California.

HIGH SCHOOL, Alcalanes, California, 1938, was designed by Ernest J. Kump, who had received his Master of Architecture degree from Harvard in 1933. He became well known for his school designs, of which he did a great number, all in the philosophy of the Functionalists and all using fresh ideas.

*CROW ISLAND SCHOOL, Winnetka, Illinois (Figure 6.5), 1939–1940, was designed by Perkins and Will, in association with Eliel and Eero Saarinen. Here is a completely straightforward design for a one-storied, economical school building that was completely utilitarian yet possessing aesthetic refinement.

From 1940 onward and during World War II, the United States experienced a complete cessation of all except war construction. By the time civilian building was resumed, hundreds, if not thousands, of new school buildings were needed and built. All were then designed in the Functional mode, and the Crow Island School was a favored model.

OTHER BUILDINGS

**TABERNACLE CHURCH, Columbus, Indiana, 1940–1942, by Eliel Saarinen, started a new trend in church design in America. Somewhat

Figure 6.5 Crow Island School, Winnetka, Illinois, 1939–1940; Perkins and Will, Architects, in association with Eliel and Eero Saarinen. Photograph by Hedrick-Blessing, Chicago.

reminiscent of the many contemporary churches in Switzerland, this ensemble of church and Sunday school is a masterpiece of space and composition. It was built on a downtown site having streets on four sides. The plot seemed almost too small, but Saarinen excavated the exposed part of the lot to basement level and created a sunken garden. The Sunday school wing bridges over this area, creating a beautiful effect. The exterior is dominated by a simple rectangular bell tower. The patterns of brickwork are most subtle, and the interior lighting most effective.

**MUSEUM OF MODERN ART, 11 West 53rd Street, between Fifth and Sixth Avenues, New York City (Figure 6.6), 1939, designed by Philip L. Goodwin and Edward Durell Stone, is situated on a crowded city lot in the heart of midtown Manhattan. It was cleverly designed for

Figure 6.6 Museum of Modern Art, New York City, 1939; Philip L. Goodwin and Edward D. Stone, Architects. Photograph by Wurtz Bros., donated by Edward D. Stone Associates.

utmost flexibility and has movable partitions in the gallery portions. A sculpture garden is located to the rear of the building. The museum is five stories high with a lounge and roof terrace on top. The facade on 53rd Street is of diffusing glass and white marble set in a rectangular grid of steel.

In 1951, a narrow addition of black steel and glass, by Philip Johnson, was added on the west side. Although this addition is not an extension of the original design, it complements it beautifully. Another wing was added on the east side by Johnson, in 1964.

**DODGE TRUCK PLANT, Chrysler Corporation, Detroit, Michigan (Figure 6.7), 1938, by Albert Kahn, Inc., of Detroit, is a masterpiece of industrial architecture. Here daylighting was one of the important problems, and the inside area has widely spaced, thin, steel columns that support bent beams for the roof. These beams provided clerestory windows that cantilever out to the side walls and light the central floor space. Exterior curtain walls, which are almost entirely of glass in steel sash, have bulkheads and overglass fillers of brick. These fillers of brick are of two layers with a 2 inch airspace between them.

OHIO STEEL FOUNDRY, Lima, Ohio, 1940, by Albert Kahn, Inc., uses the same design as the Dodge Truck Plant, with only slight modifications.

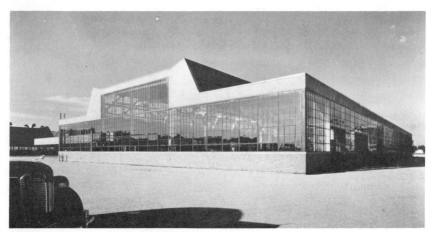

Figure 6.7 Dodge Truck Plant, Chrysler Corporation, Detroit, Michigan, 1938; Albert Kahn, Inc., Architect. Photograph by Hedrich-Blessing, Chicago.

7

THE POST-WORLD WAR II JET AGE

City Planning and Urban Renewal
1950–

Since World War II the replanning and rebuilding of our cities have become major problems for architects, engineers, sociologists, and politicians. Even before the war it was evident that our cities were becoming overly congested and obsolete. They had been built in a pedestrian age in which it was necessary to locate most activities in or near the centers. Manufacturing, wholesaling, retailing, banking, professional, and commercial offices, local government buildings, police and fire departments, railway stations, churches, schools, and residences—all were located within walking distance of each other. These were of necessity as closely centered as possible, although in those days walking one or two miles to and from work was not considered an inconvenience.

Large cities became crowded upward; the skyscraper was developed for offices and light manufacturing. Multistoried apartment buildings became necessary. As cities began to decentralize with regard to residences, streetcars and suburban trains came into being, with elevated and underground railways penetrating the hearts of great cities like London, New York, Boston, Philadelphia, and Chicago. Then came the automobile. By the post-World War II period many city dwellers owned one or even two automobiles, and this traffic was concentrated into, through, and around the downtown cores. It soon proved that our cities had to be redesigned.

Many factories and other commercial enterprises moved to the countryside, or at least to suburban sites, which offered better light and air; room to expand; convenience for truck transportation, rapidly becoming the chief mode of shipping; and above all adequate automobile

245

parking space for its customers and workers. Other buildings requiring this decentralization were some types of offices and administrative centers; hospitals, health, and medical centers; colleges, universities, and research centers; and most of all, shopping centers, which require plenty of parking space. Many people followed this outflux because of employment opportunities; others moved to the suburbs and countryside to escape urban blight and to make their homes in areas having a better social environment, space, light, and air. All were dependent on the central core: its offices, banks, and other central facilities, but not everyone wanted to live there.

It is evident that most parts of our old cities must be redesigned and rebuilt to provide for changing activities. The hearts of our cities today contain slums—ghettos where old lofts, flats, and obsolete apartment buildings are occupied by the poor and unemployed and their families. Sociologists and politicians are suggesting vast new housing projects to rehabilitate these areas, but this replanning must take into consideration the type and adequacy of employment in these areas. It is of no use to plan new low-income housing if untrained employment is dwindling or has disappeared from the central core. It is better to build such housing in the satellite centers and move the people to where there are jobs. In our older cities most unemployed slum dwellers have no means of getting to a job that may be 20 or 40 miles away.

In redesigning the central cores it is necessary that they be opened up for light and air. Parklike shopping malls and landscaped plazas should be provided for office workers. Plenty of automobile parking space, maybe underground, should be provided, as well as high-rise apartment buildings for those people who prefer to live in the central district.

City planning has thus become the science of foreseeing and planning for the changes that are necessary to rehabilitate the central cores of our cities, then anticipating and placing centers surrounding the central core, and making proper connections thereto. Many suburbs have already been built, some in the nineteenth century; but great urban growth, necessitates more surrounding developments, and better transportation must be provided. Some of these suburbs are dormitory areas for the central cores; some are dependent subcenters for manufacturing or other purposes. Their purpose and form must be anticipated and properly planned for human needs. Proper zoning for long-term development must keep in mind what is most logical for occupancy of each zone. Zoning must be part of planning and completely consistent with the projected economy of the area. Planning without regulatory, enforceable zoning is futile, as is zoning that does not anticipate logical future changes and growth.

After the various centers and satellite neighborhoods surrounding the central core, the most important factor in metropolitan planning is transportation. Fast means of travel must be provided to service the central core. It is an axiom among city planners that 45 minutes is the absolute limit for transportation time that the average person will comfortably allow between home and job. Transportation may start with the private automobile, but the presence of too many cars downtown strangles traffic. One solution is to park cars at suburban stations and take express trains or buses into the central core. There, from one or more conveniently located downtown stops, a person should be able to walk to places of employment. This is not a new problem, or a new solution, but it needs more development.

Superhighways must connect the satellite centers, and circling the total should be a highway that can bypass all of the centers and lead to transcontinental highways for trucks as well as for pleasure cars. No doubt more superarteries will need to be built into the central cities for trucks, particularly for cities that are shipping centers on a body of water, and others may be necessary for express buses, which can be hazardous if mixed with pleasure cars.

City planning is a very complicated science that deals with every aspect of community life. It must be done on a metropolitan scale and should have some direct authority. The trouble is that most communities are separate political entities that are unwilling to cooperate with their neighbors unless for special advantages. Many European cities have metropolitan commissions that are able to tackle planning problems on a broad scale and execute them through legislative authority; this is particularly true in Holland and the Scandinavian countries. Stockholm's planning office is now over 300 years old.

In the United States these problems are often discussed, but usually only by laymen commissions without centralized authority. Laymen commissions are important, and perhaps it is good that these commissions are only advisory to legislative political bodies; however they should coordinate with a central metropolitan office of planning or be replaced by the central office. This central office should consist of architects whose primary training is in the field of planning, along with civil engineers, landscape architects, and economic experts. These offices should also have consultants in law, banking, real estate, business, education, and sociology. The goal of these planners should be to project all of the future problems and their solutions, whether for a neighborhood, a suburb, or the whole metropolitan area. Planning is for change, and change is never static. Planning is to satisfy future human needs, and these vary as conditions change. There can never be one final plan.

Maps of these metropolitan areas will generally resemble spokes of a wheel emanating from a central hub, with green spaces in between each spoke for park and recreational purposes. However the exact form of each city depends on the geographic and geologic location, the economic base, climate, and politics. Cities having the hub on a large body of water will take the shape of a half wheel, like the shape of Chicago, San Francisco, and many other port cities. Or the city may elongate as a strip of outlying towns along a corridor between two metropolitan centers. As in architecture generally the form should not be imposed from without, but should evolve from conditions within.

It is the function of metropolitan planners to know and anticipate these conditions, and aid in developing their forms so that a pleasant and proper environment results. Then the development that takes place will be in the hands of the administrative divisions of each central city, and each satellite suburb and neighborhood will develop its own environment down to each individual building of each owner and his architect. But all will be in accordance with the metropolitan plan.

There are a few instances in which entirely new cities have been planned and built in new locations for a specific use. Three of these are *Chandigarh, new capitol of Punjab, India, 1951–1956, by Le Corbusier in collaboration with Jane Drew, Maxwell Fry, and Pierre Janneret, Le Corbusier's brother; **Brasilia, new capitol of Brazil, 1957–1965, by Lucio Costa assisted by Oscar Niemeyer; and **Cumbernauld, Scotland, 1958–1967, by L. Hugh Wilson, A. G. McCulloch, and Dudley R. Leaker, architects for the Cumbernauld Development Corporation. This last is a self-supporting industrial community designed to relieve the congestion of Glasgow, Scotland, some miles away.

New satellite towns have also been planned and built. These include Harlow, England, near London, 1848–1856; *Tapiola, Finland, not too far from Helsingfors, 1952–1965; and *Vallingby, Sweden, near Stockholm, 1956–1960. These are primarily bedroom towns although industry is planned so that they can eventually be self-supporting. Cuatitlan, Mexico, northeast of Mexico City, is being planned and built for 1.5 million people, as a satellite to the capital, which is already the largest and fastest growing city in the Western Hemisphere.

AN EARLY EXAMPLE OF A PLANNED CITY

However let us discuss one example of city planning that took place in the United States from 1930 to 1931, Radburn, New Jersey. This has set a pattern for many cities since that time, particularly their residential sections.[1]

RADBURN, New Jersey, 1930–1931, was designed by Clarence S. Stein and Henry Wright, architects for the City Housing Corporation of New York City. It is noted for its street plan, which completely separates pedestrian from automobile traffic. Residential neighborhoods were planned with traffic arteries around the outside and automobile cul-de-sacs running off these arteries to a depth of approximately eight lots. These lots open in back to green areas that have sidewalks leading to neighborhood schools, shops, and supermarkets. These green areas serving for park and play are private to each group of lots opening off of them. Radburn is a bedroom town for New York City; however it set a standard for neighborhood planning that can hardly be surpassed.

REPLANNING AND RENEWAL

There are cities in the United States in which some of these problems are being solved. Washington, D.C., the nation's capital city, and its suburbs in Virginia and Maryland voted a large bond issue in 1968 to institute and build a fast-moving rapid transit commuter system. A Metropolitan Authority that has status has been established. May it be hoped that this pilot project will open the way for other solutions throughout the country.[2]

No doubt the biggest error of the past three or four decades has been the concentration of much of the public works in the hands of the

---

[1] Unfortunately Radburn has not had the influence in the United States that it should have had. Many of its ideas for the separation of automobile and pedestrian traffic have been used by foreign planners for cities and neighborhoods abroad, and gradually after nearly 40 years is being noticed and used in new city plans in America.

[2] The first section of Washington's subway was opened in March, 1976.

federal government. A case illustrating lack of public discipline and the futility of federal spending without local responsibility is the Pruitt-Igoe housing project in St. Louis. This was built in 1955 to house 10,000 people, and consisted of 35 eleven-storied buildings that cost $36 million. Since its completion $5 million has been spent on social services and $13.8 million on attempts at renovations. Repair costs due to vandalism have been estimated at $1,700 per day. In 1969 there were 10 murders, 14 rapes, and more than 100 assaults in this project. Tenants have moved out in droves. By August, 1973, only 587 families occupied this project designed for 3800 units. Now it is being razed, and the cost of wrecking has been placed at $2.5 million.[2]

In recent years the United States government has appropriated huge sums of money for urban renewal and housing, mainly for low-rental housing. However the several appropriations they have made have created new branches of government—new bureaus—in addition to those already established. Washington Post columnist William Raspberry has pointed out that agencies dealing with antipoverty projects, as well as those of slum clearance and urban renewal, include (1) the Department of Housing and Urban Development (HUD); (2) the Department of Health, Education and Welfare (HEW); (3) the United Planning Organization (UPO); (4) the Model Cities Commission (MCC); and (5) the Model Inner City Organization (MICO).[3] Competition between these bureaus has been inevitable, and much federal aid for urban renewal of American cities has been ineffectual.

Nevertheless things are not all bad, and a few fine solutions have been worked out for cities throughout the country.

DETROIT, Michigan, has had a city planning commission for many years, and while some of their plans have gone unheeded, Detroit has cleaned up its waterfront and built some traffic arteries through and around the city. Charles A. Blessing, FAIA, headed its planning division, for many years, until retirement in 1974. Traffic flow is fairly well solved, and the inner city is gradually being rebuilt. Henry Ford II is heading a citizen group that is financing and building a large new commercial center on the Detroit River contiguous to the downtown core to be known as Renaissance Center. Housing is being studied, and there is

[2] Jenkins Lloyd Jones, syndicated newspaper column, September 15, 1973.
[3] Gilmore, Kenneth O., "The Great Challenge: Making Our Government Work," *Reader's Digest*, February 1969.

hope that it will be built for a balanced population. Many of the present ghetto dwellers will have to move to the suburbs where the factories are being relocated.

LOS ANGELES, California, has done a job similar to that done in Detroit, with traffic arteries through and around the city. It is rebuilding its central core and tying in the many suburbs that surround the city. Sadly, this city that used to be noted for its sunshine and blue skies is now cursed by a smog that is largely caused by the automobile. This problem is being studied before all others and must be solved to prevent the city dwellers from literally choking. No doubt, in the spirit of the West, it will be solved.

**PHILADELPHIA, Pennsylvania, under its planning commission, from 1947 onward has been developing different parts of the city at different times into an evolving overall plan. Early motivation for this work was stimulated through the efforts of Charles E. Peterson, architect, and two organizations to which he belonged, namely, the Philadelphia Society for the Preservation of Landmarks, and the Society Hill Area Neighborhood Association. In 1947 the Philadelphia Planning Commission staged a Better Philadelphia Exhibition in which a plan of the Society Hill district and its many historical landmarks, including Independence Hall, was shown. This 1947 plan was designed by Edmund N. Bacon, architect, who presented the concept, that with a few minor changes has been used since. This plan emphasizes the importance of preserving the historical area before it is too late and the need to clear out objectionable encroachments that have crowded in over the years. Even before World War II, in 1940 and 1944, architect Roy Larson had proposed that extensive clearings and green areas be created around Independence Hall, extending eastward to include the old Second Bank of the United States, and the old Stock Exchange. He also proposed a few high-rise buildings in between.

In 1957, after a lapse of time during which Society Hill further deteriorated, a team of architects consisting of Vincent Kling, Roy Larson, and Oskar Stonorov was hired to suggest a comprehensive plan for the district, including the waterfront on the Delaware River. Their plan was a refinement of the Larson plan of 1944. But there was still a group of citizenry who wanted Society Hill restored without change and who deplored the idea of including high-rise buildings. Meanwhile a Redevelopment Authority had been constituted by the city and given special powers and money to act. In 1958 it hired Preston Andrade, architect, to work with Mr. von Moltke of the Planning Commission specifically to refine and define the 1957 plans of Kling, Larson, and Stonorov and to make provisions to carry them out. By this time it was pretty well agreed that the introduction of high-rise apartments on two open sites on Society Hill would not ruin the district. However it was not until a competition was held and won in 1960 by William Zeckendorf and his architect, Ieoh Ming Pei, that the idea was finally accepted by the city. Actually Pei carried out the ideas of the earlier plans, but to appease the critics he introduced a buffer group of town houses between the Early Federal residences and the skyscrapers. As carried out, these town houses are neither Federal in design nor contemporary, and the area would have been better if they had never been built. The transitional town houses fit with neither the Federal buildings nor the high-rise apartment building.

But the several Colonial and Federal buildings surrounding Independence Hall have been saved and restored, and the area has been beautifully landscaped. Actually the landscaping has been overdone and is not too historically accurate, but it has opened up the area by giving it pleasant green lawns and trees, and it complies with the thoughts of the average American regarding the proper settings for these buildings. Society Hill, with its rows of Colonial and Federal houses, has been saved and is gradually being bought up and restored by individual householders. Society Hill is again an elite section of Philadelphia. Among the many fine residences is the *Samuel Powell House,* 1765, open to visitors at selected times. Also on the hill are several famous Colonial churches: *Christ Church, St. Mary's Chapel,* and *Old St. Peter's,* with its beautiful Palladian window.

At the west end of the central core of Philadelphia is the Pennsylvania Railroad area and its declining grandiose station. Here several thousand commuters in the past filtered in and out of the city through narrow streets clogged with the trucks and automobiles of a worn-out wholesale district. The redoing of this area, known as the "Penn Center Project," went through an evolving development from 1952 to 1966. Now it is a four block area in which commuters arrive underground and enter a submerged pedestrian way leading straight to City Hall and the commercial areas beyond. This pedestrian way, which is open to the sky at three points, is pleasant and very efficient. At street level are new office buildings and modern hotels plus a new boulevarded traffic artery that leads out of the city. At the time this section was planned, the old City Hall (French Empire style) seemed destined to destruction, but it was eventually saved and completely renovated. Traffic has been routed through and around it, and its famous high tower remains the central point of the city.

Directly between City Hall and Society Hill is Market Street East, the real core of the city, with famous department stores and congested traffic. Philadelphia's antiquated subway runs under this street, feeding the financial and commercial areas contiguous to Market Street. Most of the buildings lining this street have become old, shoddy, and obsolete. Now planning attention is focused here. A submerged pedestrian way open to the sky has been suggested as a continuation of the Penn Center scheme; the subway stations are to be updated, and the subway itself made more efficient. Most of the surface vehicular traffic is to be rerouted, and new buildings will be erected. Romaldo Giurgola, architect, has presented an ultrascheme that has several levels of both pedestrian and vehicular traffic, as well as parking spaces in the very heart of the area. But although Giurgola's scheme has a great deal of merit, it would mean almost the complete destruction of the area before rebuilding could be started and accomplished. In 1967 the Philadelphia Redevelopment Authority hired Skidmore, Owings and Merrill, architects of New York City, to tackle the problem with a more easily accomplished solution.

No doubt in a few years Philadelphia, America's oldest metropolis, will be its most modern and beautiful.

**"GOLDEN TRIANGLE," Pittsburgh, Pennsylvania, 1952–1956, was done by the Pittsburgh Regional Planning Board (1941) under Richard Mellon, President, assisted by Dave Lawrence, Mayor of Pittsburgh. The Golden Triangle, where the Allegheny and Monongahela Rivers join to form the Ohio, was the site of the original settlement of Pittsburgh. This old riverfront area had become an obsolete section of the city, littered with abandoned factories and worn-out warehouses. However since the planning by Richard Mellon and colleagues, this area has been entirely opened up and landscaped. Beautiful sites have been laid out for skyscrapers. Access boulevards have circled the area. Parking structures have been built, one of them under Mellon Square.

Before the start of the project it was necessary to get state legislative action (1945–1946) for (1) large-scale real estate investments, (2) municipal parking authority, (3) urban redevelopment authority to condemn land and to replan and rebuild on it, and (4) countywide smoke and pollution control. Pittsburgh, at the headwaters of a great river transportation system and near large deposits of bituminous coal, had become the greatest iron- and steel-producing center in the world at the cost of smoke that at times almost obscured the sun. Now that problem has been solved, and the city is practically free of smoke, soot and smog.

With all of these things accomplished, Mellon and Lawrence hit the wealthy business people of Pittsburgh with the plea to invest in the inner city of Pittsburgh. Aluminum Company of America (ALCOA) was one of the first to comply; although it had purchased property in New York City and had had plans to move there, it reconsidered and built its central office building in Pittsburgh. Nine skyscraper office buildings have subsequently been built in the Triangle, including the headquarters of U.S. Steel.

*AMPHITHEATER, Pittsburgh, 1956, by Mitchell and Ritchey, local architects, was made possible by a generous gift by Edward Kaufman, owner of the leading department store in the city. This theater was built primarily for symphony concerts and opera "under the stars." A magnificent auditorium, it has a complete stage and a circular seating area for 9500 people. Its plastic folding roof can be rotated open or shut in a matter of minutes.

*UTAH STATE OFFICE BUILDING AND UTAH STATE PLAZA, Salt Lake City, Utah (Figure 7.1), 1971, were designed by Harold K. Beecher, architect. The plaza is located between the old capitol building and the new six-storied office building. A covered walkway crossing the plaza connects the office building and the capitol. A very attractive restaurant serves the public as well as the state workers. Under the plaza, which is actually elevated above the old street level, is parking space for cars of state officers and workers.

CULLEN CENTER, Houston, Texas, 1960, was designed by Welton Becket and Associates, architects of Los Angeles. This is a $5\frac{1}{2}$ block area covering 12 acres in the southwest portion of Houston's central business district and is located at the crossroads of two inner-city freeway traffic arteries. It was master planned for development over several years, starting with a large, rectangular 22-storied office building, and all was financed by private capital for profit. It embraces four underground levels with two assigned to car parking and space for mechanical equipment. The ground surface area is for pedestrians and has landscaped plazas, shops,

Figure 7.1 Utah State Office Building and Utah State Plaza, Salt Lake City, Utah, 1971; Harold K. Beecher, Architect. Photograph courtesy of Harold K. Beecher.

and walkways. The first floor area one floor up, also for pedestrians, has additional shops, restaurants, and other facilities. Above this are office towers and in one portion a hotel. In concept it is not dissimilar to Haymarket Square in Stockholm, Sweden, although the latter is more complex with its terminal subway facilities and underground market. Cullen Center will tie in with the Greater Houston City Plan, yet to be completed.

*CONSTITUTION PLAZA, Hartford, Connecticut, 1964, was designed by Charles Dubose, coordinating architect, with Sasaki, Dawson, Demay and Associates, landscape architects. A beautiful pedestrian mall in the center of Hartford, it extends a distance of three city blocks and ties into a submerged automobile thruway at one end. At the other end is a 70 foot rough-granite-faced clock tower. The ensemble contains formal settings of large potted trees, a fountain, decorative lights, and poles holding gaily colored flags. Underneath are a huge parking structure and pedestrian walkways to the various buildings on each side of the mall.

Canada too has taken steps to improve its cities, and the influence of its city planning has been felt in the United States.

*DOMINION CENTER, Vancouver, British Columbia, Canada, 1966, designed by Erickson and Massey, comprises three contiguous square blocks in the center of the city. This center has a three-level traffic artery, huge underground parking facility, and a large office building for the dominion government. Vancouver is experiencing tremendous growth, and other parts of the central city are also being replanned.

TORONTO, Ontario, Canada, has also been redeveloping its central areas. A beautiful new city hall with a great plaza in front has been built, and new traffic arteries have been cut through and around the city, with a subway to eliminate downtown congestion.

*MONTREAL, Quebec, Canada, has been undergoing great changes due to long range planning (1967–1969) under the leadership of its forward-looking mayor, Jean Drapeau. These improvements have been expedited in great part by Expo '67, but the general planning was more profound than that. Redevelopment, Place Ville Marie, started in the central core at the railroad terminal. Air rights were used to build great office buildings and hotels over the tracks. Traffic arteries connecting the outlying districts were cut through and formed into a newly modified street pattern. A subway system that speeded traffic to and through the central city was planned and built. Montreal was given new life and room to breathe.

FOUR NEW TOWNS

In addition to Radburn, mentioned heretofore in this chapter, new satellite towns have been built in most parts of the United States.

SUN CITY, Arizona, 1954–1960, designed and built by a real estate corporation for profit, is a city primarily for retired people and offers a complete environment with a country club atmosphere. It boasts its own golf course, clubhouse, and other recreational facilities, as well as its own civic center and shopping plaza. Housing primarily consists of single family residences that are sold to the occupants on a condominium basis. The city is entirely financed by private capital and has proven so successful to both the owners and the dwellers that two similar Sun Cities have been built, one in Florida, the other in California. These Sun Cities are very attractive and are so well managed that they have been sold out almost as soon as they have been finished, with the result that in the late 1960s several additions were added.

**RESTON, Virginia, 1963–1965, designed by Whittlesey and Conklin, planners, was conceived as a profit-making private enterprise by the Reston Real Estate Corporation under Robert E. Simon, Jr., with Gulf Oil Corporation as first mortgagor. A satellite city to Washington, D.C., it is located 17 miles west of the capitol, near Dulles Airport. The airport highway and parallel railroad bisect the site from east to west, and highway Route 602 runs north and south along its western limit. Local auto traffic is directed around the city by way of a loop artery.

A civic center is situated near the railroad station, which is at the intersection of the two main highways. Some land along the railroad and near Dulles Airport Highway is zoned for light industry, and it is hoped that Reston will become self-supporting as time goes on.

The city is made up of seven neighborhoods, each with its own school and neighborhood shopping facilities. It covers a 10 square mile site of which 1500 acres is reserved for recreation. Like Radburn, New Jersey, pedestrian traffic within each neighborhood is separate from vehicular traffic, thus allowing safe travel for children to and from school, and unimpeded pedestrian access to neighborhood shops and other services.

Before Reston could be built, Simons, aided by his planners, had to develop and get passed by the county board a model density zoning ordinance called "Residential Planning Community." This ordinance permits a mixture of housing and commercial usage, with introduction of high-rise apartments close to single family and row houses, provided that there are open land areas and a high proportion of land devoted to public use. It also permits clustering of single family dwellings to create larger open areas and preserve trees.

The city is very distinctive for its diversified forms of buildings and for its many small but interesting innovations. Its street and walkway lighting is unusual in design, as well as very efficient.

*COLUMBIA, Maryland, 1966–1968, was designed by a diversified group under the direction of James W. Rouse, a Baltimore mortgage banker, who, together with several insurance companies and Chase National Bank of New York, is putting up the money. The costs are estimated to be over $100 million. The city, located on the corridor between Baltimore and Washington, D.C., is being planned to house 125,000 people by 1980. It will be managed by the Columbia Association, a nonprofit organization having representation from within the city, and owners of each piece of property will pay an annual assessment for city upkeep.

It will eventually have seven sections, or villages, each with its distinctive village green and shopping center, high school, and churches. Each village will be made up of several neighborhoods of 2000 people or more, and each neighborhood will have an elementary school, a general store for convenient purchases, a recreation building with swimming pool, and a preschool day-care center. Houses ranging in price from $15,000 to $70,000 as well as condominiums are being built for sale, and medium- and high-rent apartments are being constructed. Space is being provided for factories, and at least 17, with a total of 4000 jobs, are now assured. Contiguous acreage is also available, and this is being zoned for industry.

The general layout of Columbia, particularly its neighborhoods, is remindful of Radburn and of Reston, Virginia, not many miles away. Vehicular and pedestrian traffic within neighborhoods is kept separate, and much space is allowed for green areas, playgrounds, and parks.

Mr. Rouse consulted with over a hundred people, from psychiatrists to sociologists, bankers, architects, and landscape planners, while formulating this project. He has said that he wants Columbia to be a city "for people," not just a solution for housing and jobs. He hopes to create an environment that promotes real neighborliness and hopes that every citizen will be his own policeman and show his pride in his community.

SOUL CITY, North Carolina, 1970, is being promoted by Floyd B. McKissick, a former Durham, North Carolina, lawyer and Negro leader. Although planned primarily for blacks, it will be open to all. It will provide space for industry, and it is hoped that several companies having

Negro management and labor will settle there, James W. Rouse of Baltimore is being consulted, and options on 1800 acres have been taken. The initial costs have been estimated at $25 million, and federal financial assistance is being sought. Preliminary plans are excellent; it is to be hoped they will be carried out without too much interference from government bureaus.

THE JET AGE

The International Structural, (Miesian) Style
1950–1970

The post-World War II period brought the spread of wealth. Blue-collar workers now make an average of $10,000 per year, and many reach over twice that amount. Almost every family has an automobile, and some have two or three; most have television sets and comfortable homes that have all of the latest gadgets. Many have summer cottages on lakes, rivers, or in the mountains, motorboats, sailboats, and other recreational luxuries to go with them. Of course there have been and still are inequalities, and minority groups have been unable to share fully in this affluence. However governments are now taking care of the poor better than ever before. Inflation and several serious recessions have slowed the rise in the living standards of all Americans.

This affluence has extended to construction—it has been a most prolific and sophisticated era of building. This may have been the culmination of our civilization, although the limits are not in sight at this time. Many new industrially fabricated materials have been introduced into building construction such as fiberglass and plastics of all kinds; also bituminous rubber, anodized aluminum, stainless steel, epoxy cements, and new paints. The list has grown almost daily during the 1950 decade. The fluorescent tube has brought about a revolution in electric lighting and has all but turned nighttime into day. This has made windows unnecessary except for psychological reasons. (It is true that some of the occupants in buildings in which windows have been eliminated, have been plagued by claustrophobia. To some people the inability to look outside can be frustrating to the point of illness) Chemical refrigerants have been perfected, leading to the wide use of air conditioning and cooling.

With all of this at hand—seemingly unlimited materials and unprecedented affluence—it is no wonder that so much building has been done. However it might seem odd that the International structural style, also known as *Structuralism* and popularly called the *Miesian style,* was in vogue. It might have been expected that an extravagant, highly decorative style would have resulted.

The International Structural or Functional style glorifies the structure, the steel fabric unobscured by veneer. However most building codes did not allow the structural steel to be exposed and demanded 2–4 inches of concrete fireproofing or at least 4 inches of masonry cover over all steel structural members. Therefore the structural columns were usually set back from the exterior surfaces, and a metal grid and glass curtain wall was hung over the outside. This grid followed the structural pattern behind it, and to the casual observer appeared to be part of the structure itself. In the hands of an artist like Mies van der Rohe, this grillage was refined to a patternlike tracery that was beautiful as well as functional. The glass, which could be clear or opaque, might be so articulated that the facade became a sheer surface of plaidlike design.

During the 1950s and early 1960s Gropius reached retirement age and turned most of his practice over to Architect's Collaborative, a Boston firm of which he was senior partner. Mies van der Rohe was in the ascendency. Others such as Gordon Bunshaft, of Skidmore, Owings and Merrill's New York office, were masters of the same philosophy, but Mies was given credit for the style. It is an absurdity that his form of architecture was so vehemently designated by Mies as the "absence of style," and that the very word *style* made him launch into tirades of argument against the word. To him there was a deep philosophy behind his surface designs and the open planning, which he kept as simple as possible. His open spaces could be subdivided in many different ways to suit the whims and needs of the various people who might occupy the spaces. He believed in the ultimate in flexibility and applied his famous dictum, "More is less, and less is more." Many students mouthed this phrase, but few understood it.

Hundreds of office buildings in New York City and elsewhere were built during this era. Although most are trite and insensitive, they represent a mode that was popular until 1970. The style still has its followers but is now definitely on the wane. Possibly it was too subtle, too sophisticated, to be performed by the rank and file of architects.

Opposed to the International Structuralists was another group having another philosophy that was growing and becoming popular during this era. These were the *Emotionalists*, headed by Le Corbusier of France. Their goal was to mold structure to produce sculptural form—to appeal to the eye emotionally through form, to appeal to man's aesthetic sense. For this reason Thomas Creighton, editor of *Progressive Architecture*, in a discussion of this philosophy and style in September and October, 1959, gave it the descriptive name of "The New Sensualism." Since then the name *Sensualist Architecture*, as well as *Emotionalism*, has been used as an appropriate name for this style.

SKYSCRAPERS

It used to be said that skyscrapers are solely an American institution, but since World War II they have been built all over the world, mostly in the metal and glass style. Some were of reinforced concrete frame, some had solid masonry walls on one side or another; but the day of the monumental skyscraper had passed. These metal and glass skyscrapers are curtain wall buildings, a form no longer exclusively American. Skyscrapers have been built in England, Denmark, Germany, Italy, Japan, Australia, South Africa, Brazil, and Mexico. Skyscraper office buildings and hotels greet the eye everywhere. There is great similarity, and some are aesthetically better than others, as is to be expected. The BASF Office Building in Ludwigshafen is the tallest building in Germany. The breathtaking Post Office Tower of London, built in 1966, is 650 feet high, and although it could not be classified as International Structural design in the usual sense, it would not have been accepted in England before World War II. Copenhagen has a new SAS Building (Scandinavian Air System) that is 35 stories high and beautifully proportioned. Sidney, Australia, completed a 50-storied office tower in 1968, and in 1965 Mexico City, in spite of mud subsoil and the threat of earthquakes, built its Latin-American Tower, 35-storied commercial building. Chicago has completed its John Hancock Building of 100 stories (1965), a quite ugly but very high example, and has now completed its Sears Tower (1975), which will top them all at 110 stories. The new Chase Manhattan Bank building in Lower Manhattan is 60-stories high. The World Trade Center, also in New York City, has twin towers, each having sheer surfaces of glass and steel curtain walls, that rise 110 stories, a height of 1350 feet, making them the tallest buildings in the world.

The following descriptions of steel and glass skyscrapers in the United States include only a few of the dozens of examples that have been recognized. These have been chosen for having individuality of structure, for being a first in the field, or for being internationally famous, such as the United Nations Secretariat. Truly this era will go down in history as the epoch of the skyscraping steel and glass cage.

*EQUITABLE BUILDING, Portland, Oregon, 1948, designed by Pietro Belluschi, was one of the first office buildings to be built following World War II. The 12-storied fully expressed structure is thoroughly mechanized with heating and air conditioning operated by heat pumps. The exterior columns and beams are faced with aluminum in the upper stories, and the horizontal rectangular infillings are of greenish glass. The high columns on the ground floor, which is occupied by the Equitable Savings and Loan Association, are veneered with polished granite.

**UNITED NATIONS HEADQUARTERS, United Nations Plaza (between 42nd and 48th Streets), New York City (Figure 8.1), 1947–1963, was designed by Wallace K. Harrison and a team of 14 architects, including Le Corbusier of France, Oscar Niemeyer of Brazil, Sven Markelius of Sweden, and architects from 10 other countries. However Harrison served as director of the project, and much of the design is attributed to his office. The headquarters complex has two main buildings, the Secretariat and the General Assembly Building. The Secretariat certainly belongs to the Structuralist style. The 35-storied steel and glass curtain walled rectangular building has solid ends veneered with white marble. It is oriented with its long axis running north and south so that one glass wall faces east, overlooking the East River, and the opposite wall faces west over the city. In summer, however, offices on the west side become unbearably hot from early afternoon onward; even with air conditioning the system cannot compete with the sun's rays. Most of the offices on the west side have therefore become workrooms that are used only during morning hours. The building is sleek and beautiful and stands as a symbol of the United Nations ideals.

The General Assembly Building, which contains a large auditorium in which the representatives of all nations meet, is expressive of its function

Figure 8.1 United Nations Secretariat, New York City, 1947–1950; Wallace K. Harrison, Architect, director of a team of 14 international architects; Miesian style. Photograph courtesy of the United Nations.

in form with sweeping curves and domical construction. It should probably be classified as an emotional structure. Certainly it is not structural in the Miesian sense; however it fits in very well with the Secretariat and forms a beautiful foil to it.

A library, by Harrison, Abramovitz and Harris, was added in 1963.

PRUDENTIAL LIFE INSURANCE BUILDING, Wilshire Boulevard, Los Angeles, California, 1948, was designed by Wurdeman and Becket, architects. Perhaps this building should not be classified as a skyscraper, as it stands only eight stories high above a plaza and court. However it has all of the elements of a skyscraper and is no doubt the first office building in the United States in which an attempt was made to screen the sun. The main frontages are glass curtain walls behind sun screens; other walls are of dressed limestone.

*LAKE SHORE APARTMENT HOUSES, Chicago, Illinois (Figure 8.2), 1949–1951, were designed by Mies van der Rohe as luxury apartments. The buildings, twin towers overlooking Lake Michigan to the east and north, are identical in shape but are placed at right angles to each other. The structural steelwork is fireproofed with concrete, which was necessary to meet the building code requirement, but curtain wall framing of black-painted steel is set on the faces, outlining the structure behind. The infilling of the outside curtain walls is entirely of plate glass in aluminum frames, and the structural columns are exposed at the ground level. The design is very tailored, very sophisticated, and very elegant; however, as is necessary with this style, it is impossible to accommodate window design to the function of the spaces behind the facade. Living area windows have the same amount of glass as do bedrooms. The black steel appears quite severe in contrast to the yellow-lined drapes that are required in all windows. However these buildings are beautiful, particularly in comparison with the neighboring conglomerate group of 1920 terra-cotta apartment buildings in Baroque and other pseudohistorical designs.[1]

---

[1] It is interesting that although Mies van der Rohe has been the foremost proponent of the Structuralist group and the foremost preacher of "structural integrity," he used reinforced concrete for the actual structure of his nearby Esplanade Apartments, which have similar exterior curtain walls of black-painted steel.

Figure 8.2 Lake Shore Apartments, Chicago, Illinois, 1949–1951; Mies van der Rohe, Designer; Miesian style. Photograph by Balthazar Korab, Troy, Michigan.

**LEVER HOUSE, 390 Park Avenue (between 53rd and 54th Streets), New York City (Figure 8.3), 1950–1952, by Skidmore, Owings and Merrill's New York office, is the headquarters of the Lever Brothers Company. The 22-storied rectilinear block of steel and glass covers about a third of its lot and appears to sit on top of a 2-storied steel and glass structure. This base structure, which extends over the remaining two

Figure 8.3 Lever House, New York City, 1950–1952; Skidmore, Owings and Merrill, New York Office; Gordon Bunshaft, Designer; Miesian style. Photograph rented from the Bettmann Archive, Inc.

thirds of the lot, has a large open court free of the main building. The space is entirely open at sidewalk level so that pedestrians can freely circulate there. The roof of this 2-storied structure has an employees' garden.

The curtain walls of the tall portion present sheer unbroken surfaces of glass set in metal grids totally screening the structural fabric behind. A very sensitive piece of design, this structure was hailed as a masterpiece by the American Institute of Architects at its New York City convention in 1952. At long last the United States architects recognized that structure could be beautiful and that the old pseudosophisticated Eclectic approach was a thing of the past. The preachings of Louis Sullivan and the goals of the Chicago School, which had been generally ignored for 50 years, were at last recognized and accepted.

*MILE HIGH BUILDING, Denver, Colorado, 1954–1956, designed by Ieoh Ming Pei, is a 22-storied office building of steel and glass. It is named for Denver, which boasts of being 5280 feet above sea level; therefore the building was built a mile high. The main columns are on the surface here and run from sidewalk to roof. Between these are intermediate white mullions and spandrels that contrast with the dark-colored structural members, forming a beautiful plaidlike design.

Next to this building at ground level, and part of the same complex, is a geodesic dome, which is used as a bank. The composition also includes a rectangular pool with flowerlike spray and a plaza with sculpture. The ensemble is very slick, very beautiful, and very sophisticated.

*INLAND STEEL BUILDING, Chicago, Illinois, 1957–1958, by Skidmore, Owings and Merrill's Chicago office, was designed by Walter Netsch. It is a 19-storied office building of steel and glass. Transverse beams supporting the floors are set between strongly marked exterior stanchions that are exposed on the long facades. These stanchions, encased in stainless steel on the exterior, allow clear interior floor spaces without columns. A tower at the back carries all of the elevators, stairways, and service facilities so that the working floor areas can be open or divided as desired. It is a beautifully proportioned building that shimmers.

**SEAGRAM BUILDING, 375 Park Avenue (between 52nd and 53rd Streets, New York City (Figure 8.4), 1956–1958, was designed by Mies van

Figure 8.4 Seagram Building, New York City, 1956–1957; Mies van der Rohe, Designer; in association with Philip Johnson; Miesian style. Photograph by Ezra Stoller (Esto).

der Rohe in association with Philip Johnson. This 38-storied building has a penthouse that carries the sheer facades 4 stories higher to shield the mechanical equipment from view. In concept it is similar to the main block of Lever House, though here the curtain wall fins are of bronze and the glass is amber to block the sun's rays. It covers approximately half of the corner site, which contains two small reflecting pools and a planting space, though most of the plaza is uninterrupted paving. The entire ensemble is extreme; a most sensitive piece of design. It was certainly so rated by the assessor's office, which tacked on an inflated value over actual costs, "because of prestige value due to exquisite design."

BLUE CROSS–BLUE SHIELD BUILDING, Boston Massachusetts, 1959–1970, designed by Paul Rudolph, is included here because it is an interesting experiment in the expression of semiexposed plumbing pipes and ductwork. These are channeled on the outside of the building and made to blend with the structure—a stunt without too much validity, though cleverly handled. The building, 11 stories high on a 2-storied base, has an elegant entrance floor that is entirely glass. Public rooms and a restaurant lie under the podiumlike platform that appears to support the building.

*PAN AM BUILDING, 200 Park Avenue, New York City, 1961–1963, was designed by Emery Roth and Sons, architects, with Walter Gropius and Pietro Belluschi as consultants. Built over air rights contiguous to Grand Central Station, the structure has a commanding view looking north and south on Park Avenue. The building is a colossal rectangle, the ends of which are pointed, of 60 stories that rise out of a complex of other buildings. It is amazing how well the traffic flow has been worked out in this congested neighborhood; there is direct access to the two flanking streets as well as to the concourse of Grand Central Station. The construction of this all steel and glass building was a remarkable engineering feat: it was built over the Grand Central tracks without delaying or stopping a train during the construction. The building is quite distinguished, particularly the main lobby, which is noted for its wire sculpture by Richard Lippold. This sculpture soars to a height of 30 feet and is 60 feet long. It shimmers in the interior lights and almost appears to vibrate into musical sounds.

**CHICAGO CIVIC CENTER, Chicago, Illinois (Figure 8.5), 1964–1967, was designed by C. F. Murphy Associates; Skidmore, Owings and

Figure 8.5 Chicago Civic Center, Chicago, Illinois, 1964–1967; C. F. Murphy Associates, Architects; Jacques Bronson, Designer; Skidmore, Owings and Merrill with Loebl, Schlossman, Bennett and Dart, Consultants; Miesian style. Photograph by Hedrich-Blessing, Chicago.

Merrill with Loebl, Schlossman, Bennett and Dart were consultants. Jacques Bronson of C. F. Murphy Associates was the designer. This 26-storied rectangular tower covers approximately half of the area of its site, a city block in the center of the Loop. It is a Miesian steel and glass structure that is very sensitively proportioned. The exterior metal is an oxidizing, high-strength, low-alloy steel developed by the United States Steel Company. The material slowly oxidizes to a brownish rust color after erection and is guaranteed not to change or deteriorate further. The effect is as beautiful as the bronze veneering on the Seagram Building in New York City and, of course, was much cheaper. It is a wonderful technical advance over ordinary steel, which must be kept painted if exposed to the elements; or stainless steel, which is very expensive and difficult to apply, or other metal veneerings such as aluminum, which may corode.

One of the features of the Center is the 50 foot high, grotesque sculptural piece by Picasso, which stands in the small plaza in front of the building. Chicagoans have named it "The Thing." Built of the same oxidizing steel used on the building it is held together by steel rods that are part of the design.

CIVIC AND OTHER BUILDINGS

**ILLINOIS INSTITUTE OF TECHNOLOGY, Chicago, Illinois, 1946–1956, was designed by Mies van der Rohe. Soon after he had arrived at the school to become Professor of Architecture, it was decided that a new campus would be designed for that institution. That was in 1939. Three square blocks on South Wabash Avenue between 31st and 34th Streets were set aside as the site: a slum area that needed to be cleared. Before construction could be started, World War II was raging in Europe, and construction was postponed until 1946.

The plot plan is symmetrical, almost classic in its axial treatment. The buildings, all one and two stories high, are structures of black-painted steel infilled with glass or one-toned light-colored brick. The steelwork is sensitively organized, and all detail is meticulously worked out. The first impression most people receive is one of starkness to the extreme; however as one lives with it and studies it, it becomes more and more subtle and profound. It is truly a masterpiece. It is not that here one finds marble and ebony as in the Tugendat House in Czechoslovakia, which he designed, or in his German Pavilion at the 1929 Spanish Exposition in Barcelona—long since destroyed. Here are only iron and brick, but put together with such refinement and resulting Mondrian-like effect, that it is beautiful, even though plain to the extreme.

CROWN HALL, I. I. T., (Figure 8.6), 1952, the building for the Department of Architecture, was constructed with a load-bearing frame of trusses every sixth module, thus allowing complete open floor space within. The distinctive *Chapel*, 1952, is described under churches (see Religious Buildings p. 278).

ATTLEBOROUGH HIGH SCHOOL, Attleborough, Massachusetts, 1948, designed by Walter Gropius and TAC (The Architects Collaborative), is similar to Impington College, Cambridgeshire, England, which

Figure 8.6 Crown Hall, Illinois Institute of Technology, Chicago, Illinois 1952; Mies van der Rohe, Architect; Miesian style. Photograph by Balthazar Korab, Troy, Michigan.

Gropius designed in 1936. It was one of the first one-storied school complexes having classrooms, gymnasiums, locker rooms, lunchroom, library, and offices laid out in a semicampus plan along connecting corridors or covered passageways. Ebrele Smith, architect of Detroit, and Ernest Kump, in California, developed similar solutions for school designs without reference to Gropius, and from this time on this type of functional school building became the standard. Architects worked closely with educational consultants to develop efficient solutions for modern education (see Chapter 6).

HARVARD GRADUATE CENTER, Cambridge, Massachusetts, 1949–1950, by Walter Gropius and TAC, consists of a group of two-and three-storied buildings comprising seven dormitories and a commons building, all grouped around a series of courtyards. The Commons Building, of steel construction, is curved in plan and one story in height. The dormitories are of reinforced concrete. Light-colored brick was used to veneer most of the curtain walls.

Though not an outstanding design, it set a trend away from the older collegiate styles. Up until this time Harvard had been "colonial" and pseudoclassic; the University of Illinois was painfully Georgian; Yale, Princeton, University of Chicago, Duke University, and the University of Washington, Seattle, to name only a few, were Oxfordian Gothic. Harvard's Graduate Center was strictly Industrialized Midcentury Modern—or International, Miesian Style. It blended with the environment and was comfortable.

**GENERAL MOTORS TECHNICAL CENTER, Warren (suburb of Detroit), Michigan (Figure 8.7), 1948–1955, was designed by Eliel and Eero Saarinen in collaboration with Smith, Hinchman and Grylls, Detroit architects. This is the experimental research center for General Motors Corporation. It is a vast acreage of flat land with a complex of very carefully disposed buildings, all in the steel and glass mode of the Internationalists. The center of the composition, a shallow 5-acre, rectangular lagoon, not only adds reflective beauty to the composition, but is a reservoir for water in case of fire. A row of geyserlike fountains plays along a stretch near one end of one side of this lagoon. The long sides of the several buildings tend to be a bit monotonous in their repetitious compositions of black steel and greenish glass to reduce glare; however the monotony is relieved by the ends of the buildings, which are of

Figure 8.7 General Motors Technical Center, Warren, Michigan, 1948–1952; Eliel and Eero Saarinen, Designers; Smith, Hinchman and Grylls, Architects.

enameled brick in bright colors like those of the brick of ancient Babylon. One building has an end of fire-bright vermilion, another of sunflower yellow, while still another is of deep violet blue. The effect is magnificent.

Some of the interiors are startling, particularly the entrance to the Employees' Restaurant, with its Bertoia Screen; also the lobbies of the Executives' Building and the Design-Styling Building, with their suspended stairways. The entire complex down to the finest detail has the appearance of utmost efficiency, but in a formal sort of way.

In addition to the buildings described above, there are two elements that are not in the Miesian style. One is the shimmering stainless steel water tower, which looks like a giant mushroom on a trifoil elongated stem. This sits in the lagoon and is a magnificent accent piece. The other element is a thin-shelled dome, the Arena, where new models of General Motors' products are presented to VIPs and the press. Although this building is located apart from the main ensemble, it can be seen at the far end of the lagoon.

*FORD ADMINISTRATION BUILDING, Dearborn (suburb of Detroit), Michigan, 1954–1955, was designed by the Chicago office of Skidmore, Owings and Merrill. The site is a large parklike area facing Michigan Avenue, a principal east-west thoroughfare out of Detroit. The building has a long rectangular plan, stands 12 stories high, and is all of glass curtain wall construction. On top are a restaurant, lounge, and roof garden for executives and office workers. On the ground floor is a fine lobby containing a beautiful sculptural mural by Thomas F. McClure, Professor of Sculpture at the University of Michigan. The building is handsome in its proportions and refinements of detail. However it is an example of a glass-cage building that has its principal elevation facing south—on hot summer days even air conditioning and glareproof green glass can hardly compete with the heat of the sun. In the summer offices on this side of the building have to be vacated from midafternoon onward, especially during the golfing season.

DEERE AND COMPANY ADMINISTRATION CENTER, Moline, Illinois (Figure 8.8), 1955–1957, was designed by Eero Saarinen and Associates. The site is a pond-spotted valley overlooking the Rock River, which is about a mile distant. The Center is composed of two buildings on two levels. The upper one, housing the offices of Deere

Figure 8.8 Deere and Company Administrative Center, Moline, Illinois, 1955–1957; Eero Saarinen and Associates, Architects; Miesian style. Photograph by Balthazar Korab, Troy, Michigan.

and Company, makers of farm machinery, is the more important. The second one houses designing, engineering, and research. The main building, which looks out over its own little lake, is six stories high; the upper five stories have continuous balconylike sunshades all around. The exterior is of glass and exposed copper-alloyed steel that oxidizes to a deep brown color (see Chicago Civic Center). The buildings, beautifully proportioned and meticulously detailed, have been called Saarinen's masterpiece.

CONNECTICUT GENERAL LIFE INSURANCE COMPANY, Bloomfield (near Hartford), Connecticut, by Skidmore, Owings and Merrill, is a large three-storied office building with two appendages: one, in front, is the public reception building; and the one to the rear is the employee's restaurant. The main building is approached from the west, and the public reception building is attached to the southwest corner. The site is a semiwooded and parklike acreage that has natural ponds and small streams. A large parking area is on the south side of the building.

*AVON PRODUCTS, INC., Southeastern Branch Facilities, Atlanta, Georgia (Figure 8.9), 1968–1969, by Sol King, FAIA, architect, and Albert

Figure 8.9 Avon Products, Inc., Southeastern Branch Facilities, Atlanta, Georgia, 1968–1969; Sol King, FAIA, Architect, Albert Kahn, Inc., Associated; Miesian style. Photograph by Forster Studio, Detroit, Courtesy of Sol King, FAIA.

Kahn Associates. The owner wished to provide a pleasant environment for his employees and visitors, and though this set of buildings is primarily a warehouse and distributing center, by means of its setting it is a handsome ensemble. The buildings were planned to take advantage of the view offered by the site, which consists of natural trees and natural landscaping, augmented by a man-made lake with water jet and two pools flanking the lobby pavilion. Large windows allow full views of the surroundings. The ensemble received an Honor Award from the Michigan Society of Architects in 1970 and, the following year, a Citation for Excellence from the Atlanta Civic Design Commission.

*REYNOLDS METAL COMPANY GENERAL OFFICE BUILDING, Richmond, Virginia, 1956–1958, designed by Skidmore, Owings and Merrill, is located on a large wooded plot on the outskirts of Richmond. It has beautiful landscaping with trees, open air, sunlight, and water relating the building to the site; it creates a handsome environment. The building, like the Connecticut Life Insurance Offices, is three stories high, and is a large hollow square. The center court, which contains a fountain, is paved in rich red brick. On the ground floor a colonnade rests on a large, paved podium. The upper two stories, of glass curtain wall construction, contain the offices. All of the exterior metal is weatherproof aluminum, which adds shimmer to the design. It is a very refined composition, very classic in its symmetry and very beautiful in its setting. One feature of the glass upper stories is the automatic, sun-controlled, vertical louvers on the east, south, and west walls of the exterior and courtyard. These louvers rest on continuous balconylike overhangs at each floor and roof, and accent the horizontal aspect of the composition.

Frederick D. Nichols and William B. O'Neall, both eminent authorities, listed this structure as the "finest building of the century in Virginia."[2] Certainly it is the epitome of the Industrial Age, yet it is human and classically dignified.

RELIGIOUS BUILDINGS

---

*CHAPEL, Illinois Institute of Technology, Chicago, Illinois (Figure 8.10), 1952, by Mies van der Rohe, is the essence of simplicity. A rec-

[2] *Architecture in Virginia, 1776–1958: The Old Dominion's Twelve Best Buildings,* Virginia Museum of Fine Arts, 1958.

Figure 8.10 Chapel, Illinois Institute of Technology, Chicago, 1952; Mies van der Rohe, Architect; Miesian style. Photograph by Balthazar Korab, Troy, Michigan.

tangular steel-framed building with infilling of light tan brick, it is laid out on an 18 foot module and is approximately 30 feet wide across the front. This front has an 18 foot center bay of clear glass divided into three parts and having an additional one-third module width on each side. This five-part grid front is of black steel. The flat roof is framed with a grid of exposed steel beams that ties into the front and carries prefabricated concrete components that are corrugated undersides. Looking into the chapel from the outside, one sees a simple altar with a large metal cross, set against a plain drapery, hanging in back of it. In back of the drapery are a sacristy and chaplain's office.

KNESSES TIFERETH ISRAEL SYNAGOGUE, Port Chester, New York, 1954, by Philip Johnson, is a rectangular steel-framed building approximately 55 feet wide, 135 feet long, and 40 feet high. This is divided into seven bays and is very Miesian in its regularity. The steel frame is black with white infilling, and both are set off by an allover pattern of staggered vertical glass openings on the front and back sides. In front and entering the rectangle at midpoint is a vestibule, oval in plan, about 20 feet high, and capped by a low dome. In back of the main mass is a school wing with offices and kitchen facilities. The large worship room, multipurpose in arrangement, has an 8 foot movable screen. This divides the room so that the end serving as a worship area, which normally seats 250, can be enlarged by removal of the screen to seat 700 on high holy days. The oval vestibule and its suspended white plasticlike ceiling, which looks like stretched canvas, lighten what would otherwise be a dour expression.

This synagogue could perhaps be classified as Emotional in style because of the shape of the vestibule and the interior floating ceiling. These show that Johnson must have had a momentary flight of imagination out of the realm of Mies. Certainly it is a very interesting building, not beautiful in the usual sense, but of sensitive character.

**CHAPEL, Air Force Academy, Colorado Springs, Colorado (Figures 8.11 and 8.12), 1962–1963, by Skidmore, Owings and Merrill's Chicago office, was designed by Walter Netsch. It is A-shaped and fabricated of a system of light steel, aluminum-covered trusses connected at the top. Although this building is not in the boxlike idiom of Mies van der Rohe, it is the epitome of the Structuralist style; the entire steel structure is exposed. The design is not conservative; in fact it is quite emotional. A furor resulted in 1958 when the first sketches were prepared, and the drawings and model presented to a Congressional committee for an appropriation. Legislators and press alike criticized the design as too radical and inappropriate. It was four years before the controversy finally subsided and money was given for construction. Perhaps the exterior, with its 17 finlike metal-covered tetrahedral trusses, is too jagged, like too many sails on a boat, and perhaps the interior is somewhat unemotional in its need for more color or interest. However the condemnation

Figure 8.11 Exterior: Air Force Academy Chapel, Colorado Springs, Colorado, 1962–1963; Skidmore, Owings, and Merrill, Chicago Office, Architects. Photograph by Balthazar Korab, Troy, Michigan.

by a few members of Congress now seems only a tempest in a teapot. Certainly the finished building has an exciting form, rising as it does 150 feet to the top of the 17 spires. It is distinctive as the fulcrum of this newest of military academies in the United States. The other academy buildings are quite miesian in their construction and appearance.

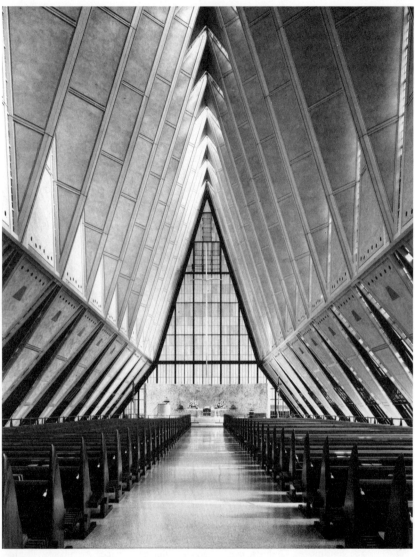

Figure 8.12 Interior: Air Force Academy Chapel, Colorado Springs, Colorado, 1962–1963; Skidmore, Owings and Merrill, Chicago Office, Architects. Photograph by Balthazar Korab, Troy, Michigan.

Although this outline has listed only three examples of churches done in the Structuralist style, no doubt there were more. However as religious worship in general is an emotional experience, most church building committees prefer emotional architecture.

BUCKMINSTER FULLER'S GEODESIC DOME

The geodesic dome, developed by R. Buckminster Fuller, is one of the principal contributions of the post-World War II era. It is built of hexagonal panels framed by equal lengths of steel or aluminum struts. Each strut is only a few feet long, with the length depending on the span of the dome. Three each of these struts are set so as to form equal angles, and brought together and pinned to form a joint; then the loose ends of these struts are joined in a threesome to other struts, and the process is repeated until the domical structural form is completed. The struts are light in weight and only strong enough to stand a small compressive weight. The hexagonal open space between struts may be divided into three equal diamond shapes or six triangles, and these spaces may be filled with transparent plastic or sheet metal, depending on whether the dome is to be skylighted or solid.

Mathematically it is impossible to calculate either the exact stresses of these struts, whether in tension or compression, or the stresses caused by live or dead loads, wind, rain, or snow. The struts must be of such size and weight that they can be fabricated and fitted together easily, yet strong enough to resist lateral bending when the weight of one or two men is placed on them. They are then strong enough to bear the natural loads such as wind, rain, or snow that may be placed on the panels. There is no mathematical way to determine the sizes or connections of these struts.

However by this simple method of forming hexagonal panels bordered by equal lengths of struts and fitting them together in domical form, or even in spheres, domes spanning 20 to 400 feet can be built, and Fuller says that 400 feet is by no means the limit.

AUDITORIUM, Hawaiian Village Hotel, Honolulu, Hawaii, 1957, was designed by Donald Richter and Donald La Rue, engineers, in consultation with R. Buckminster Fuller. This aluminum geodesic dome was prefabricated by Henry J. Kaiser in California in one of his several factories, then packaged and shipped to Kaiser's Hawaiian Village Hotel, where it was erected and ready for use in 34 days. It contains 575 panels of diamond-shaped sheet aluminum over an aluminum frame of geodesic design. The structure seats 1800 people and was opened with a gala performance by the Honolulu Symphony. It received worldwide publicity at the time.

*AMERICAN SOCIETY OF METALS HEADQUARTERS, Metal Park (23 miles south of Cleveland, Ohio, 1959–1960, was designed by John Terence Kelly, architect, with Buckminster Fuller as consultant. It is a large geodesic dome with plastic infilling and sun regulated louvers, it spans 390 feet. Inside is a separate structure of two levels of offices, public spaces, meeting rooms, and an auditorium. The top level features a Mineral Garden with over 350 specimens beautifully displayed. At the time it was built this was the largest geodesic dome in existence, and it still is.

**UNITED STATES PAVILION, Expo '67, Montreal, Canada, 1967, was designed by Buckminster Fuller with Sadoa, Inc.; Geometrics, Inc.; and Cambridge Seven Associates, Inc. This pavilion, a huge geodesic sphere that is 20 stories high and 250 feet in spherical diameter, looks like a huge bubble. The minirailroad of the exposition threaded through the sphere, and one of its stations was located inside. The whole outside is of transparent plastic, in the daytime the sun shimmers on its surface, and at night the dome glows from its interior lighting. On the interior are several stories connected by elevators that are built free of the exterior shell. It houses a 300 seat theater that showed continuous movies of life in the United States; also displays of fine arts, folk art, and technology. On the top floor of these displays, open to the dome, was an outer space exhibit and a simulated lunar landscape with full-scale lunar vehicles. This was reached by a continuous 125 foot long escalators, said to be the longest in the world.

Since the exposition in 1967, this great bubble, as well as many other important buildings with their displays, has been retained and reopened each summer.

CUSTOM RESIDENCES

Most of the houses described here were built during the 1950s. They were chosen because they seemed to be pacesetters at the time they were built. Since then a few having the same general idea have been constructed throughout the United States, but these residences were primarily luxury houses for a sophisticated clientele and did not greatly influence house design in general.

ROBINSON HOUSE, Williamston, Massachusetts, 1946, by Marcel Breuer, has an H plan, with entrance in the middle section, and two wings: one for living and entertaining, one for bedrooms. The structure is chiefly of wood with a variety of butterfly and flat roofs, but some of the walls are of New England fieldstone; mostly these are screen walls, though some are carried into the main structure.

KAUFMANN Residence, Palm Springs, California, 1947, was designed by Richard Neutra. This house in the desert has an open plan having four wings, and sidewalls are of glass. There is a beautiful relationship between the interior and exterior, which has a swimming pool and magnificent distant view.

*PHILIP JOHNSON HOUSE, New Canaan, Connecticut (Figure 8.13), 1949, was, of course, designed and furnished by him. The house has two parts: one having an entirely glass exterior, and one of brick. The main house of glass contains the master apartment with living area, dining space, and sleeping area surrounding a center core containing bath and service space. The brick portion has a studio and guest bedrooms. The site is wooded and fenced for complete privacy, and the two buildings form part of a composition that includes formal garden, sculpture, and swimming pool. The main house is most carefully furnished and arranged so that not a chair or ashtray can ever be out of place. It is very sophisticated.

*EAMES HOUSE, Santa Monica, California, 1949, was designed by Charles Eames, industrial designer, and his wife, Ray, as a study in house design using standard industrial components. It is a two-storied house with bedrooms that open onto a mezzanine overlooking a high living room. The main structure is steel framed and has sliding glass doors. It is a very clever composition. Bright colors have been used, and the house has an extreme, yet gay appearance.

Figure 8.13 Philip Johnson's Glass House, New Canaan, Connecticut, 1949;
Philip Johnson, Architect; Miesian style. Photograph by Yukio Futagawa.

**DR. EDITH FARNSWORTH HOUSE, Plano (about 40 miles northwest of Chicago), Illinois, 1950, was designed by Mies van der Rohe. This
is a white-painted steel cagelike house set on steel stilts above the surrounding wooded terrain, which often floods in springtime from a
nearby river. It was built as a country retreat. The outside curtain walls
are of plate glass, like the Philip Johnson house, and there is a central
core containing bathrooms and utility spaces. The living areas surrounding the core are partially screened by storage walls. The floor, a continuous plane of polished travertine, is reached by travertine steps leading from a raised travertine terrace.

W. R. HEALY HOUSE, Sarasota, Florida, 1950, was designed by Paul
Rudolph and Ralph S. Twitchell, his older partner, who had a great

deal to do with his early training. Ralph Twitchell did ultramodern, Miesian-type houses in and around Sarasota even before World War II; most were more livable and more human than this one, which seems to have been planned as a structural stunt. It is set off the ground on concrete posts and framed by steel columns that are steadied by steel cables in tension. A simple rectangle, it features a concave flexible roof that has a watertight plastic covering. It has the appearance of a portable house. It is very much tied down and was designed to withstand hurricanes even better than the average structure.

*NOYES HOUSE, New Canaan, Connecticut, 1954, was designed by Eliot Noyes, architect and industrial designer, for his own residence. It rivals the close-by Philip Johnson glass house and also stands in a wooded site. The house is planned around a central patio and has two parts—one informal, for his children; the other formal, for adult living and entertaining. The sidewalls are of rough fieldstone although most of the structure is of steel and glass. It is open in front and in back, as well as around the patio.

*PROFESSOR WILLIAM MUSCHENHEIM HOUSE, Ann Arbor, Michigan (Figure 8.14), 1955, was designed by the owner, a professor of architecture at the University of Michigan. It is a modular design in steel and wood frame with infillings of glass and plywood. The building is trilevel and lends itself beautifully to its hillside location, particularly the informal garden to the rear. This garden is overlooked by an all-glass wall of the living room and dining area. The exterior has a distinctly Mondrian quality. The interior is ultramodern yet warm and human, with books, plants, family pets, and in cool weather a sparkling fire on a brick hearth under an iron canopy.

There are a number of similar medium-sized, one-family residences in and around most of our Universities, particularly those universities that support architectural schools. These include the Gropius and Walter Bogner residences in Lincoln, Massachusetts; the Herbert Johe, Walter Sanders, and Robert Metcalf houses in the Ann Arbor, Michigan, area; the Professor Richard Williams House in Champaign, Illinois; and others south and west.

Figure 8.14 Professor William Muschenheim House, Ann Arbor, Michigan, 1955; William Muschenheim, Architect; Miesian style. Photograph by William Muschenheim.

PREFABRICATED

This was the age of the International Structural (Miesian) style for commercial buildings and for a few residences built for an ultrasophisticated sector of society. Very little of this styling was used in other residential buildings, most of which adopted the pseudohistorical styling of the past. Even apartments that were Miesian on the exterior had interiors that were, more often than not, decorated in some historical or eclectic style. However there were houses that were contemporary in style, with large windows looking toward a view. These were built on suburban lots with studied landscaping and blacktopped drives.

The vast majority of houses were built and designed by contractors or speculators who bought large plots and developed subdivisions. They used multiple building methods, developed very efficient uses of labor, and bought their materials wholesale. On the whole they produced very well built houses that had all of the latest conveniences and gadgets. Most of these houses were in the $30,000–$60,000 class.

Among the great advantages of this was that people seeking a new home could inspect completed houses and choose from among many types without going through the long drawn-out process of planning and building a custom-built house. A good architecturally planned, custom-built house usually takes two years or more to complete and costs more.

In style these tract houses were conservative and followed semihistorical lines. There were one-storied, ranch-type colonials, half-timbered English cottages, two-storied Georgian columnar houses of pseudo-Southern style, and others. Some had attached garages with dovecotes on top, although the pigeons were excluded by blocked and black-painted holes. Others had shutters without hinges nailed next to the windows and other eye-catching tricks.

These houses were often well planned and contained all of the amenities such as automatic heat, air conditioning, colorful bathrooms, and beautiful kitchens. The local furniture and department stores gave advice on interior decorating. The magazines *House and Garden* and *House Beautiful* showed stereotyped decorative schemes and the latest thing in mass-produced furniture. This was all indicative of relative affluence.

Much research and experimentation have gone into the development of prefabricated houses. Although their goal has been economy, factory overhead expenses including sales costs have usually eaten up the cost advantages of factory efficiency. Craft unions such as the American Federation of Labor (AFL) have fought the factory unions such as Congress of Industrial Organizations (CIO) and United Auto Workers (UAW) over factory-fabricated houses. Many times factory houses have been torn apart and reassembled to meet their labor rules. At the instigation of the unions, city building departments have often ruled against prefabricated houses requiring the use of only on-site craft methods of construction on property under their jurisdiction.

Nevertheless prefabricated houses, apartments, and all other types of buildings are being experimented with. The reason is, of course, that custom-type houses and apartments can no longer be built at prices that the common man can afford. Craft labor has priced itself out of the market of lower and middle class housing. Politicians perhaps inspired by the huge labor vote, say that government subsidy is the answer. The real answer seems to lie in the development of cheaper and more efficient ways of building through the use of factory automation. But this is not easily accomplished.

ALADDIN BUILT HOUSES, 1910–1920 (see Chapter 3).

BUBBLE HOUSES, Hobe Sound, Florida, were designed by Eliot Noyes, architect, although he used a method of construction that was patented by Walter Neff in 1940. They are, as the name implies, bubbles in shape. Each house is 30 feet in diameter and 14 feet high. The interior space is divided into either one bedroom or two bedroom arrangements. Over 1200 have been built in South America, Africa, and Pakistan.

The method of construction is simple in theory. A circular foundation is laid and a deflated balloonlike envelope stretched thereon. This envelope is then inflated to a rigid bubble form that acts as centering for steel mesh, which is laid over. A 2 inch layer of concrete mixture is then gunned over this steel fabric and allowed to set for 24 hours. After this the air is released from the balloon, and the envelope is removed and cleaned for reuse. Fiberglass insulation is then sprayed onto the concrete surface, and over this another 2 inch reinforced concrete shell is laid on. Front and back sides of the bubble shape are left open and filled with vertical steel mullions, glass sash, and doors. Interior arrangements are built inside.

Perhaps these "bubble houses" should not be classified as prefabricated houses; however the shells are not standard construction, and they are designed to be built in quantity in an assembly-line type of operation.

MOBILE HOMES, 1950 onward, were initially developed as factory-built trailer types of vacation houses in the late 1930s and began to come into general use during and immediately after World War II. Soon, however, they developed into "mobile homes," which could be transported by truck to semipermanent locations.

Many people are now living in such mobile homes, particularly young married couples, transient workers, and retired people. They range in price from $8000 to $30,000 although most are in the $8000–$15,000 bracket. Like automobiles, they are manufactured with exteriors of enameled sheet metal or anodized aluminum. Insulated against heat and cold, their interiors include all the amenities of a compact residence. They are heated and cooled in various ways. Some sleep two and some can sleep four or more. Some have built-ins such as sofas and dinettes. All have kitchens and one or more baths.

Mobile home parks laid out near most cities have spaces that can be rented. These provide metered utility hookups, and many also provide community houses with laundries, playgrounds, swimming pools, and in some instances community lounge rooms. Thus people can live in their individually owned home and move with a minimum of disruption if change of employment so dictates. Retired people can spend the winters in the southern states and the summers in the North, escaping high rent and high capital investment.

Maybe mobile homes should not be classified as architecture; however since they are competing in the housing and residential market, they must be so considered. They are encroaching on the architectural field although their design has been taken over by industrial designers who understand industry and factory production better than do architects.

MAGNOLIA HOMES, 1967, are manufactured by Magnolia Homes, Incorporated, Vicksburg, Mississippi, and a branch factory in Virginia. These house units are factory built by a company that first built trailer houses, then mobile homes, and now portable living units. These portable units can be placed on prepared sites in a matter of hours and have several possibilities of exterior treatment. Each living unit is 12 feet wide and 56 feet long. (The dimensions are limited by highway regulations.) Each unit has a living room, two bedrooms, a kitchenette, and bath. It has its own furnace and air conditioner, is factory carpeted and furnished, and can be set up either as a small individual house or assembled into small one-storied apartments of several units. It is flat roofed, and several may be stacked in two-storied apartments by use of a crane; also by fabricating steel frames they may be stacked higher.[3]

One hundred of these Magnolia Houses have been set up in Chicago, and similar projects are being given the green light in Detroit, Baltimore, Washington, D.C., and Atlanta, Georgia. The federal government's Department of Housing and Urban Development is watching closely. New ideas are developing rapidly. This is no doubt one of the answers to low-cost housing.

[3] Variants of this method of unit building have been successfully tried in houses as well as other types of buildings. Notable is the Hilton Hotel in San Antonio, Texas, which was built in record time to be ready for the opening of the San Antonio Exposition, "Hemisfair," in 1968. Concrete cubelike units complete with furnishings were factory built and transported to the site. Here they were lifted by crane and connected to the 12-storied frame. The hotel was started in October, 1967, and opened in April, 1968.

THE JET AGE

The Emotional ("Sensual") Style 1960–

CIVIC AND OTHER BUILDINGS

Although the Miesian style seemed appropriate for office buildings, factories, and other commercial structures, it never achieved any great popularity for civic, residential, or religious architecture. No doubt this was due to the great influence of Le Corbusier, leader of the Emotional-style group. Possibly it was a natural reaction to the starkness of the Miesian style—the war-ravaged world wanted something more human and exciting. Whatever the causes, the architectural world turned gradually to an aesthetic approach, almost forgetting function in the quest for exotic structural shapes: multiple cubes, domes, and sculptural forms of all kinds. Fortunately the world plunged into an era of great affluence and could afford the luxury of exotic shapes and extravagant structures. Notice should be taken of the Olympic Pool and Ice Rink in Tokyo by Tange; the new Opera House in Sydney, Australia, by the Danish architect, Jorn Utson; and the churches and other works by Candela in Mexico.

The phenomenon of change is not new in history; however when an architectural style does change, it is not due alone to one or two leaders such as Frank Lloyd Wright of the United States and Le Corbusier of France, but to the profound changes in the philosophy and way of life of the world. It is evident now, years later, that a new day dawned after World War II. About 1950 the world, particularly the United States, was thrown into an age of atomic power, into a jet age in which one is able to circle the world in a matter of hours and explore outer space. It was a computer age, also an age of welfare governments and new concepts of religion. Great advancements were made in science, and this was no less true in the technology of building.

Frank Lloyd Wright and Le Corbusier were among the first to espouse a new philosophy in architecture, and they became prophets of the style, expressed in Wright's Guggenheim Museum in New York City, originally designed in the early 1940s, and Le Corbusier's Unité d'Habitation, Marseilles, France, 1947. Joseph Hudnut, Dean of the School of Architecture of Harvard University, was one of the first to propagandize for a change in architectural philosophy. Though he was a great admirer of Walter Gropius, and it was he who had brought Gropius to Harvard in 1937, in the late 1940s he began to break with the somewhat austere Gropius philosophy. He was never able to define what he was asking for, except that he wanted "human quality, more aesthetics, more curves, more color."

It was soon recognized that in this fourth phase of the industrial age, the era of automation and nuclear science, rigorously adhering to the Miesian space frame was very limiting. Now there were thin-shelled domes and vaults of reinforced concrete or plastic; both materials could be formed into many varying shapes. Eduardo Torroja in Spain, Robert Maillart in Switzerland, and Pier Luigi Nervi in Italy had already shown the way. A whole new world of aesthetic forms was opened to the architect. Then too, tensioned steel could be used to suspend roofs and other parts of buildings, and steel and plastics could be formed into geodesic domes of almost unlimited spans, as demonstrated by R. Buckminster Fuller. Architecture could now assume exciting sculptural shapes—cubical, bulbous, rectilinear, or curvilinear.

Some of the so-called masterpieces of this era, like many buildings of the Renaissance, do not function very well. They are not "machines for living," but are emotionally exciting.

In this era architectural designers found that almost anything was possible in the attempt to create exciting forms. The Sensualists, particularly since 1960, were the fashionable group. Perhaps some of their designs were frivolous in their quest for attention, but man's quest for beauty has ever been one of his weaknesses.

In searching for a name for this style, or for the philosophy that prompted its conception, several suggestions come to mind. To the layman, it is *modern,* which means almost anything that cannot be classified as historical. *Contemporary* may also be used in the same sense.

Thomas Creighton, as stated earlier, wrote about this style and its philosophy under the title of "The New Sensualism." *Structural Exhibitionism*, another title that has been used, no doubt expresses a part of the philosophy that is inherent in a great deal of the work. *Sculptural Architecture* is another term that fits many cases, as do *Romantic* and *Emotional*. However the term that seems to describe both this architecture and the philosophy which conceived it is the one used in the heading above, the *Emotional ("Sensual") Style*. Certainly this architecture is structure that is bent to emotionalized form.

*BAKER HOUSE (Student Dormitory), Massachusetts Institute of Technology, Cambridge, Massachusetts, 1947–1949, by Alvar Aalto, would be monotonous if the plan did not undulate in the shape of a large Greek sigma. The building, which is three stories high, overlooks the Charles River, and every student room has a view; toilets and showers are at the rear. The story is told that one-way glass was specified for the toilet and shower rooms but that it was installed with the one-way view in the wrong direction. Subsequently this was corrected.

*UNIVERSITY ART CENTER, Fayettesville, Arkansas, 1949–1951, was designed by Edward Durell Stone in association with Haralson and Mott. The setting is a small city in the beautiful Ozark mountains. The main mass of the ensemble, a three-storied rectangular wing for offices and studios, is of glass curtain wall construction with horizontal projecting grilles for sunshades. In addition to this wing there is a 300 seat theater which is convertible to several arrangements and has as good or better stage equipment than many of New York theaters. The group also includes a 250 seat concert hall, an outdoor theater, a 10,000 book library, and a glass-enclosed exhibition hall. The ensemble is beautifully composed, and it is this composition that gives the main building its distinction.

*BAY ROC HOTEL, Montego Bay, Jamaica, 1952–1953, was designed by Edward Durell Stone in association with Stanley M. Torkelson and John Donald Tuttle. The hotel has a holiday spirit that dramatizes its tropical seashore setting. Its plan is divided into three areas: (1) a central services and administrative section with a tentlike circular dining area, a bar, and an open lobby lounge surrounding a circular, richly landscaped, open-air courtyard; (2) a two-level block of bedrooms to the west, facing the sea; (3) a row of guest cottages to the east of the main section, along the curve of the oceanfront. This vacation paradise is both sophisticated and informal, remindful of Carpo Crespi in Mexico. The antithesis of the Riviera, Miami Beach, Waikiki, and Acapulco, it is like what the South Sea isles are imagined to be and generally aren't. The hotel is a place to enjoy all the comforts: sunshine, breezes, and the sea. During the evenings a Latin American orchestra provides music for dancing on a palm terrace, but there is no casino or night club.

NORTH CAROLINA STATE FAIR Pavilion, Raleigh, North Carolina, 1953–1954, was designed by Matthew Nowicki in collaboration with Fred Severud and William H. Dietrick. This is a large oval building formed by two oblique-angled parabolic arches that curve upward and intersect. Viewed from the side, these arches form a huge flat X. A light covering skin is carried by steel cables suspended from these two opposing arches, and most of the roof is also carried by steel in suspension. It was a very economical building structurally and quite exciting in form.

This structural concept has since been used in other buildings, notably for an Exhibition Hall in Karlsruhe, Germany, and in the Conference Hall, Interbau Exhibition, Berlin, Germany, 1955–1957 (see p. 296).

LAMBERT-ST. LOUIS AIRPORT, St. Louis, Missouri, 1953–1955, was designed by Hellmuth, Yamasaki and Leinweber. This rectangular building has a ground floor devoted to plane services and freight, and an upper level for passengers. This upper level is formed by three identical groin-vaulted domes, 110 feet on each side. Because these vaults are framed by diagonal and edge-strengthening ribs, their infilling needed to be only 4 inches thick however these were greatly overdesigned. These framing ribs are placed on top and are not visible from the inside. The domical roofs are covered with copper over insulation. The exposed arches of the groined vaults are infilled with glass; triangular spaces left between the joining of the three domes are also filled with glass. This air terminal is very comfortable, and the great passenger concourse (upper level) is clear and very beautiful.

KRESGE AUDITORIUM, Massachusetts Institute of Technology, Cambridge Massachusetts, 1954–1955, by Eero Saarinen and Associates, is a three-cornered, thin-shelled dome that rests on three triangular points placed 155 feet apart. The resulting shape generally describes the fan-shaped auditorium within, although it is evident that it took a bit of doing to fit the interior into this tricornered domical shape. This auditorium is located in an open area on the campus and does not seem to relate to any of the close-by buildings. Even the nearest, the Kresge Chapel, is unrelated. In itself the building is a simple and interesting form, and quite exciting to photograph.

**CONFERENCE HALL, Interbau Exposition, West Berlin, Germany, 1955–1957, was designed by Hugh Stubbins and Associates, architects of Boston, Massachusetts, with Fred Severud, structural engineer. Werner Duettmann and Frans Mocken of Berlin were the supervising architects. The building was a gift from the United States to West Berlin as a symbol of one of the West's most cherished possessions, free speech. It is located in the Tier Garten of West Berlin at the edge of the River Spree, at the very edge of the famous Berlin Wall.

The principal unit, the auditorium, sits on the terraced roof of a huge, square, platformlike ground story which houses a large foyer. In this ground floor are a restaurant with lounge and bar, a small theater, and an exhibition hall. There are, of course, the usual service rooms in addition to a number of conference rooms. In front of the building is a large reflecting pool, and on the left the Spree River. People are generally led into the ground floor foyer from the front, then by an inside grand stairway to the large terrace above that the auditorium rests on. An imposing exterior stairway leads directly to the terrace and auditorium.

The main feature, of course, is the auditorium, which is circular and covered by a large swinglike concrete vault that is supported by two cross arches similar to those of the Stock Pavilion in Raleigh, North Carolina. These arches spring from two common supports and spread out as they mount upward over each side of the auditorium. A circular ring of concrete between the arches seems to outline the auditorium walls. However, though this ring has structural value, it is not exposed and does not count in the design. A thin-shelled concrete roof hung between the arches covers the ring.

The two mammoth arches dominate the scene. Under them the circular auditorium, which seats 1250 people, is quite hidden; nevertheless it is a very dramatic and beautiful building. The structure has been criticized as overdone and not purely functional, but it was the most outstanding building at the Interbau Exposition of 1957 and continues to be West Berlin's most beautiful edifice.

*MARY COOPER JEWETT ARTS CENTER, Wellesley College, Wellesley, Massachusetts, 1955–1957, was designed by Paul Rudolph, associated with Anderson, Beckwith and Haible. The landscape architects were Sasaki and Novak. This building completes a quadrangle of an older set of buildings designed in the Tudor Gothic manner, popularly known as Collegiate Gothic. The site of the center is on the downhill side of this quadrangle, which at this point has a drop of approximately 20 feet. The plan concept can be separated into three parts: (1) a square auditorium section also containing a library and classrooms; (2) an Exhibition Gallery, which forms a bridge over an axial walkway to the courtyard of the quadrangle on the upper level; and (3) a four-storied administration, classroom, and studio section, which may be called the main unit. The latter is a long rectangular wing that juts into the quadrangle and forms the fourth side of the courtyard.

The art center is designed on a 15 foot module, which was used on the older Gothic-styled buildings, and sets an intimate scale with them. The auditorium section as well as the rectangular main portion are topped with prismlike skylights to recall the pinnacles of the Gothic group. The main unit has two-storied, projecting vertical screen panels of enameled aluminum, "a kind of built-in ivy," which screen the windows of the upper two floors. The ensemble complements the older parts of the campus; it is quiet, yet it attracts attention. It is probably Rudolph's best work.

**UNITED STATES EMBASSY, New Delhi, India (Figures 9.1 and 9.2), 1955–1957, was designed by Edward Durell Stone. The plan is a simple rectangle with 8 gold-plated steel columns on the front and back, and 17 on the sides. It actually has classic proportions similar to those of the Parthenon in Athens, and though it has a wide, overhanging, flat roof and shows modern steel construction, the classic touch is unmistakable. On the interior two stories of offices surround a large rectangular garden pool. Outside curtainlike grilles of white tile and glass lie behind the peripheral golden columns. These grilles screen the offices immediately behind them.

This classic building sits on a podiumlike ground floor base given over to services and a garage for 22 cars. In front of this podium is a circular water garden in which an abundance of lotus bloom most of the year. This pool forms the center of a circular drive to the front steps. Between the two center front columns, which define the entrance, hangs a large seal of the United States.

Figure 9.1   United States Embassy, New Delhi, India, 1955–1957; Exterior; Edward D. Stone, Architect, New York City; Emotional structural style. Photograph courtesy of Edward D. Stone Associates.

*UNITED STATES PAVILION (now destroyed), Brussels World Fair, Belgium, 1958, was designed by Edward Durell Stone. It was a circular building 300 feet in diameter and covered the approximate area of the Colosseum in Rome. This building, though circular, used the same proportions as the embassy in New Delhi and is suggestive of it. The roof construction resembled that of a flattened bicycle wheel, with an outer compression ring connected to an inner ring by steel rods in tension. The flat outer ring, which projected about 10 feet, rested on two concentric rows of polished steel columns; between them was a honeycomb screen wall of aluminum sealed in a plastic skin. The roof was covered by translucent plastic over metal mesh. Like the embassy in New Delhi, a huge Seal of the United States was suspended between columns over the front entrance.

The clear interior space, about 30 feet high, featured a garden pool surrounded by existing willow trees. A mezzanine floor around the circumference contained a few exhibits, but generally it was a building in which to relax and rest. A style show with beautiful girls was a feature attraction several times during the day and evening; there was also a cinema in which visitors were given an interesting travel view of the United States: its cities, commerce, and factories; its farms, plains, rivers, lakes, and mountains; its universities and cultural centers. It was a total revelation, very well done, quiet, and not at all tiring.

Figure 9.2 United States Embassy, New Dehli, India, 1955–1957; Interior; Edward D. Stone, Architect, New York City; Emotional structural style. Photograph courtesy of Edward D. Stone Associates.

In front of the building was a large paved plaza having flags and a huge, circular, shallow pool with geyserlike fountains. This pool was so inviting that on hot days many weary and footsore visitors sat on the edge and dangled their feet in the water.

At this time a number of critics made derisive remarks about Stone and his screen walls; and screen curtain walls did become a cliché for a few years, not only with Stone but with Yamasaki and others. However this cliché was used so beautifully, particularly in these two buildings, that it leaves the criticism quite without substance.

**INGALLS HOCKEY RINK, Yale University, New Haven, Connecticut (Figure 9.3), 1957–1958, by Eero Saarinen, is a building that shows a willful attempt to warp structure to a desired form in order to create a strong emotional effect. Yet the form here in no way hinders the functional use of the building; in fact it enhances it. The building is planned around a standard hockey rink having spectator seats on each side. These seats rise upward and are present in greatest number along the center section. Entrances are at each end. To devise a form that would enclose this volume, Saarinen designed a great center spine of reinforced concrete that undulates upward in the center like a great caterpillar, with head and tail lifted upward to accent the entrances at each end. From this structural spine the roof swells outward to cover the seats at each side and accommodate the curving plan. The result is one of the most exciting sports buildings of the age. It is equaled only by Nervi's *Pallazetto dello Sport in Rome,* erected for the 1960 Olympics, and *Tange's Swimming Pool and Ice Rink in Tokyo,* erected for the 1964 Olympics.

*MCGREGOR MEMORIAL CONFERENCE CENTER, Wayne University, Detroit, Michigan, 1957–1958, by Minoru Yamasaki, was built as

Figure 9.3 Ingalls Hockey Rink, Yale University, New Haven, Connecticut, 1957–1958; Eero Saarinen, Architect; Emotional structural style. Photograph by Ezra Stoller (Esto).

a conference center with public lounge, auditorium, and a number of all-purpose rooms. It is a simple blocklike rectangle in form, relatively small and very delicately detailed. The ends of the building are of white marble veneer except the entrances at each end, which are featured by glass set in triangular shapes that reach up and over the length of the building. The sides are of glass and have delicate aluminum grilles that act as sunshades. The interior on the first floor has a two-storied lobby lounge in the center and is capped by the aforementioned skylight. At the sides are offices and service rooms. Surrounding the high lounge on the second floor are conference rooms that can also be used for dining purposes; however kitchen facilities are quite inadequate. In the basement is an auditorium seating approximately 300; this is reached by an inadequate stair and hallway.

Nevertheless the building is a gem of beauty, particularly the exterior. It is partly surrounded by the University Fine Arts Building, which forms two sides of a courtyard. A skillfully designed Japanese garden and lotus pool emphasize the crystalline beauty of the white marble and glass center. No one seems to care whether a conference luncheon is served box-lunch style; the lounge and the exterior and garden pool are ecstatically beautiful.

*RICHARD'S MEDICAL RESEARCH CENTER, University of Pennsylvania, Philadelphia, Pennsylvania, 1957–1960, was designed by Louis I. Kahn. The building, of reinforced concrete construction, is six stories high and consists of five square units set in tandem and joined by short middle corridors. A sixth unit, the entrance bay, with doorways on two corners is set in front, off center of the general alignment. Above these entrance doorways, and in the corners of the other units, are wraparound windows of pseudo-Mondrian design. The ensemble is of brick veneer and features high stair towers and tall intake air stacks that vie with one another for prominence.

*TRANS WORLD AIRLINES TERMINAL, Kennedy Airport, New York City, 1960, by Eero Saarinen and Associates, is a study of plastic form executed in reinforced concrete. It consists of a central dome with two half-domes, one on each side opening outward and both attached like wings. It has been compared to a huge bird in flight, an appropriate form for an airline. The interior is a beautiful clear space accented by glass sides and the vaulted ceiling overhead. Circulation is usually good, although access to the planes from the terminal building can be criticized. This is via long wormlike tubes—insisted on by the airline engineers, contrary to the advice of Saarinen. He is quoted as wanting and having designed moving lounges that would have shuttled back and forth between planes and terminal, and three years later he used such a system in the Dulles Airport for Washington, D.C. The building is interesting and beautiful; however it has become crowded between other and larger airline terminals. Instead of a bird in flight it now has more of the appearance of a sitting duck. It lacks scale in its environment, a shame because it should be set off by itself.

*FOOTHILL JUNIOR COLLEGE, Los Altos, California, 1960, was designed by Ernest Kump in association with Masten and Bird. Sasaki, Walker and Associates were the landscape architects. As the name implies, this school is located in the Los Altos hills, and occupies a 122 acre site. Designed for 3500 students, this is a complex of more than 20 low-roofed buildings of cedar shingle covering. The structures are of redwood supported by walls of rough aggregate concrete combined with native stone. Although the buildings show Spanish influence, they are not eclectic. They have a wonderful naturalness. Each building is a simple square or rectangle, each has wide and low-hanging eaves all around, and each has a roof rising to a square or rectangular mastabalike penthouse at the top. Each penthouse encloses the mechanical equipment for each unit, which is independent in structure and equipment from that of its neighbor. In the plot plan automobile and pedestrian traffic are completely separate, and no parking is allowed on the campus.

*SCIENCE PAVILION, Century 21 Exposition, Seattle, Washington, 1963, was designed by Minoru Yamasaki. This U-shaped pavilion fronted onto a patio that was an integral part of the design. The patio featured a geyserlike fountain under a huge complex of skeletonized Gothic-shaped arches. It was particularly beautiful at night, when floodlighted with lights of changing colors. In fact this fountain and arch display was so beautiful and breathtaking at all times, that many people neglected to enter the building to see the scientific exhibition. To them this was the display.

**DULLES INTERNATIONAL AIRPORT, Washington, D.C. (Figure 9.4), 1961–1963, was designed by Eero Saarinen and Associates, with

Figure 9.4 Dulles International Airport, Washington, D. C., 1961–1963; Eero Saarinen and Associates, Architects; Ellery Hustat and Burnham Kelley, Consultants; Emotional structural style. Photograph by Ezra Stoller (Esto).

Ellery Hustat and Burnham Kelley, consultants. This was the last major building that Eero Saarinen designed before his untimely death in 1962, at the crest of his career.

In outward appearance the building is a simple rectangle topped by a huge concave roof running lengthwise. This roof appears much like a large canvas tarpaulin supported by poles. Much higher on one side than on the other, it is supported by huge struts that lean outward to assume the exact line of compression, just as do the poles at the outside of a large tent. On close examination this building is not simple. The base handles services and incoming passengers, and the top story has the ticket offices and great concourse with the usual conveniences. Here all passengers depart. Gates line one complete side and parts of the side opposite. From these gates departing passengers enter portable lounges mounted on truck chassis, which on signal move out to designated planes. These lounges are entered on the concourse floor level, which is also the level of the great jet airliners. These moving lounges are one of the features of this airport.

Deplaning passengers arrive at the airport at ground level. A large parking lot is located adjacent to the building, and there are many services at this level; however departing plane passengers are led directly to escalators that go to the great concourse above.

Deplaning passengers are transported by moving lounges but arrive at an intermediate level on which there is baggage pickup. It represents a masterful job of planning and a masterful design all around.

*TORONTO CITY HALL, Toronto, Canada, 1960–1963, was designed by Viljo Revell in association with John B. Parkin, who were awarded the commission as a result of an international competition. It is recognized that this building is Canadian and not American; however it is so close to the United States, and so important, that it could not be left out.) This building stands in a plaza with a reflecting pool in front that serves as a skating rink in winter. Three parabolic, thin concrete arches lined with lights fly across this pool. The roof of a high first story lobby forms a great podiumlike terrace above. This podium can be mounted from the outside by a ramp that ascends from one side. It is a beautiful setting for ceremonials, which can be viewed from the front plaza. Set back on this podium is a domical saucerlike council chamber, which is partially surrounded by two segmental office towers of slightly varying height. These segments of circular towers having windows only on one side are very effective. Although they are, of course, stationary, they are so dynamic in form that one almost expects them to rotate at any time, bypassing or crushing one another. It is an excellent piece of design, well worked out functionally as well as aesthetically.

*TYRONE GUTHRIE THEATER, Minneapolis, Minnesota (Figure 9.5), 1962–1963, by Ralph Rapson and Associates, was built for the Minnesota Theater Company, a permanent repertory group. The design is based on the Elizabethan theater, with open stage in the center and seats on three sides. In this respect it is similar to the Shakespearian Theater at Stratford, Ontario, which was built in 1961. However behind the open stage is a shallow rear stage with fly loft that permits scenic backgrounds if desired. The seating is steeply pitched, and there is a small balcony so that no seat is farther than 55 feet from the stage platform. The balcony, placed asymmetrically in front at one side, joins a balconied orchestra space. All seats are upholstered in bright colors—ten different hues—with tickets to match. These produce a confettilike appearance, and even without people this theater does not appear empty. The audi-

Figure 9.5 Tyrone Guthrie Theater, Minneapolis, Minnesota, 1962–1963; Ralph Rapson and Associates; Emotional structural style. Photograph furnished by Ralph Rapson and Associates.

torium ceiling is cleverly designed with a galaxy of large square and rectangular panels suspended to give a floating effect. They conceal air ducts and lighting galleries so that the stage can be viewed from different angles. Truly this theater was designed from the inside out.

The *entre act* space is mostly on the balcony level and is a "floating concourse" between slightly sloping interior walls and an exterior screen wall of glass. The entrance lobby is under this. The walls are white, the carpeting is charcoal, the doors are bright red or orange, and white bubble fixtures are hung at different levels throughout these two spaces.

The exterior walls are fronted by freestanding screens of thin concrete which form a framework of rectangular openings of off-white color. Behind these screens are the actual exterior walls of glass and black steel framework, which thus make the thin concrete screens appear almost like cutout pieces of cardboard. At the top of the screens are flagpole holders, which were added with the idea that banners would fly on opening days, thus giving the whole a gala appearance; however these flags have never been supplied. Nevertheless it is all very gay and has an appearance of impermanence that is appropriate for a playhouse. Certainly here the play is the thing.

GATEWAY ARCH, JEFFERSON NATIONAL EXPANSION MEMO-RIAL, St. Louis, Missouri, 1959–1965, was designed by Eero Saarinen and Associates. The commission for the designing of this arch for the Mississippi riverfront park was awarded to Saarinen as a result of an international competition held in 1947. The park takes the place of an old riverfront section of the city in which wharves, factories, wholesale houses, stores, and saloons once stood. It is now an open meadow. The arch symbolizes the Gateway to the West. It has a clear span of 630 feet and rises in parabolic form to a height of 630 feet. Built entirely of stainless steel, it is hollow and has elevators and stairs inside to the apex, where lookout windows allow magnificent views both to the west and east. There is no doubt that this arch is astonishing for its size and its slick and shimmering beauty. The park site is supposed to tie into and form a setting for the Old Cathedral and the famous old Court House, but it doesn't. The arch stands alone without relation to anything near by. It is without a base and lacks scale. It needs something to give it human quality, maybe a large paved terrace with blocklike abutting walls. No one can believe on first viewing this arch, even from a short disance, that it is as large as it is.

*SALK INSTITUTE OF BIOLOGICAL RESEARCH, La Jolla, California, 1967–1968, was designed by Louis I. Kahn and is no doubt his masterpiece of the galaxy of fine buildings and groups that he has done. It is a fine composition of many parts made up in a series of cubical forms with strong voids and solids. The voids, of course, are the windows and balconies; the solids are geometrical panels of concrete. Bays jut in and out. The main composition is a rectangular court that has identical pavilionlike structures on each side. This court is entered by twin flghts of steps in formal arrangement to the court level, which is 8 feet above the street level. In the court are reflecting pools and rectangular planting boxes. It is all very axial and classic in plan, but here any reference to past history stops. The structures are very much of this era in design and technology; they have excellent scale and are emotionally satisfying.

RELIGIOUS BUILDINGS

Throughout history religious buildings have been highly emotional in design—from the temples of ancient Egypt to the Rococo heavenly dreams of eighteenth century Bavaria. All religions deal with human emotions either in the service or the physical environment, or both. Churches are places for worship and prayer; places of escape from worldly trials and tribulations. They must appeal to the senses in their form and color, and in their music, ritual, and sermons.

Appendages to the sanctuary must be planned to take care of the business of the church, to educate the young in religious history and living, and to provide clubhouse facilities for auxiliary groups of the parish. However it is the sanctuary that is most important. It is here that a person should feel that he is in an environment of the Infinite. Here should be a place to seek solace in communion with God.

*BAHAI TEMPLE, Wilmette, north of Chicago, Illinois, 1912–1953, was designed by Louis Bourgois, architect of Chicago. It is on Sheridan Road overlooking Lake Michigan, on a fairly large site that is profusely landscaped with flowers. Begun in 1912, this temple design was 40 years ahead of its time; however construction progressed slowly. World War I intervened, and for lack of money work was not resumed until late in the 1920s. The great financial depression in 1930 caused work to stop for over seven years, and this was soon followed by World War II. The structure was finally finished in 1953.

It is a reinforced concrete structure having a six pointed star plan. Concrete ribs rising from the points of the star sweep upward to the apex of a pointed central dome. Infilling between the ribs is of glass set in cast concrete of filagreed tracery design. The building generally has an oriental expression but cannot be connected with any one Oriental style. However it does express the Bahai philosophy, which has a great deal in common with Oriental philosophy, particularly that of India. It is an extraordinary building.

*CHRIST LUTHERAN CHURCH, Minneapolis, Minnesota, 1948–1951, by Saarinen, Saarinen and Associates, is quite similar to the earlier church in Columbus, Indiana (see Tabernacle Church (p. 241) Functional Style, between World Wars) although this one does not have a sunken garden. It has the same general components of a longitudinally rectangular church, a tall rectangular tower, soft-colored brick inside and out, and trim of Indiana limestone. The seats, pulpit, altar railing, and lecturn are all of natural birch.

To some the sanctuary of this church is more beautiful than that of the Columbus model, particularly because of its simple chancel end, which has a thin metal cross mounted on the wall over a tablelike altar and which receives light from a tall side window that is cleverly screened from view from the nave. The left side walls of the sanctuary undulate slightly as if to wave the eyes of the worshiper toward the cross and the altar.

*LORD OF LIGHT LUTHERAN STUDENT CHAPEL AND CENTER, Ann Arbor, Michigan (Figure 9.6), 1949–1951, by Ralph W. Hammett, is a three-purpose building: a chapel, student recreation center, and apartment for the resident pastor. It is under the general administra-

Figure 9.6 Lord of Light Lutheran Student Chapel and Center, Ann Arbor, Michigan, 1949–1951; sponsored by the American Lutheran Church and the Lutheran Church in America; Ralph W. Hammett, Architect; Emotional Structural style. Photograph by Ralph W. Hammett.

tion of the National Lutheran Council, a joint venture of the American Lutheran Church and the Lutheran Church in America. The building was paid for primarily by local friends and students. It is on a small lot in the center of the university community and is planned on three levels. The ground level, which includes lounge room, library alcove, recreation room, and kitchen, and its small yard are for the students. An intermediate level houses the chapel, which seats 150. The top level is an apartment with complete living facilities and three bedrooms for guests and student assistants. Most of the building is of cement block trimmed with stained redwood, but the front of the chapel and small tower is of native fieldstone.

On the stone front, which reflects the single pitched form of the chapel roof, there is a large rough-sawn oak cross that sets out about 6 inches from the wall. Neon tubing on the back of the cross is lighted at night. It is very effective. On the interior of the chapel the stone wall has a simple silver cross mounted on its surface. It serves as the background for a freestanding altar table. The chancel is also accented by a specially designed pipe organ with exposed pipes.

**WAYFARER'S CHAPEL, Palos Verdes, California (Figure 9.7), 1951, was designed by John Lloyd Wright, son of Frank Lloyd Wright. This chapel stands on an isolated, commanding promontory overlooking the Pacific Ocean. The building is a simple rectangle in plan, supported by four laminated wood trusses, as if to form a simple basilica. However the walls on all sides are of plate glass set in large geometrical frames of Y and circular shapes. These allow those attending services to see the magnificent works of nature around them and to drink in to the full the wonders of God.

*FIRST PRESBYTERIAN CHURCH, Cottage Grove, Oregon, 1951, by Pietro Belluschi, is one of several outstanding churches designed and built by him. Others are Zion Lutheran Church and Central Lutheran Church, Portland, Oregon; and Church of the Redeemer, Baltimore, Maryland. These churches echo the same influences seen in the Finnish work of Alvar Aalto. It is interesting that Belluschi is of Italian descent and was not very much aware of Aalto at the time these buildings were designed. However, Belluschi's home state, Oregon, is lumber country like Finland, and he became intrigued by the use of lumber as did Aalto. For this reason it is not odd that their results are so similar in character.

Figure 9.7 Wayfarer's Chapel, Palos Verdes, California, 1951; John Lloyd Wright, Architect, Emotional Structural Style. Photograph by Ronald Wiener.

**KRESGE CHAPEL, Massachusetts Institute of Technology, Cambridge, Massachusetts (Figures 9.8 and 9.9), 1954–1955, was designed by Eero Saarinen. This nonsectarian chapel dedicated to the Infinite God is a circular silolike structure in soft red brick, both inside and out. It is masterfully handled, particularly on the interior, in which a white marble block, simulating an altar, is elevated on a few steps and lighted from a circular skylight in the high ceiling above. Behind this altarlike block, which is without decoration or appointments of any kind, is a Harry Bertoia screen of freehanging cardlike metal chips. These twinkle as they slowly move about and catch the light from above. Another subtlety is the undulating interior wall treatment, as well as the cylindrical shaft resting on small arches of various sizes. A glow of light is admitted through these arches by way of a shallow and narrow moat that is both inside and outside the building. A pipe organ, toned to the small interior, is elevated over the entranceway opposite the altar.

The entrance is a corridorlike appendage fastened to the circular chapel like a handle and connected to several offices. The immediate site is nicely landscaped and partly hidden by a grove of trees, and though the chapel does not relate to any other part of the campus, it is a thing apart and creates its own environment. It is a beautiful example of Emotional-styled architecture, quietly and beautifully dedicated to all religions.

*CONCORDIA CHAPEL, Concordia College, Fort Wayne, Indiana, 1955–1956, designed by Eero Saarinen, is the chapel of a college for the training of Lutheran ministers (Missouri Synod). The entire group was designed by Saarinen and built at one time. The chapel is a simple rectangle in plan with a steeply pitched roof that rises from the ground and forms an A shape. There is a freestanding, spikelike spire to the left and toward the rear. The front and back walls, interior and exterior, are finished with special diamond-shaped brick of a soft red color, with mortar joints aligned and varied so as to form larger diamond shapes. These walls are beautiful studies of subtle patterns that reflect the A shape of the building. At the peak of the roof is a skylight running the length of the building. A choir loft with exposed organ pipes lies over the narthex to the rear of the sanctuary.

**CHAPEL OF THE HOLY CROSS, Sedona, Arizona (Figure 9.10), 1956, was designed by Robert S. Anshen and William S. Allen. This

Figure 9.8 Exterior: Kresge Chapel, Massachusetts Institute of Technology, Cambridge, Massachusetts, 1954–1955; Eero Saarinen, Architect; Emotional Structural style. Photograph by Joseph W. Molitor, Ossining, New York.

Figure 9.9 Interior: Kresge Chapel, Massachusetts Institute of Technology, Cambridge, Massachusetts, 1954–1955; Eero Saarinen, Architect; Emotional Structural Style. Photograph by Joseph W. Molitor, Ossining, New York.

Figure 9.10 Chapel of the Holy Cross, Sedona, Arizona, 1956; Robert S. Anshen and William S. Allen, Architects; Emotional structural style. Photograph by Julius Shulman, Los Angeles.

chapel stands at the crest of a rock formation, a small acropolis, and looks out over a magnificent view of desert and mountains. It is strangely isolated, and to ascend to the top of the rock visitors must park their cars and walk via a circuitous concrete ramp up and around half of the mound. The chapel is very simple in form but subtle in execution. It is rectangular in plan and built of concrete. The sides are solid and splay out slightly from the top to bottom. The chancel end of the chapel, which is higher than the entrance end, supports a huge concrete cross that rises out of the rock hillside far below the floor line. The effect is one of the cross holding up that end of the building. Although the sides of the building are solid, both ends are of glass. The glass of the chancel end is in a muted color to eliminate glare. The roof is pierced with glass insets that give a starlike effect on the inside. Artificial lighting is also used, as well as candles on the altar. Both the exterior and interior effects are very dramatic.

**ST. JOHN'S ABBEY CHURCH, Collegeville, Minnesota (Figures 9.11 and 9.12), 1960, was designed by Marcel Breuer and Associates. This dramatic concrete building is conspicuous for its great signlike carillon gateway, which stands in front of the entrance, and for a great decorative front wall of pierced concrete grillage. The interior of the main chapel is fan shaped and features a large chancel for liturgy and a monk's choir. Both chancel and the sound of the male voices are magnificent. A beautiful pipe organ and loft are at the back of the sanctuary over the narthex. The ground floor below contains two small chapels, very quiet in tone and very beautiful.

Since 1960 the Emotional Structural group developed forms that are even more emotional. No longer did form follow structure—structure was made to follow form, all for emotional effect. There seemed to be no

Figure 9.11 Exterior: St. John's Abbey Church, Collegeville, Minnesota, 1960; Marcel Breuer and Associates, Architects; Emotional structural style. Photograph by Bill Hedrich, Hedrich-Blessing, Chicago.

Figure 9.12 Interior: St. John's Abbey Church, Collegeville, Minnesota,1960; Marcel Breuer and Associates, Architects; Emotional structural style. Photograph by Shin Koyama.

limit in the attempt to design something different, to outdo Le Corbusier in exotic sculptural shapes. Not all designers were motivated by this philosophy, of course, but in the anxiety to be noticed, to be heard as well as seen, many architects used structure as a means of developing exotic shapes and letting their imaginations run wild.

*FIRST PRESBYTERIAN CHURCH, Stamford, Connecticut (Figures 9.13 and 9.14), 1960, designed by Wallace K. Harrison and Max Abramovitz, in association with Sherwood, Mills and Smith, is an especially interesting study in framing, as well as the use of stained glass. The general shape might be described as similar to that of steep-sided mansard roof sitting directly on the ground. The sloping walls are of reinforced concrete covered with slate shingles. In the nave section of the church the

Figure 9.13 Exterior: First Presbyterian Church, Stamford, Connecticut, 1960; Walace K. Harrison and Max Abramovitz, Architects; Emotional structural (sensual) style. Photograph by Joseph W. Molitor, Ossining, New York.

sides fold in and out, forming triangular patterns. These triangularlike bays are filled with stained glass set in geometrical concrete tracery. The stained glass, by Gabriel Loire, is in deep colors, predominately blue. From the inside this gives the impression that the center of the church, as well as the high end, is entirely of stained glass.

**SHAAREY ZEDEK SYNAGOGUE, Southfield (a suburb of Detroit), Michigan (Figure 9.15), 1960–1962, was designed by Albert Kahn, Inc., in association with Percival Goodman. Mr. Goodman is an outstanding authority on synagogue architecture and has designed more of these than any other architect. This synagogue stands prominently on a high lot overlooking Northwest Highway. The main worship room is squarish in plan set diagonally to the main axis of the ensemble. The main auditorium is arranged so that it can be set up in several different ways to accommodate different-size crowds. The ensemble, which includes classrooms, offices, and other necessary auxiliaries, is generally low in form but fits in well with the synagogue proper, which rises to a high prowlike triangular end. This end, which points out over the highway, is

Figure 9.14 Detail, Exterior glass in concrete tracery: First Presbyterian Church Stamford, Connecticut, 1960; Wallace K. Harrison and Max Abramovitz, Architects; Emotional structural ("sensual") style. Photograph by Joseph W. Molitor, Ossining, New York.

Figure 9.15 Shaarey Zedek Synagogue, Southfield (a suburb of Detroit), Michigan, 1960–1962; Albert Kahn, Inc., Architects, in association with Percival Goodman; Emotional structural style. Photograph by Balthazar Korab, Troy, Michigan.

spectacularly large and dramatic. This form is equally dramatic on the interior. It has a band of beautiful and meaningful stained glass panels which follow the rake of the roof and frame two great panels suggestive of the Laws of Moses. These in turn flank a stainless steel plaque representing the Tree of Life.

*NORTH SHORE CONGREGATION ISRAEL, Glencoe, Illinois, 1964–1965, by Minoru Yamasaki, is one of the most exotic religious buildings of its decade. It is simple in plan, a rectangular building with large lobby connecting a school and office section. The sanctuary seats almost 600, with additional spaces at each side for 160 more. The sanctuary can be opened into the lobby on high holy days to seat 400–500 more. This rectangular building is surrounded by a Gothic-like cloistered enclosure of poured concrete, which has an 8 foot screen wall between the arches. The main building, which dominates all of this, is a white concrete structure of vaultlike elements. These very delicately designed elements appear like the petals of a flower arranged to simulate Gothic-like vault construction. The tips of these petallike forms lean inward and touch at the crest. The open roof spaces between their stems are filled with tracery and glass skylights so that the roof appears to be open from the inside. The sidewalls—the spaces between the stems of these petallike vaults—are high, pointed arch forms filled with concrete traceried panels of glass. The end wall of the temple is approximately 75 feet wide and assumes the shape of a huge arch. On the interior this forms the background for the bimah and other ritual appointments. The Torah cabinet is framed by a high and sharply pointed niche with a tubular light, the Ner Tamid, hanging above it.

*CHAPEL, CONCORDIA LUTHERAN JUNIOR COLLEGE (Missouri Synod), Ann Arbor, Michigan, 1965–1967, was designed by Vincent Kling and Associates. This college provides the first two years of seminary and liberal arts study. The campus, consisting of classrooms, gymnasium, dormitories, and chapel, was all designed at one time for a student body of 1000–1200. It forms a beautiful ensemble on the northern bank of the Huron River, east of the city. The outstanding building is the chapel, which is triangular in shape. Entrances are at two of the corners with the chancel occupying the third angle, thus giving a fan-shaped auditorium with seating conveniently arranged for 800. A steeply pitched roof that seems to float above a band of stained glass windows rises to a small open belfry having a spire and cross at the top. At the meeting of the three sides of the roof are continuous strips of stained glass that seem to lace the roof together from bottom to top. Behind the chancel and freestanding altar there is an additional panel of stained glass. The outer walls of the building are only 7 feet 6 inches high plus the height of the strip of glass, which is 2 feet 6 inches. This chapel is a true place of prayer, yet it is also a place in which happy hallelujahs are in order. In addition to being used as a chapel, it is used for convocations, lectures, and concerts.

**TEMPLE BETH ZION, Buffalo, New York, 1966–1968, was designed by Max Abramovitz, architect. The temple itself is a white marble building of circular form, made up of 10 large scalloplike panels. These panels flare outward "like a man's arms raised in prayer." Off of the temple is an elongated, two-storied educational and fellowship wing containing 20 classrooms, administrative offices, a library, and a chapel for small religious services, weddings, and funerals. There is also a fellowship room that seats 1000 people, with attached kitchen, fully equipped stage, and projection room.

The interior of the temple, which has a seating capacity of 1000, is extremely beautiful and meaningful. There is a feeling of openness, and the encircling sidewalls which lean outward give an added feeling of exhaltation, particularly when the great pipe organ is played.

Over the main entrance on the west is a magnificent stained glass window by Ben Shahn, depicting the 150th psalm, and to the east behind the altar is a similar window with a massive upturned hand symbolizing creation. The altar is dominated by 30 foot high commandment Tablets of the Law, also designed and executed by Ben Shahn. The 10 symbols representing the commandments are of glass mosaic, and the tablets are garnished with gold leaf. These tablets on each side of the altar frame the Holy Ark, with the Eternal Light above.

*ST. PAUL'S BY THE SEA, Jacksonville Florida, 1967, is the work of Ellis, Ingram and Associates. It is a double-ended boatlike form made by two sweeping concentric curves. Each end has a narthex, and inside a freestanding altar is placed on axis, nearer one end than to the other. The two curved walls are of poured concrete and slightly inclined. The forms for the concrete have been left rough with the patterned form marks showing. One wall sweeps up to a high pointed end, where a thin metal cross provides a nice accent to the building. No light is admitted to the church except by the multiple glass doors at the two ends. The interior is artificially lighted by a galaxy of inserted ceiling lights and, of course, by the altar candles. This building occupies a site quite by itself and does not conflict with its neighborhood.

*UNIVERSITY LUTHERAN CHURCH AND STUDENT CENTER, Lawrence, Kansas, 1968, was designed by Ramey and Jones, architects. This is a square, entirely poured concrete building that occupies the top of a rough wooded knoll. A square church in the center of the plan, has a long altar table and large free space dominating the sanctuary. Recreation rooms, library, offices, and other necessary adjuncts surround the church and complete the square form. Although the building is in no way a plagiarism of Le Corbusier's monastery La Tourette, near Lyon in

France, it is similar in spirit. It has a monastic look, is of rough concrete, and blends in with its rustic hilltop setting. The dominating feature of the exterior composition is a circular-topped bell tower, which marks the on-axis main entrance.

ZUMBRO LUTHERAN CHURCH, Rochester, Minnesota, 1968–1969, by Thorson and Thorson, architects, is a bold composition set on a sloping lot. It is two stories plus basement in height and has an entrance at each of the two top floors from the sloping side street. On the main floor, off the upper corner of the lot, is the sanctuary. This is a large, square room set diagonally so that the main entrance is from a corner opposite the chancel. This chancel has a huge, freestanding table with bold pulpit and lectern in cardinal red, black, and white. On the walls over the chancel are biblical quotations in red on a buff background. The ceiling reflects the roof lines of the sanctuary, which is pyramidal in form. In front of the sanctuary is the narthex, which has ample coat hanging space, and around it are corridors opening into classrooms, offices, a library, and a parlor. Over the narthex at the back of the sanctuary is a balcony containing choir loft and pipe organ.

On the basement level two floors down, though not completely underground because of the slope of the lot, are classrooms and, under the sanctuary in the center, a large, high-ceilinged all-purpose room with attached kitchen and other facilities. The intermediate floor has other classrooms and services. An elevator connects these two lower floors. This is a very bold composition, very compact and very well planned. It is a sweeping, uninhibited expression.

**WASHINGTON TEMPLE (MORMON), Washington, D.C. (Figure 9.16), 1970–1974, was designed by Markham, Beecher, Fetzer and Wilcox, Inc., a firm made up of four individual practicing architects who were brought together to design and carry out this building. The site is located in Kensington, Maryland, outside the confines of the District of Columbia, but in the metropolitan Washington area, and the building is a landmark of the nation's capital. The site covers 57 acres, quite heavily wooded and rising to a mound in the center, on which the temple is placed. The building is an elongated hexagon, almost diamond shaped, and has square towers protruding from each of the six corners. Each tower is topped by a vertically set rectilinear mass, which in turn is topped by a tall, very thin spire. Four of these towers are of the same

Figure 9.16 Washington Mormon Temple, Washington, D.C., 1970–1974; Markham, Beecher, Fetzer and Wilcox, Inc., Architects; Emotional structural style, but based on the original temple in Salt Lake City. Photograph courtesy of the architects.

height, but two toward the front are higher. One, highest of all, is capped by a statute of the angel Maroni blowing his trumpet. The whole composition is of white Alabama marble, and the walls between the towers are marked by strong repetitious verticals from ground to top of parapet. There is glass between some of these verticals, but other than that windows are not part of the composition.

The building is six stories high and has a spacious lobby on the ground level, also a baptistry, kitchen, and cafeteria. The middle four floors contain offices, conference rooms, and special suites. Most of the top floor is taken up by the large Solemn Assembly Hall. This room, which is actually the sanctuary, is reached by fast elevators from the ground floor lobby. Nonmembers of the Mormon Church are not allowed on the upper floors. Total space in the building is 160,000 square feet, and the total cost was $15 million.

Two features in the lobby are the large crystal chandelier and a huge mural. The chandelier is made up of 10,000 pieces of cut glass from Czechoslovakia that have been embedded in a 10 by 6 foot oval frame made by the Metals Manufacturing Company of Salt Lake City. The mural painting, 40 feet long and 12 feet high, takes up one entire wall of the lobby. This painting, which depicts the Second Coming of Christ, is by John Scott.

BUILDINGS BY ALDEN B. DOW

Alden B. Dow of Midland, Michigan, has enjoyed a fine practice over the years, and although he is a member of the board of directors of the Dow Chemical Company, his architectural profession is his first love. His work is emotional and romantic, but always practical in its function and within the budget. His office is attached to and part of his residence; however the two look out in different directions and there is no conflict. Dow is always open to fresh ideas, and it is an inspiration to work for and with him; however, when the project is finished, it is a Dow design. His practice has embraced residences, churches, colleges, commercial buildings, and even factories.

**ST. JOHN'S EPISCOPAL CHURCH, Midland, Michigan (Figure 9.17), 1951–1952, is one of Dow's more conservative designs. It has an L-shaped plan on two sides of a cloisterlike court. A social hall is located on the right side as one enters this cloister, and the sanctuary is at the end as one walks along the left cloister walk. The nave looks out onto this court through large windows. The plan is typically Anglican, with choir and pipe organ in front of the altar area, and lectern and pulpit in front of the choir. Here a communion rail separates the chancel from the nave. The nave seats 500. One of the features of this church is the narthex, which has a large stairwell and staircase at the front. This opens the main floor to the Sunday school portion below. At this point the lot falls away so that the downhill side of the Sunday school is on a lower level. This narthex and stairway are featured by a prow-shaped end of the building that has glass extending from the lower level to the

Figure 9.17 St. John's Episcopal Church, Midland, Michigan, 1951–1952; Alden B. Dow, Architect; Emotional structural style. Photograph given by Alden B. Dow.

ceiling of the narthex. Both exterior and interior are done in soft red colored brick. The roofs and ceilings are peaked, and the exterior features a tall detached chimney to the rear that also serves as a tower.

*DEARBORN PRESBYTERIAN CHURCH, Dearborn, Michigan (Figures 9.18 and 9.19), 1964, is an extremely interesting composition. A long horizontal mass accents the entrance walkway along the front of the Sunday school section and continues past a sharp vertical marking the altar section within. Much of the plan is worked out on a triangular module, and the detail, particularly on the interior, is alive with the idea of trinity. In front a high altar window is featured.

*MRS. JOSEPHINE ASHMUN HOUSE, Midland, Michigan (Figure 9.20), 1951, is an interesting diagonal composition arising from its A-frame shape. It is set on a concerte base at ground level, and the brick exterior is carried inside with a brick floor of rich brown color. A rectangular appendage, the entrance vestibule, is of common brick and wraps around one corner; it has a flat roof and forms a strong contrast to the A-frame. The house is set in a small clearing of dense woods, and

Figure 9.18 Exterior: Dearborn Presbyterian Church, Dearborn, Mighigan, 1964; Alden B. Dow, Architect; Emotional structural style. Photograph by Hedrich-Blessing.

the wood frame and wood siding are stained brown so as to blend with the surroundings.

*JOHN RIECKER RESIDENCE, Midland, Michigan (Figures 9.21 and 9.22), 1956, is a horizontal composition of brick walls and flat multiple-beam roof frame. It has the appearance of a craft-built house, particularly the large living room, which is library, game room, and family room all combined into one. This room has exposed framing that forms an intricate ceiling pattern.

MIDLAND CENTER FOR THE ARTS, Midland, Michigan (Figure 9.23), 1971, is a rectangular building embracing an exhibition hall, theater, dressing rooms, and studios. Perhaps it is not an outstanding architectural design: however, it is typical of a type of building that became very popular at this time.

Figure 9.19 Interior: Dearborn Presbyterian Church, Dearborn, Michigan, 1964; Alden B. Dow, Architect; Emotional structural style. Photograph by Hedrich-Blessing.

**ALDEN B. DOW RESIDENCE AND ARCHITECTURAL OFFICE, Midland, Michigan (Figure 9.24), 1935–1941, was designed by the owner. Figure shows the exterior view of the office conference room, whose floor is below the water level. Connected to the office proper and the office entrance by wide steps, it is an enticing feature both from the inside and out.

Figure 9.20 A-Frame House of Mrs. Josephine Ashmun, Midland, Michigan, 1951, Alden B. Dow, Architect; Emotional structural style. Photograph by Bill Hedrich, Hedrich-Blessing.

Figure 9.21 Exterior: John Riecker Residence, Midland, Michigan, 1956; Alden B. Dow, Architect; Emotional structural style. Photograph by Bill Hedrich. Hedrich-Blessing.

Figure 9.22 Interior: John Riecker Residence, Midland, Michigan, 1956; Alden B. Dow, Architect; Emotional structural style. Photograph by Bill Hedrich. Hedrich-Blessing.

Figure 9.23 Midland Center for the Arts, Midland, Michigan, 1971; Alden B. Dow, Architect; Emotional structural style. Photograph by Harr, Hedrich-Blessing.

Figure 9.24 Alden B. Dow Residence and Architectural Office, Midland, Michigan, 1935–1941; Alden B. Dow, Architect; Emotional structural style. Photograph by Bill Blessing, Hedrich-Blessing.

10

THE JET AGE AND BEYOND
The Brutal Style
1960–

The Brutal style was a phase of the Emotional structural style, the second phase of the philosophy of the Sensual style. This very pronounced and very emphatic phase became increasingly popular toward the end of the 1960s and will probably become the leading style of the next decade or two. It has tended toward sensationalism in the 1970s, using anything to get attention. During this period it was not the conservative that got attention, but the bizarre and shocking. The leading designers and architects have sought attention in the architectural press by sensational designs. Whereas the earlier sensualist designs of the 1950s were feminine and flowerlike, almost Art Nouveau in inspiration, this latest turn has been the antithesis. The Brutal style, if separate style it is, uses strong unadorned, forms almost like the bones of a mammoth skeleton. The planning and main concepts are usually axial, almost classic, and like the classic they depend on repetitive detail: columns, blocklike triglyphs, and dentils. But whereas classic forms and detail are delicate and refined, in the Brutal Style they are large and forceful. The style is strong, muscular, and masculine.

Le Corbusier's last works can be recognized as belonging to this style, particularly his last important design, the *Dominican Monastery, La Tourette, near Lyons, France, 1956–1959.*

Maybe the advent of this new expression marked the end of the post-World War II era and the beginning of a new phase. Certainly there has been a change in the philosophy of life in government, law, and order, and even religion. There has been a radical change in dress for both men and women, a radical change in hair styling, and more: a new permissiveness in morals, law enforcement, and discipline.

Certainly architecture has been affected by these changes. In the residential field relatively few individual homes were built. This was caused not only by initial high costs but also rising upkeep costs, high interest rates and high taxes. Many wage earners and retired people turned to mobile homes, which were cheaper and quite comfortable, as well as mobile. Apartment living became popular, even in small towns, and condominium apartment complexes were purchased for their cost and upkeep advantages. As ever, architecture is reflecting the profound psychological changes in society, particularly among our young people.

The term *brutal* as applied to art and architecture is not meant to be derogatory but simply descriptive. It is used to denote a style that is strong, blocky, and masculine. The best works of art are thrilling, exciting, very masculine, often brutal in appearance, but smooth and rhythmic. So are the better architectural works: blocky and strong, not given to curving forms or frivolous ornaments.

Large plain surfaces are the rule, often combined with overhanging upper portions, in fact, overhanging blocky forms are one of the characteristics of the style. The material used for exteriors may be brick but most often is concrete that has been troweled smooth. It is a very functional style. If the plan dictates that a special room is best served by a particular location and thereby must protrude from the other elements, then it does protrude and it is the designer's responsibility to see that it is an aesthetic element. Large plain surfaces sometimes must be relieved by rhythmic accents such as vertical matchlike struts on each side of vertical windows. These are of the same material as the walls to which they are attached, concrete or brick. Thus the style can be said to be thoroughly forthright and clean, even though strong and brutal. It can be beautiful.

The question can be asked: "Is this the latest phase of the Emotional ("Sensual") style, or is it an entirely new phase?" Certainly this brutal style of the present decade has individual merit, but whether it is simply a faddish tangent remains to be seen. At least it is strong, with its plain surfaces and deep shadows. It is not trivial.

Before the general discussion of the Brutal Style is closed, one design motive should be mentioned and described. This is the use of encircling colonnades that contain a new form of column. Maybe this motive is separate and distinct from the Brutal style although contemporary with it, and maybe it was adopted for its formality and pseudoelegance. The columnar effect is reminiscent of classic, though the detail and column structure are new and different. These columns, usually of white reinforced concrete, are not cylindrical but often have the shape of a Greek cross. They taper to almost a point at the bottom where they are pinned to the foundation. From there they swell to about one-third their height and then gradually narrow—like the entasis of classic columns—for the remaining two-thirds of their height. At the top attachment is usually made to a flat slab roof without overhang. A safe ratio of length over radius (l/r) is maintained by an overatio at the one-third point, so that these columns are buckleproof and elegant. There were several variations of this columnar design cliché, which was semipopular during the period. An outstanding example is its use in Avery Fisher Hall in Lincoln Center, New York City.

PUBLIC BUILDINGS

---

*CARPENTER CENTER FOR THE VISUAL ARTS, Harvard University, Cambridge, Massachusetts, 1961–1963, was designed by Le Corbusier; Sert, Jackson and Gourley were the supervising architects. The building is tucked in between Fogg Museum of Fine Arts and the Harvard Faculty Club, two buildings of classic eclectic style on a back street off Harvard Yard. The central core of the plan is nearly square, approximately 80 by 90 feet, and has two bulbous protuberances swelling out from opposite corners. One of these projecting shapes, at the second floor level, houses a studio workshop. Its roof becomes a terrace on the third floor level. The other is a studio workshop on the opposite third floor level. There is a clever interplay of spaces and shapes. The whole building is supported on stiltlike columns which are round throughout the structure and are spaced on a 15 by 25 foot module. Construction is of reinforced concrete whose outer surfaces are smooth and white. Extraneous ramps from both sides bisect the building at the third floor and entry may be made there; however the building is entered more directly on the ground level. The building may lack unity in composition, which seems to have been intended, but is clever and bold in its integration of forms.

**UNIVERSITY REFORMED CHURCH, Ann Arbor, Michigan (Figure 10.1), 1961–1962, by Birkerts and Straub, Architects, was designed by Gunnar Birkerts. It is a tall, narrow, rectangular building of poured con-

Figure 10.1 University Reformed Church, Ann Arbor, Michigan, 1961–1962; Birkerts and Straub, Architects; Brutal style. Photograph by Balthazar Korab, Troy, Michigan.

crete. As seen from the campus, this church presents a tall blank wall divided into two vertical rectangles. The site on which it is placed, at the end of a university street, is placed on axis with that street. The lot is 66 feet wide and about 350 feet long and runs between two thoroughfares. It slopes from front to back, with the campus at the upper level. The building plan is a long rectangle having entrance at midpoint. Here a two-storied educational wing is planned tandem with the sanctuary wing. The church seats 500 and has a social hall beneath. It is compact and very well organized.

The structure, as stated, is poured concrete with controlled aggregate. Narrow and deep bents run across the sanctuary on the interior and rise in three steps from each side wall. Concrete fins are placed at regimented close intervals between the bent beams at the side walls, and colored glass skylights are placed there. These very effectively light the sanctuary; otherwise there are no windows. The design is very severe but most effective, and there is no doubt that it is a church.

Figure 10.2 Boston City Hall, Boston, Massachusetts, 1962–1969; Kallmann, McKinnell and Knowles, Architects; Brutal style. Photograph by Balthazar Korab.

**BOSTON CITY HALL, Boston, Massachusetts (Figure 10.2), 1962–1969, was the result of a national competition won by Gerhard M. Kallmann, Noel M. McKinnell and Edward F. Knowles, architects. Later they associated with Campbell, Aldrich and Nulty, architects.

City Hall square is essentially a trapezoid on the scale of St. Mark's Plaza in Venice, though lacking the openness and interest of the latter. It extends roughly from the Old State House to Fanuel Hall and the Old Quincy Market, having absorbed old Scully Square, which is no more. The site was decided on before the competition and was laid out by I. M. Pei Associates for the Boston Redevelopment Authority. The plot has a two-storied difference in levels between upper and lower areas. The space requirements and the circulatory patterns were prepared by Becker and Becker, space engineers, and made part of the competition program. The finished building and exterior spaces adhered to these requirements very well.

The building is eight stories high at most points and has entrances on the first and third floors to conform to the varying street levels. Major public services are on the second and third floors. The interior circulation is excellent. The structure is essentially poured-in-place concrete and except for paving brick in the plazas surrounding the building and red quarry tile floors in the lobbies and corridors, all else is concrete with a monolithic character. This is not a building of marble veneers and crystal chandeliers. Nevertheless it is not overpowering. The building is broken up by beamed ceiling patterns, human-scaled windows, doors, and stairways.

The exterior is in the Brutal style of 1970. The upper three stories are stepped out, and a heavy dentillike pattern accents the encircling rows of windows. Elements such as the council chamber and the reference library are expressed on the exterior; in fact the architects have attempted to express almost every important plan element, perhaps too much so. The exterior shows strong influence of Le Corbusier's later works, particularly La Tourette in France. It is not a quiet building but certainly is an exciting one.

ART AND ARCHITECTURE BUILDING, Yale University, New Haven Connecticut, 1963, was designed by Paul Rudolph. The exterior, a masterful composition of seven stories in rough textured concrete, is a combination of strong verticals interlaced with horizontals and many balconylike projections at different levels. It is a building much talked about for its exterior composition. The interior, however, is disappointing. The chief element here was a multistoried interior court having balconied work spaces at each level, from which students used to drop things onto other students' desks below. These victims built plywood protections over their desks, so that the effect was a miniature shantytown with bad light and circulation. In 1968 this debris caught fire, and the result was disastrous. The interior has been remodeled, but the faults could not be completely rectified.

*SHAPERO HALL OF PHARMACY, Wayne State University, Detroit, Michigan, 1965, Paulsen and Gardner, architects, is an unusual four-storied building that is half again as large on the top floor as it is at the bottom. It is built of cast concrete with interesting but conservative detail. A two-storied base supporting the building is masked by a square-columned colonnade that runs through two floors. The first floor contains a lobby and a lecture hall, as well as access to the floors above. The second floor, which juts out to the face of the supporting columns, contains classrooms and offices. The third floor overhangs abruptly, as does the fourth floor in turn, thus causing the building to look like an inverted stepped pyramid. An early example of the Brutal style, it appears quite radical next to its low, ground-hugging neighbors.

*CHAMBER OF COMMERCE OFFICE, Traverse City, Michigan (Figure 10.3), 1965, was designed by Paul A. Hazelton, architect of Traverse City. It was desired to locate the building adjacent to the parkway paralleling the shore of Grand Traverse Bay, and close to the business district only one block away, as well as to take advantage of the municipal parking lot adjacent to the site. This made it necessary to design a pedestallike building having a cantilevered main floor, as the actual site was very small—for all practical purposes only large enough for a hot-dog stand, which was prohibited by zoning. However all worked out to the advantage of the Chamber of Commerce. In their building raised from the ground and having glass all around, they have a commanding view of the waterfront, the City Zoo, the City Marina, and the business district—all conducive to Chamber of Commerce activities. Zoned heating and cooling have made the building very comfortable both summer and winter.

*LIBRARY OF TOUGALOO COLLEGE, Tougaloo, Mississippi (Figure 10.4), 1965, by Gunnar Birkerts and Associates, is an addition to a centry-old Negro college near Jackson, Mississippi. The school now has only a few hundred students but plans to expand to 1250 in the immediate future. Birkerts was asked to plan a new campus, starting with a library and classroom building, and to incorporate a couple of old buildings that will eventually be destroyed. The site of the college is a hillside that can be divided into three areas: the top, where the present campus is located, and two heavily wooded lower levels. The shifting clay subsoil demanded special structural considerations, and utmost economy was a primary demand. These considerations brought about the decision to adopt a standard module and system of construction that would be adaptable to many conditions. A 30 foot module was worked out. Caissons of poured concrete of bell-bottom design support reinforced con-

Figure 10.3 Chamber of Commerce Office, Traverse City, Michigan, 1965; Paul A. Hazelton, Architect; Brutal style. Photograph by architect.

crete columns up to a decided level; above this are precast concrete columns that tie into concrete beams and floors. It is interesting how this 30 foot module for column spacing can be adapted to flexible planning for classrooms, lecture halls, and dormitory suites.

**WICHITA PUBLIC LIBRARY, Wichita, Kansas (Figure 10.5), 1966–1967, by Schaefer, Schirmer and Associates, is an excellent example of the Brutal style and is also very beautiful. It is a three-storied horizontal composition having large plain surfaces of smooth concrete and plate

Figure 10.4 Library of Tougaloo College, Tougaloo, Mississippi, 1965; Gunnar Birkerts and Associates, Architects; Brutal style. Photograph by Balthazar, Korab, donated by Gunnar Birkerts.

glass. The building is set on a podium, which reduced the amount of excavation and allowed space for book storage in a basement above the groundwater level. It provided for 110,000 books and a future capacity of 450,000. The entrance is on center of one of the long sides. The interiors are very open, with most spaces defined by the library furnishings. A large reading area for the public is placed in the center, and this is under the control of a central desk near the entrance where books can be checked in and out. Offices of the library administration are easily accessible, and a second floor is open to the public. The book stacks in the basement are closed to the public, but all reference materials are easily accessible from the reading areas. The exterior elements and details are well balanced and composed.

*PALACIO DEL RIO, Hilton Hotel, San Antonio, Texas (Figure 10.6), 1967–1968, was designed by Cerna, Garza and Associates, with Feigenspan and Pinnell, structural engineers. Construction was started in October, 1967, and the hotel was finished and ready to open for "Hemis-

Figure 10.5 Wichita Public Library, Wichita, Kansas, 1966–1967; Schaefer, Schirmer and Associates, Architects; Brutal style. Photograph by Julius Shulman, Los Angeles, California.

fair," San Antonio's World Exposition, in May 1968. This remarkable record-breaking achievement was accomplished by the contractor and promoter of this building, H. B. Zachery, who constructed the 21-storied steel frame at the same time that he fabricated the concrete cube rooms outside the city. These cubes were then transported to the site, where they were lifted into place—already carpeted and furnished—and permanently fastened onto the frame. It was a tremendous advertising stunt, which the citizenry enjoyed and it accomplished its greater purpose of having the building ready when the fair opened: both on time.

The main entrance to the hotel is at street level, directly across the main thoroughfare from the fair and San Antonio's Convention Hall and Convention Center, including its spectacular tower with revolving top. The rear of the building boasts a beautiful terrace and outlook onto the famous San Antonio River walk.

*CAMPUS CENTER BUILDING AND DORMITORY, General Motors Institute, Flint, Michigan, 1968–1969, was designed by Tarapata, MacMahon and Paulsen, Associates. This is an excellent example of the Brutal style. The bulk of the building seems to rest on a ground-story podium whose terrace opens onto the main campus. The first two stories above the podium, the first floor and mezzanine, have the appearance of widely spaced pairs of extra strong pylons with glass in between. The third, fourth, and fifth stories, which house student residence rooms, are treated as one large, overhanging block divided into a repetitive pattern

Figure 10.6 Palacio del Rio, Hilton Hotel, San Antonio, Texas, 1967–1968; Cerna, Garza and Associates, Architects of San Antonio; Feigenspan and Pinnell, Structural Engineers; H. B. Zachary, Promoter and Contractor; Photograph by Zinteraff, furnished by CGR, Inc.

of small vertical rectangles. These run through two stories and are topped by a series of large horizontal fifth floor windows. A mastabalike copper attic story, set back from the front and sides, acts as a cap over all. The main exterior material is red sand-molded brick. The building contains public rooms and offices, lobbies and lounges, dining areas, recreation, and conference rooms, as well as the dormitory rooms above. There is also a large multipurpose room for dances, banquets, and other occasions. It is an outstanding building in every respect.

*MICHIGAN ELECTRIC POOL CENTER, South Wagner Road, Ann Arbor, Michigan, by Smith, Hinchman and Grylls, architects, Detroit, is owned and operated jointly by the Detroit Edison Company and Consumers Power Company. It is an all-concrete building that sits on rolling terrain. The surfaces are striated vertically in a strong pattern, and the main masses boldly overhang a base story. This facility centralizes the generation and transmission of more than 10 million kilowatts of power and allows the exchange of electrical power among Michigan, Indiana, and Ohio. It contains automatic monitoring and computer equipment that enables transfer of power without interruption from one source to another.

*NORTHWESTERN UNIVERSITY LIBRARY, Evanston, Illinois, 1968–1970, was designed by Walter Netsch of Skidmore, Owings and Merrill's Chicago office. An addition to the older Deering Library, it is made up of three almost identical buildings called towers, tied to the older building by an umbilical cord-like connection that threads diagonally to and through each building. Each building is used for a different type of research. In the center of each square, each of which is five stories high, is a skylighted circular space on the top floors. The stacks radiate from these circular spaces, and carrels, study rooms, typing rooms, and seminar spaces are located on the periphery. The library is designed for three types of users: undergraduate students; graduate students, and faculty. The sequence of stacks in the three buildings is repeated twelve times in each tower, and each level provides for 120,000 volumes. The three towers have a combined capacity of 1600 carrels, 18 seminar rooms, 136 faculty studies, 50 faculty carrels, and 18 typing rooms. Corridors linking the three towers at major levels contain exhibit spaces, checkout stations, stair, and elevator lobbies, and toilets.

The exteriors of the towers, all of rough concrete, have exposed columns running through the two lower floors, with the three upper floors overhanging in a multitudinous collection of vertical rectangles that appear to telescope as they overlap upward at each floor. The effect is very busy, and though it picks up the scale of the old Deering Library, it almost runs away with itself. It tries to express every in-and-out division of the interior: carrels, study rooms, and so forth, for no particular purpose. The plans of the towers are beautifully integrated, and the interiors are very quiet and beautiful in arrangement, color, and furnishings. The exterior, however, seems to have gone too far toward sensationalism.

*LYNDON BAINES JOHNSON LIBRARY, University of Texas, Austin, Texas, 1970, was designed by the New York office of Skidmore, Owings and Merrill, with Gordon Bunshaft, chief designer, and in association with Max Brooks, Barr Braeber and White. It houses the papers and documents of Lyndon Baines Johnson's political career from 1935 to 1969. The squarish rectangular building of Italian travertine rises eight stories and rests on a paved terrace that is next to a long two-storied building, Sidney W. Richardson Hall: built at the same time and overlooked by the library. This hall houses the Lyndon Baines Johnson School of Public Affairs, the Eugene C. Barker Texas History Center, the Texas Historical Association, and the Institute of Latin American Studies.

The library building itself is a severely simple composition of two parallel upright slabs (200 by 65 feet) set 90 feet apart and supporting an overhanging top story of horizontal design. The large space framed by these slabs is a plain surface. The upright slabs are subtle in their curving entasis, and the creamy-white travertine has a very pleasing texture. The interiors are simple and monumental on the first and second floors, and very businesslike and utilitarian on the third through the seventh floors. The top floor meeting rooms and a front section that duplicates LBJ's executive offices in the White House, even the Oval Room, though at slightly smaller scale.

**OAKLAND MUSEUM, Oakland, California (Figure 10.7), was designed by Kevin Roche, John Dinkeloo, Associates, successors to Eero Saarinen and Associates. It is a three-part museum of art, cultural history, and natural history, situated on a four-block sloping site which has been transformed into a formal terraced park. The museum spaces, which are distributed underneath these terraces, have openings here and there by way of loggialike galleries and blocky beige-colored concrete

Figure 10.7 Oakland Museum, Oakland, California, 1970; Kevin Roche, John Dinkeloo, Associates, Architects. Daniel U. Kiley, Landscape Architect. The Museum spaces are distributed beneath these terraces with openings here and there by way of loggialike galleries. Photograph furnished by Kevin Roche, John Dinkeloo, Associates.

retaining walls. Daniel U. Kiley was the landscape architect, and the ensemble shows close collaboration between the architecture and the landscape work. The site has magnificent plantings of indigenous ground covers, ferns, vines, aquatic plants, espaliers, cedars, and redwood trees. There are also pergolas, fountains, pools, and wide walkways. Certainly the concept is revolutionary, if not brutal.

The interior displays were carefully selected by Gordon Ashby, working with the curators and Kevin Roche. Most displays are independent of the building proper by means of freestanding screens and elegant cases. The screens are mostly of walnut with other surfaces of black anodized aluminum or of beige or white epoxy paint. The different sections are interesting and arranged so as not to be as tiring as those of most museums. They vie with the terraced spaces outside for interest and beauty. The whole ensemble was built for just under $10 million, which seems a bargain price for so much.

*GEORGE GUND HALL, Graduate School of Design, Harvard University, Cambridge, Massachusetts, 1970–1971, was designed by John

Andrews, architect of Toronto, Canada. It is built in five succeeding levels above a ground floor which houses a large and spacious library. The building has a stepped roof that is continuous over its length. Fifteen steps leading to this roof have vertical glass risers, and these give the appearance of a large bleacher stand. The roof follows the general slope of the receding floor spaces within, which are all open and receive their daylight from the risers of the roof steps. Each interior level has studio space with faculty offices and seminar rooms, and the studio spaces are so arranged that the entire work spaces can be seen from any one point.

The building is very utilitarian. It has a certain elegance, but actually makes little pretense of being more than a work space for student architects, landscape architects, and planners. Here they are not pocketed away from one another, but are thrown together so that all students can see what the others are doing.

SHERATON ISLAND INN, Goat Island on Narragansett Bay, Newport, Rhode Island, 1970–1971, was designed by Warner, Burns, Toan and Lunde, architects. This is an interesting composition of sculpture-like forms: cubes, rectangles, and sweeping roofs that rise nine floors. The complex dominates the landscape—or seascape—and contains all of the amenities of good living. Although it has 100 guest rooms, it is primarily for the in-and-out clientele who patronize the several restaurants, bars, and public lounges.

*AMERICAN INSTITUTE OF ARCHITECTS' NATIONAL HEADQUARTERS, Washington, D.C. (Figure 10.8), 1970–1972, was designed by Norman Fletcher of TAC (The Architects Collaborative). It is a seven-storied concrete building which forms an obtuse L shape on two sides of the five-sided garden of the Octagon House. The lower walls of this new building are of brick to match and to tie in with the eighteenth century Octagon House, which it complements, and the upper portions are of concrete. Each floor is accented by horizontal windows with continuous balcony-like spandrels that run the length of the building. It contrasts with the Octagon but also acts as a fitting background for it. There is a large lobby on the ground floor, as well as a library and exhibition space. On the second floor is a social hall, a large boardroom, and execuitve offices; the upper floors are divided into general offices, with one floor devoted to conference rooms.

Figure 10.8 American Institute of Architects' National Headquarters, Washington, D.C., 1970–1072; Norman Fletcher of TAC (The Architects Collaborative, Inc.,) Designer. Photograph by Ezra Stoller (Esto).

**FEDERAL RESERVE BANK, Minneapolis, Minnesota (Figure 10.9), 1970–1972, by Gunnar Birkerts and Associates, is built on the principle of a suspension bridge. It covers a large city block, and except for the two supporting pylons and an elevator core for six elevators at one side of the center, the ground level is uninterrupted. This ground level is a paved public area but does not lead into the building; this is one build-

Figure 10.9 Federal Reserve Bank, Minneapolis, Minnesota, 1970–1972; Gunnar Birkerts and Associates, Architects; Brutal style. Photograph by Balthazar Korab, given by Gunnar Birkerts.

ing that is not open to the public. Suspended above this ground level, and starting 20 feet up, are 10 floors of offices, supported by two bridge-like trusses at the top. These trusses form an eleventh floor, which contains mechanical equipment.

Structurally the building appears to be a *tour de force*; however it is so very logical in analysis that this may be a concept for future large buildings to follow. In theory it is simple: two pylons support a rectangle of steel and glass. There are no bumps or protuberances, and the great parabolic catenaries are brutal in concept. Because much of the construction is of steel in tension, the amount of steel required for the supports was reduced; however the clear span of the floors (66 feet) is excessive, and some of this gain was canceled out by the steel necessary to construct these long spans. The floor areas are free from columns and are therefore very efficient for office arrangement. Each floor provides approximately 20,000 square feet of uninterrupted space.

The huge cables are made up of catenary members of steel in the shape of wide-flange I beams, laced with 4 inch cables, three on each side. These form two upside-down parabolas, one on each side of the building, 66 feet apart and hanging from the tops of the pylons. On the outside areas bounded by these catenary cables there is 1 inch of insulating glass supported by 1 by 8 inch steel hangers. Inside the great parabolas the glass is set back about 4 feet from the outer edge of the catenary cables, and great vertical steel fins, 4 feet in depth, appear to hang from a steel apron at the eleventh floor. These fins are built out from 8 inch wide flange columns and act as continuous vertical window frames. All insulating glass is clear, and all exposed steel is painted black; thus seen from certain angles the great upside-down parabolas appear solid black, whereas between the steel fins there is complete sight through the clear glass surfaces.

There is provision for six more floors in the future, over the top of the eleventh floor trusses. These will be supported by the trusses as well as by two arches, which will rise from the pylons, quite the reverse of the catenary cables below.

In addition to the superstructure described above, there is a block square underground space of three levels that houses security operations. This area is reached by motor trucks, which drive down to security loading and unloading zones. It is the roof of this underground space that forms the public area at ground level, which is paved with closely fitted Cold Spring granite.

The architecturally trained professionals in the office of Gunnar Birkerts, were also assisted by Skilling, Helle, Christianson and Robertson, structural engineers; by foundation engineers Shannon and Wilson, Inc.; and by Jaros, Baum and Rolles, mechanical engineers. Landscape architects were Charles Wood and Associates.

MUMMER'S THEATER, Oklahoma City, Oklahoma (Figure 10.10), 1968–1970, was designed by John Johansen, assisted by David Hayes, stage designer. It is a Siamese-like building that is broken up into many masses: rectilinear and cylindrical. It is the epitome of the Brutal style. Each mass has a smooth concrete surface, and each is a different primary or secondary color. The parts, about 30 different exterior shapes, have the appearance of being tied together by round pipes painted bright red. These pipes carry air from a central heating and cooling mechanism housed in a rectilinear penthouse that tops the ensemble. On seeing this building, one asks the question: "What is it, or what are they?"

They are primarily two theaters, both small by usual standards; however Oklahoma City has a large auditorium. The larger theater seats 592 people in raised panellike groups that thrust out from a foyer opening off the lobby. These panels of seats radiate from one side of a round stage and are separated by alleylike entrances from the basement, in which the dressing rooms, an actors' assembly hall, and offices are located. The smaller theater is an arena type and seats 240 people for

Figure 10.10 Mummer's Theater, Oklahoma City, Oklahoma, 1968–1970; John Johansen, Architect, assisted by David Hayes, Stage Designer; Brutal style. Photograph by Balthazar Korab.

lectures and recitals. All interiors are finished—or unfinished—in rough concrete and rough boards. It is the antithesis of the Baroque theater of plaster garlands and crystal chandeliers. However the acoustics are good, the sight lines excellent, the chair seats comfortable, and the lighting effects perfect. Nevertheless on the exterior it is a queer ensemble that leaves the viewer quite breathless. It is raucous! Eventually it will be part of a Tivoli-like center.

EDUCATIONAL FACILITIES BUILDING, HARVARD'S SCHOOL OF PUBLIC HEALTH, Cambridge, Massachusetts (Figure 10.11), 1968–1971, was designed by William Kessler and Associates. It is a 10-storied building on a trapezoidal lot that varies from 95 to 240 feet on a side. Because the site is jammed in between older buildings and the program required 142,000 square feet of interior space, it had to be a multistoried building. The surrounding buildings, most of them part of the Harvard Public Health School, are generally of classic design and built of smooth Indiana limestone. Therefore one problem was to either use Indiana limestone for this building or find a fitting substitute. Kessler used panels of copolymer thermosetting resin and sand matrix, a plastic material that could be cast at the factory into 3 inch thick panels 5 by 12 feet with 3 foot ribbed portions at one end. These 3 foot ribbed sections were used to designate the floor structure and spandrels between windows at the different floor levels. The structure is steel with concrete over steel for the floors. To fit the site the upper five floors are rectangular, approximately 35 by 125 feet, and from this rectangular portion the lower five floors fan out in five steps to the lot lines. The ground floor fills the site.

The lower floors contain lecture rooms, teaching laboratories, foyers and exhibit spaces, and lounges; also a kitchen and several dining and conference rooms. The upper floors are used for seminars, classes, teaching laboratories, data processing, epidemiology, and administration.

From the ground the exterior has different appearances from different fronts. The exterior wall panels, with their 3 foot ribbed sections leaving plain surfaces 9 feet wide, give the exterior a subtle horizontally striped appearance that is very interesting. The tall portions, of course, dominate and give the impression of twin buildings having a 10-storied vertical strip window denoting the elevator lobby and the division between parts. Two large 5-storied entrance features mark the two main entrances. The top of this building also carries out the twin motive, with the two top floors stepped out one over the other. Windows on the

Figure 10.11 Educational Facilities Building, Harvard School of Public Health, Boston, Massachusetts, 1968–1971; William Kessler and Associates of Detroit, Michigan, Architects; Brutal style. Photograph by Balthazar Korab, Troy, Michigan.

two long facades are arranged in interesting patterns. Like the other facades, the end elevations are plain and have no windows. The building is air conditioned and well lighted electrically.

*BIRMINGHAM–JEFFERSON CIVIC CENTER, Birmingham, Alabama, 1970, was designed by Geddes, Brecher, Qualls and Cunningham in association with Lawrence S. Whitten and Son. It consists of four main buildings: a large exhibition hall, a 10,900 seat colosseum, a 3000 seat concert hall, and an 800 seat theater. It cost $36.5 million.

*ART GALLERY, UNIVERSITY OF CALIFORNIA, Berkeley, California, 1970–1972, was designed by Mario J. Ciampi and Associates, with Peter Reiter, Richard Jorash and Roland Wagner. John Volkos was in charge. This building of rough concrete has a plan of five main parts that open off an entrance lobby like the leaves of a fan. These leaves, at juxtapositioned levels, are reached by ramps from the main lobby. Their blank exterior ends are separately defined and seem to float over a high basement of heavy block forms. The interior has, in addition to the five main exhibition areas, seven more, making 12 areas in all on nine different levels, which breaks the continuity from one set of exhibits to another. As the building is entered there is a great skylighted court in which unusually large sculptures can be shown. From here the entire interior scheme is evident at once. The exterior features a sculpture garden at one side.

**LILA ACHESON WALLACE WORLD OF BIRDS, Bronx Zoo, New York City (Figure 10.12), 1970–1972, was designed by Morris Kethchum, Jr., and Associates. It has 25 exhibit areas of various sizes and shapes, from rectangles with rounded corners to ovals and cylinders, all massed together in one close composition that houses a large assortment of birds from all parts of the world. Here an attempt has been made very successfully to simulate natural environments as nearly as possible. One of the most spectacular exhibits is the New World Rain Forest, where 100 varieties of tropical birds occupy a space that has simulated forest sounds and tropical rainstorms.

This World of Birds was a gift of Lila Acheson Wallace and her husband, the publishers of the Reader's Digest, to the New York Zoological Park.

Figure 10.12   Lila Acheson Wallace World of Birds, Bronx Zoo, New York City, 1970–1972; Morris Ketchum, Jr., and Associates, Architects. Photograph by Alexandre Georges; donated by New York Zoological Society.

*ATLANTIC ENVIRONMENTAL RESEARCH LABORATORIES FOR THE NATIONAL OCEANIC AND ATMOSPHERIC ADMINISTRATION, Miami, Florida, 1973, by Ferendino, Grafton, Spillis and Candela, architects, was designed by Hilario Candela. The building is three stories high with mechanical equipment forming a fourth story and a rather secluded director's office in a small penthouse on a fifth level. The ground floor is quite open and has stiltlike columns supporting the upper stories. The two upper floors, which jut out in great cubical masses, house four sets of scientists' offices on each side of each floor: four sets of senior offices and four sets of junior offices. The senior offices are oddly shaped but were tested by full-sized mock-ups during the design stage for the occupants' approval. The building is entirely of white concrete striated vertically in an effective texture. The supporting piers rest in the water of a lagoon that was dredged out on one side. This lagoon is used to test water equipment, so is more than just an aesthetic addition. The design might be classified as a bit nervous, but it is, at the least, interesting.

**RELIGIOUS-ARTS CENTER, Carthage College, Kenosha, Wisconsin (Figure 10.13), 1973–1975, designed by Architects III of Milwaukee. It houses a 2000 seat chapel and convocation center, the college music department and practice rooms, fine arts studios, and exhibition space. The building, primarily of concrete, is topped by a 69 foot stainless steel spire holding a cross. It is built into a hillside lot and has the entrance to the chapel and exhibition spaces on the upper level, and the entrance to classrooms and practice rooms on the downhill side. It is an excellent example of the straightforward Brutal style.

*MURRAY LINCOLN CAMPUS CENTER, University of Massachusetts, Amherst, Massachusetts, 1970–1973, designed by Marcel Breuer and Herbert Beckhard, architects, is an $11 million center for students,

Figure 10.13   Religious Arts Center, Carthage College, Kenosha, Wisconsin, 1973–1975; Architects III. of Milwaukee, Photograph furnished by Carthage College.

faculty, and alumni. This 10-storied rectangular building is built entirely of large, precast concrete units. It sits on a large podium and has large areas below ground; the open ground floor is at the podium terrace level. This ground floor has stiltlike columns for support of the upper floors and a stair tower at each end of the rectangle. The building contains conference spaces, dining rooms, cafeterias and snack bars, recreational facilities, a large multipurpose ballroom, and administrative offices. Fenestration is regular from the second through the fifth floors and has a double pattern on the sixth and seventh floors. The eighth and ninth stories overhang the rest of the building and have large horizontal windows set in back of an allover-patterned concrete balcony screen. Most of the exterior consists of large, precast concrete units, which frame the windows and give the effect of an overall pattern.

LABORATORY AND CLASSROOM BUILDING, New York University, University Heights, Campus, 1972–1973, was designed by Marcel Breuer and Hamilton Smith. Three elements make up the ensemble: a three-storied classroom building, an eight-storied laboratory, and an office wing that includes a library, lecture room for 180 people, exhibition spaces, and individual faculty offices. The buildings are mainly of precast concrete in large units that differ from one element to another. Some of the tower walls are of brick.

*FARMINGTON PROFESSIONAL BUILDING (Figure 10.14), 1973–1974, was designed by Rossen–Neumann Associates of Southfield (Detroit), Michigan. It is a two-storied medical office building and houses a large pediatrics clinic as well as general family practitioners and several specialists.

Construction is of steel frame with concrete floors on metal decks. Exterior walls are of brick with precast concrete trim. All windows are bronze-colored, heat-absorbing glass in bronze anodized frames. The building was given an honor award by the Detroit Chapter of the American Institute of Architects in 1975. The exterior, which is beautifully balanced is composed in the Brutal style.

**POST OFFICE AND FEDERAL OFFICE BUILDING, Saginaw, Michigan (Figure 10.15), 1974–1976, is by Smith, Hinchman and Grylls,

Figure 10.14 Farmington Professional Building, Farmington, Michigan, 1973–1974; Rossen–Neumann Associates, Architects; Brutal style. Photograph by Balthazar Korab, Troy, Michigan.

Inc. under the direction of Arthur G. Sampson, chief administrator for the General Services Administration in Washington. This has been designated by Mr. Sampson as the GSA's Environmental Building, a "living laboratory that will serve all the functions that a federal office building should, besides enhancing the environment." Most of the office floors will be slightly below grade to allow ramps to flow from the street levels to the roofs. The roofs will be used for parking and recreation, and approximately half of their area is to be landscaped with lawn, shrubs, and trees. The building will cover about half of its site of 125,500 square feet. The structure will be of reinforced concrete, and the estimated cost is $4.12 million (1974 prices, and costs are increasing). One of the features of the building will be a flat 8000 square foot solar collector panel of glass on a concrete frame. This huge panel is to be placed astride the building, facing south and tilted upward at approximately 60 degrees to catch the maximum amount of the sun's rays. This will supply solar energy to the building. Although it is an expensive element now, in time it will pay for itself by supplying energy for heating and cooling.

No doubt more and more future buildings will be submerged in whole or in part to allow savings in heat and exterior upkeep and to allow parking space and landscaping at ground level.

Figure 10.15 Post Office and Federal Building, Saginaw, Michigan, 1974–1976; Smith, Hinchman and Grylls, Inc., Detroit, Architects, under the direction of Arthur G. Sampson, Chief Administrator, General Services Administration, Supervisor; Brutal style. Photograph courtesy of Smith Hinchman and Grylls, Inc.

RESIDENCES

Although there was a great deal of residential building during this period, much of it was by speculative builders, and the trend was to reproduce pseudo-Colonial ranch types and two-storied Southern Colonial mansions that have badly proportioned classic detail.

Custom-built houses designed by architects were generally conservative. Many were of stained wood—cedar or redwood—but had large areas of glass; some were flat roofed, others had sloping roofs. Not many residences were built in Brutal style, for although the public accepted this new sensual expression for public and commercial buildings, they reverted to the styles of past years for their homes.

*PFEIFER RESIDENCE, Arizona Desert, 1972, was designed by Bruce Brooks Pfeifer, architect, from sketches made by Frank Lloyd Wright in 1938. The house is owned by Bruce Brooks Pfeifer and his father, Arthur E. Pfeifer. All of the living spaces of the house are separate circles that surround a covered courtyard. Windows facing the desert view are long bands of horizontal glass. Doors entirely of glass open onto a grand terrace; others open directly to the outdoors. The house, of white cement, presents an ensemble of circular shapes that look like a series of tanks tied together by flat roof slabs melding unobtrusively into the tops of the various circular spaces.

GELLER HOUSE II, Lawrence, Long Island, New York, 1972, by Marcel Breuer and Herbert Beckhard, is a one-storied house of concrete contained within a long, sweeping concrete arch. The front looks out from a living room that has a fireplace at one end and a dining space and kitchen at the other. The back of the house contains the owner's bedroom suite with dressing room and bath, plus two guest rooms with walk-through closets and bath. The arch is open on the two sides and has glass set into large piers and cross beams of concrete.

*STEPHEN KAPLAN RESIDENCE, East Hampton, New York, by Barbara and Julian Neski, is a fantastic plan of angles, circles, and squares that meld together remarkably into a workable and livable composition. The exterior is of bleached cedar vertical siding, carefully fitted so that the surfaces are smooth. This two-storied house is very square and blocky in form with flat roofs and open parapets. It has deeply recessed spaces forming terraces and balconies that are backed by large plates of glass that slide open. The site is wooded with trees and shrubbery, which helps carry out the strong horizontal effect.

**J. B. HANSELMAN RESIDENCE, Fort Wayne, Indiana, 1974, was designed by Michael Graves. This house is an outstanding example of the Brutal style carried into the domestic field. The two-storied house has plain surfaces offset by large horizontal glass areas. It is a stunning though simple composition of voids and solids. The site is semiwooded. This residence received an American Institute of Architects Honor Award for excellence in design at the 1975 convention in Atlanta, Georgia.

BUILDINGS FOR THE PERFORMING ARTS AND LARGE INDOOR STADIA

**LINCOLN CENTER FOR THE PERFORMING ARTS, New York City (Figure 10.16), 1962–1966, is located between Columbus and Amster-

Figure 10.16 Lincoln Center for the Performing Arts, Metropolitan Opera (left), (Avery Fisher) Hall (right), New York City, 1962–1966; Wallace K. Harrison, Coordinating Architect; Brutal style (conservative). Photograph by Bob Serating, courtesy of Harrison and Abramovitz.

dam Avenues from West 62nd to West 66th Streets. The design of the ensemble was directed by Wallace K. Harrison, who coordinated the work of the architects of the individual buildings. It has been called "an acropolis of music and theater" and cost more than $165 million. Its four main buildings, the Metropolitan Opera House, Avery Fisher Hall, the New York State Theater, and the Vivian Beaumont Theater with the library–museum, are beautifully related one to the other. They rest on a grand terrace over a vast basement garage. Unfortunately the Center is badly located in relation to the city and its transportation.[1] Public transportation for so many large auditoriums in one cluster is maddeningly inadequate. Taxis and private cars are unable to arrive and depart properly. Even with the submerged auto garage, parking space is inadequate, and no space is provided for chauffer-driven cars at street level.

[1] Just how this could have been solved in the crowded city of New York is an unanswerable question.

**METROPOLITAN OPERA HOUSE, Lincoln Center, New York City, 1964–1966, designed by Wallace K. Harrison, is the largest of the four main buildings. The design is actually very conservative, with a high vaulted portico facing the central plaza and screening a red-carpeted lobby and stairs. These stairs lead to balcony levels and a café at the top. The ceiling is gold leafed, but the main features are Austrian crystal chandeliers, which hang in the lobby as well as in the auditorium. At performance time these chandeliers are silently raised to the gold-leafed ceilings and gradually dimmed.

The auditorium and stage are equipped with every luxury and convenience: dressing rooms, chorus rooms, scene galleries, and special scene-shifting apparatus. Acoustics are good, and most sight lines are perfect.

*NEW YORK STATE THEATER, Lincoln Center, New York City, 1964, is the design of Philip Johnson and Richard Foster. It seats 2800 people and was designed primarily for ballet and orchestra performances. It is fronted by a four-storied foyer suitable for large receptions. The theater is quite Baroque in character, an assemblage of gold leaf, crystal, gold-chain drapery, and mirrors. In addition to the rich Baroque trappings the interior is accented by two white marble sculptures by Elie Nadelman.

AVERY FISHER HALL, Lincoln Center, New York City, 1962, was designed by Max Abramovitz and is the home of the New York Philharmonic Orchestra. The exterior is a composition of tall, tapered, white columns which screen an enclosure of clear glass. Features of the foyer include two metal clusters by Richard Lippold, which hang in central positions and sparkle their way to attention. This hall had acoustical difficulties that had defied simple rectification; therefore the auditorium interior was redesigned and rebuilt in 1975.

*VIVIAN BEAUMONT THEATER, Lincoln Center, New York City, 1965, by Eero Saarinen and Associates, is a 1100 seat theater for repertory dramatic productions. The exterior is accented by a massive attic story, which seems to float above a split-level glass-enclosed lobby. The interior of the theater, including the lobby, is quite neutral and only comes to life when lighted and populated with people.

THE LIBRARY–MUSEUM, by Skidmore, Owings and Merrill, in collaboration with Eero Saarinen, occupies the large attic story of the Beaumont Theater. It is actually a thing apart and shows many Skidmore, Owings and Merrill subtleties. It contains some excellent spaces and excellent audiovisual exhibits.

JONES HALL OF THE PERFORMING ARTS, Houston, Texas, 1967–1968, by Caudill–Rowlett–Scott, architects, is a circular building that fills an entire city block. It is an auditorium with all of the latest gadgets: it allows "interior configuration changes to meet the differing events with the touch of a finger." By the lowering or raising of the ceiling, the auditorium can be enlarged from 1800 to 3000 seats in a matter of minutes. The stage is beautifully equipped and is adaptable to many uses. It is the home of the Houston Symphony Orchestra, The Houston Society of the Performing Arts, and the Houston Opera, which plays a season of 20 performances here every year. It is one of the best community performing arts centers in the United States.

THE JOHN F. KENNEDY CENTER FOR THE PERFORMING ARTS, Washington, D.C., 1972–1973, was designed by Edward D. Stone and is a great triumph. Also to be mentioned are the *Performing Arts Center of the University of California* at Santa Cruz, California, and the *Performing Arts, Radio and Television*.

CENTER AT THE UNIVERSITY OF MINNESOTA, Minneapolis, Minnesota. These last two were designed by Ralph Rapson and Associates of Minneapolis.

MUSIC HALL OF HOUSTON, Texas, 1962, by Caudill-Rowlett-Scott, stands near Jones Hall and is a large auditorium of 3000 seats. It is the scene of musical events throughout the year.

**ASTRODOME, Houston, Texas, 1964–1965, located 5 miles from the center of the city, is part of a huge amusement park known as Astroworld, which has over 100 rides and shows of different kinds, including the Crystal Palace Review, a variety show rivaling the Radio City Music Hall Review in New York City. Astroworld covers a total of 200 acres and has parking for 30,000 cars.

The Astrodome is designed to house a number of different sporting events, including baseball and football. Trussed steel beams arch upward to a steel lamella frame that supports 5000 diamond-shaped plastic skylights. It has a clear span of 642 feet and a center height of 208 feet, the height of an 18 to 20-storied office building. It provides six levels of seating and accommodates 45,000–65,000 spectators depending on the event. It has heating and air conditioning provisions for all kinds of weather. The total cost was $31 million.

Next door to the Astrodome is Astrohall, a huge exhibition hall that is home of the Houston Live Stock Show, which takes place in February at the time of the Houston Rodeo. At other times it is used for large conventions.

*DALLAS ATHLETIC DOME, Dallas, Texas, 1972–1974, was built primarily for the Dallas Cowboys, Dallas' football team. This dome is equal to Houston's Astrodome in many respects and is more elegant in some of its appointments. Its special boxes were auctioned off to Dallas' business men and were then decorated and furnished to their individual specifications many of them at a cost of thousands of dollars.

*NEW ORLEANS DOME, New Orleans, Louisiana, 1972–1974, is near the center of the city and is similar to the Astrodome.

**PONTIAC STADIUM, Pontiac, Michigan (Figure 10.17), 35 miles north of Detroit, 1973–1975, was designed by O'Dell, Hewlett and Luckenbach, Inc. with Carl Luckenbach, Jr., designer in charge. It is the world's largest covered football stadium, with 80,400 seats and is the home of the Detroit Lions of the National football League. However it is not limited to football and is booked for concerts, rodeos, trade shows, and other sporting events. The stadium sits on a 135 acre site and is surrounded by paved parking for 9000 cars and 450 buses. The building itself covers 10 acres.

The chief claim to fame of this stadium is its air-supported dome, which covers the entire 10 acres. This dome, which is supported by an eight-sided exterior concrete structure, is slightly curved and rises 205 feet in the center; it is covered by an airtight fiberglass fabric that is inflated by 29 giant blowers. This fiberglass fabric is coated with Teflon, and is translucent so that the interior is daylighted without glare.

Seating consists of moulded plastic armchairs. The stadium has a fast-food service that can feed 5000 people a minute. There are 102 private

Figure 10.17 Pontiac Stadium, Pontiac, Michigan, 1973–1975; O'Dell, Hewlett and Luckenbach, Inc., Architects, Birmingham, Michigan. Photograph courtesy of O'Dell, Hewlett and Luckenbach.

air-conditioned suites, each seating from 8 to 20 persons and fully equipped. Also, at one end, is a 250 foot glass wall, which provides patrons of the 600 seat restaurant with a full-length view of the field. At the other end are an automated scoreboard and a closed-circuit television screen for replays and other information.

Of the five large covered stadiums built during the last decade, Houston's Astrodome, Dallas, New Orleans, Seattle, and the latest, Pontiac, this was the largest and the cheapest per seat. The cost of the New Orleans stadium has been given as $2333 per seat, whereas Pontiac's cost per seat is $529.

**ASSEMBLY HALL, University of Illinois, Urbana, Illinois (Figure 10.18), 1961–1963, was designed by Harrison and Abramovitz assisted by Ammann and Whitney, structural engineers. The building is a great cir-

Figure 10.18 Assembly Hall, University of Illinois, Urbana, Illinois, 1961–1963; Harrison and Abramovitz, Architects; Emotional structural style. Photograph courtesy of Harrison and Abramovitz.

cular dome of precast concrete sections that rest on the outer perimeter of a great circular hall. This stadiumlike concrete structure encircles a large arena that contains the seats and meets the outer perimeter of the dome. The total weight of the structure rests on a reinforced concrete foundation that outlines the arena. The hall, which can seat up to 19,000 spectators, is a structural accomplishment that can be classed among the wonders of the age. It is a building that adapts to many uses, from student convocations to indoor sports such as basketball and even to large circuses. Furthermore it is a beautiful structure, smooth and graceful.

*CRISLER SPORTS ARENA, University of Michigan, Ann Arbor, Michigan, 1966–1968 was designed by Daniel L. Dworsky, California, in association with Kenneth C. Black Associates of Lansing, Michigan. This building is oval and can seat up to 16,000 people. It is named for Herbert C. Crisler, a retired athletic director and football coach of the university.

*COLISEUM OF HAMPTON ROADS, Hampton, Virginia, 1970, was designed by Arthur Gould Odell, Jr., of Odell Associates, Inc. It is a cylindrical building constructed of precast Y forms on the outer circumference. These forms are attached to each other at the tops of the circle, on which a flat concrete dome rests. It is a very striking building in the Brutal style.

SKYSCRAPERS

Although the Brutal style was introduced at this time and was widely used for buildings of a few stories, it was not adaptable to skyscraper design. It could neither evolve away from the structural form nor be hung onto it naturally. Therefore we see jet age skyscrapers of sheer glass and steel in Miesian designs even though the popularity of Miesian structural expression passed its zenith in the 1950s. These jet age skyscrapers were expressive of their steel flight upward but were often clad in stone, as can be seen in the Cincinnati, Ohio, center, or in both steel/glass and stone, as in the Columbus, Ohio, center. However extreme height continued to be the goal of the jet age, whether for an office building in New York, Pittsburgh, or Chicago, or a hotel or apartment building in Atlanta, Detroit, or San Francisco.

This race for extreme height culminated in the World Trade Center (twin towers) in New York, and the Sears Tower in Chicago. Both buildings are 110 stories high and both claim to be the tallest building in the world. However the Sears Tower rises 1454 feet, whereas the World Trade Center stands 1350 feet. Both are built of metal and glass in the Miesian tradition. There seems to be no way to clothe 50-storied or higher buildings with blocky forms. Gropius did do this in his design for the Chicago Tribune Tower in 1923, but even there the forms were extraneous. Therefore the skyscrapers listed as belonging to this period of time—the jet age—bear few characteristics of the Brutal style.

*LAKE POINT TOWER, just off Lake Shore Drive, Chicago, Illinois, 1968, was designed by Schipporeit-Henrich. Its plan has three wings reaching out from a central triangular core. All surfaces are curved, and the outer curtain walls are of aluminum and glass. It rises 70 stories and is the highest apartment building in the world. It houses 900 units of one and two bedrooms, all electrically heated and cooled. The building is very slick and attractive.

*MARINA CITY APARTMENTS, Chicago, Illinois, 1963–1965, by Bertrand Goldberg Associates, are two cylindrical towers on the north side of the Chicago River, opposite downtown Chicago. The buildings are identical and contain 40 floors of apartments over 13 floors of parking spaces. The apartments are arranged around a central utility core, which houses the elevators. The exterior views of these two towers are quite startling, particularly since the vertical tiers of adjoining apartments have curved fronts giving the effect of kernels on two mammoth cobs of corn.

*BANK OF AMERICA BUILDING, San Francisco, California, 1968–1970, was designed by Wurster, Bernardi and Emmons, with Pietro Belluschi, and Skidmore, Owings and Merrill, consultants. It is 52 stories high. The facades are strongly faceted verticals that zigzag in and out from the base to the very top. The building has a few setbacks as the masses approach the top. This is the banking and office center of the world-renowned bank that ranks as the second largest, if not the largest, bank in the world. It is a very distinctive building, and perhaps its zigzag design and setbacks near the top can be said to give it Brutal quality.

**THE PEACHTREE CENTER AND HYATT REGENCY HOTEL ADDITION, Atlanta, Georgia, 1967–1976, was designed by John Portman, architect and promoter. "It all started with a hotel with a hole in the middle: and 220 foot high atrium lobby," begins one description. This hotel will reach 70 stories and for the most part will be cylindrical and sheathed in bronze-backed mirrors. It will be the tallest building in Atlanta, as well as in the entire South. The lobby underneath this cylinder will be 20 stories high, reaching a height of 220 feet; 9 stories of this will be taken up by shops, restaurants, exhibition halls, ballrooms, year-round swimming pool, gymnasium, dressing rooms, and sauna. The main shaft of this cylinder of 50 stories will be occupied by 500 hotel rooms—50 floors of 10 rooms each—and the top 3 floors will be revolving cocktail lounges and restaurants overlooking the city. Peachtree Center itself will be a cluster of buildings, each separate but connected to the hotel. It will contain a world trade center building, six multistoried office buildings, plus parking garages. All of this is constructed of reinforced concrete from forms worked out by the Symons Manufacturing Company of San Antonio, Texas.

*EMBARCADERO CENTER, San Francisco, California, 1970–1976, by John Portman and Associates, architects, is a great commercial center which, when completed, will cover 8.5 acres and is estimated to cost upwards of $200 million. It is being developed by Trammel Crow and David Rockefeller and Associates for the San Francisco Redevelopment Agency. The complex will contain a 45-storied office building, two 25-storied office buildings, one of which is now completed, and a 60-storied office tower. The center, which will overlook the bay, will also contain a 2000 seat theater, arcaded shops and plazas, and a Hyatt Hotel, The Regency.

*REGENCY HYATT HOTEL, Embarcadero Center, San Francisco, California, 1972–1973, was designed by John Portman and Associates, architects, which firm also did several new Hyatt Hotels, beginning with the one in Atlanta, Georgia. Most of these hotels feature a large and public interior court which is air conditioned but open to the sky and which features two-storied decorative elevators of glass. One side of this hotel is pyramidal, with each room having a balcony, and ascends at a 45 degree angle up 18 stories. The public interior court is a beautiful feature, and is accented by a fountain topped by a hollow sphere, 40 feet high and 35 feet in diameter. This fountain is made up of tubes of gold anodized aluminum, woven together to make a sphere of intersecting pentagons that rotate about a central axis.

Several other **HYATT HOTELS,** by John Portman, architect and promoter, are bing planned, including one in New York City.

RENAISSANCE CENTER, Detroit, Michigan, 1974–1980, which is being designed and promoted by John Portman and Associates, is to be a landscaped commercial center similar to Embarcadero Center in San Francisco and Peachtree Center in Atlanta. Financed by a group headed by Henry Ford II, it is located on the Detroit River in a large area vacated by railroad tracks, warehouses, and obsolete factories. The central building is to be a 77-storied office building, and there is to be a 70-storied Hyatt Hotel. There will also be arcades for shops and plazas.

Other skyscrapers of the period include the *Aluminum Company of America (Alcoa) Building* (Figure 10.19), 1953, and the *U.S. Steel Headquarters Building* (Figure 10.20), 1958, in the Golden Triangle of Pittsburgh; the *Phoenix Mutual Insurance Company Headquarters* (Figure 10.21), in Hartford, Connecticut, 1964; the *Columbus Center Building* (Figure 10.22), 1974, Columbus, Ohio; and the *Cincinnati Center Building* (Figure 10.23), 1975, Cincinnati, Ohio. All of these were designed by Harrison and Abramovitz architects of New York City. There is also the *Cedar Square West Group* (Figure 10.24), of tightly integrated tall buildings in Minneapolis, Minnesota, by Ralph Rapson and Associates of that city.

**WORLD TRADE CENTER, New York City (Figure 10.25), 1961–1973, was designed by Emory Roth and Sons. Malcolm Levy, architect, of the office of Emery Roth, was the resident architect on the job, Minoru Yamasaki and Associates were design consultants. These twin towers, the tallest buildings in the world, are flat-topped rectilinear shafts that stand 110 stories high. Each tower is in effect three buildings placed one on top of the other, and each has a lobby on the first, forty-fourth, and seventy-eighth floors. These lobbies have coffee bars, newsstands, and special elevator-waiting lobbies for each segment. The buildings were financed by the Port of New York Authority, which will occupy 20 stories in one of the buildings.

There are 23 express elevators, each having a capacity of 55 passengers, as well as 72 elevators in each building for local service. All elevators open on one side at the lobby levels and discharge their passengers on the opposite side at intermediate levels, thus speeding up passenger flow. The elevator systems of these buildings are heralded as being the most perfect and safest that have yet been devised. It is not possible for an elevator to get stuck between floors.

The buildings are equipped with automatic loudspeaker systems to warn of fire or other emergency anywhere in the building, and the entire building can be told of the what, where, and how of the emergency.

It will be noted that these buildings took 12 years to be built. They are located on Church Street and the West Side Highway on the Hudson

Figure 10.19 Aluminum Company of America (Alcoa) Building, Pittsburgh, Pennsylvania, 1953; Harrison and Abramovitz, Architects; Jet Age Skyscraper. Photograph courtesy of Harrison and Abramovitz.

Figure 10.20 U.S. Steel Headquarters Building, Pittsburgh, Pennsylvania, 1958; Harrison and Abramovitz, Architects; Jet Age Skyscraper. Photograph by Ezra Stoller (Esto); courtesy of Harrison and Abramovitz.

Figure 10.21 Phoenix Mutual Insurance Company Headquarters, Hartford, Connecticut, 1964; Harrison and Abramovitz, Architects; Jet Age Skyscraper. Photograph by Ezra Stoller (Esto); courtesy of Harrison and Abramovitz.

River in Lower Manhattan. They are built on filled land that was once part of the river, and much time was taken with the foundations and the large terrace site on which the buildings appear to rest.

When fully occupied, these buildings will have a daytime population of 50,000. However because of the heat loss through their glass outer surfaces, the great amount of energy required to heat or cool the building, and run the elevators will require as much electrical energy as the city of Schenectady, New York, which has a population of 100,000.[2]

[2] *U.S. News and World Report*, February 18, 1974.

Figure 10.22 Columbus Center Building, Columbus, Ohio, 1974; Harrison and Abramovitz, Architects; Jet Age Skyscraper. Photograph by Hedrich-Blessing, Chicago, Ill.

Figure 10.23 Cincinnati Center Building, Cincinnati, Ohio, 1975; Harrison and Abramovitz, Architects; Jet Age Skyscraper. Photograph by Bill Engdahl of Hedrich-Blessing, Chicago.

Figure 10.24 Cedar Square West, Minneapolis, Minnesota, 1975; Ralph Rapson and Associates, Architects; Jet Age Skyscraper. Photograph by Barton Aschman, Chicago, Illinois; courtesy of Ralph Rapson.

Figure 10.25 World Trade Center, New York City, 1961–1973; Emery Roth and Sons, Architects, with Minoru Yamasaki and Associates; Malcolm Levy, Resident Architect. Photograph by Balthazar Korab, Troy, Michigan.

SEARS TOWER, Wacker Drive and Jackson Boulevard, Chicago, Illinois (Figure 10.26), 1971–1974, by Skidmore, Owings and Merrill's Chicago office, also rated as the tallest building in the world. It rises 110 stories high, 1454 feet above ground level, is of steel and glass in a Miesian-type design. It starts as a ground level base of 68,000 square feet in area and rises 45 stories. At this point it sets back to a smaller area, which rises another 40 stories more before it sets back again at the eighty-fifth floor. From there the central shaft rises to its ultimate height of 110 stories. There is an observation floor at the 103rd level, 1353 feet above the ground, and this is serviced by two nonstop elevators.

The building has a population capacity of 16,500, including 7000 Sears employees. There are 103 high-speed elevators, including 14 double-deck units, pulled by a total of 80 miles of elevator cable.

These two projects—the World Trade Center in New York and the Sears Tower in Chicago—are no doubt the climax of building in the jet age. They are monuments to the ego of those who financed and built them, and they have great advertising value as extravaganzas of technology. Although they may be justified by the value of the land that they occupy, certainly much more economical buildings could have been built elsewhere—buildings that would be much more economical in heat and electrical energy for heating and cooling and operation of elevators. However whether they denote the end of an era or not, they are wonderful, a fitting climax to 200 years of American Architecture.

MODERN ARCHITECTURE IN COLUMBUS, INDIANA

Before this survey of architecture in the jet age is ended, a few pages should be devoted to the city of Columbus, Indiana, and its architecture since World War II. Columbus has become a showplace of modern architecture, particularly that of the Brutal style of the past two decades, and that city has gone through a veritable renaissance.

This started with the First Christian Church, designed by Eliel Saarinen and dedicated in 1942 (see p. 241). People accepted and liked the design: its simplicity, boldness, and purity. After World War II Columbus, like many other cities, found itself lacking in school buildings: the population had doubled, but no construction of new schools had taken

Figure 10.26 Sears Tower, Chicago, Illinois, 1971–1974; Skidmore, Owings and Merrill, Chicago Office, Architects. Photograph by Balthazar Korab, Troy, Michigan.

place since the Great Depression of the 1930s. However a local manufacturing company, the Cummings Engine Company, set up a special
foundation and offered to pay the architectural fees for new schools provided that only distinguished national architects were selected. The
school board accepted the offer, and 12 schools have been constructed
under this program since 1955. A number of other types of buildings
have been designed by noted architects without the benefit of the
foundation.

As a result architecture in Columbus has been the subject of feature
articles in national and international publications, and each year thousands of people visit the city to see these buildings.[3]

Among the many buildings to be noted are the following 12 schools,
each an example of the contemporary style of the time, the Brutal style.
A few other buildings in Columbus follow.

Lillian C. Schmitt Elementary School, 1957, Harry Weese, architect,
Chicago.
**Mable McDowell Elementary School,* 1960, John Carl Warnecke, archi-
tect, San Francisco.
North Side Junior High School, 1961, Harry Weese, architect, Chicago.
Parkside Elementary School, 1962, Norman Fletcher of The Architect's
Collaborative, Boston.
Bartholomew Consolidated School, Administration Building, 1963, Nor-
man Fletcher of The Architect's Collaborative, Boston.
**W. D. Richards Elementary School,* 1965, Edward Larrabee Barnes,
New York City.
Lincoln Elementary School, 1967, Gunnar Birkerts, Birmingham, Mich-
igan.
**L. Frances Smith Elementary School,* 1969, John M. Johansen, archi-
tect, New Canaan, Connecticut.
**South Side Junior High School,* 1969, Eliot Noyes, Architect, New
Canaan, Connecticut.
Mt. Healthy Elementary School, 1972, Hardy, Holzman, Pfeifer Asso-
ciates, New York City.
**East Senior High School,* 1972, Mitchell, Giurgola Associates, Phila-
delphia.

[3] In 1974 the Columbia Area Chamber of Commerce, Inc., published a guidebook, *A
Look at Architecture, Columbus, Indiana,* which is available at the Visitors' Center,
506 Fifth Street, Columbus. At this center are trained volunteer guides for visitors
who wish to see the city. There is also a guided tour by minibus.

Fodree Community School, 1973, Caudill, Rowlett, Scott, Paul Kennon and Truitt Garrison, Houston, Texas.

**North Christian Church,* 1964, by Eero Saarinen, architect, has a very distinguished design. The building is hexagonal with a low-pitched roof that rises to the center and is then accentuated by a slender spire rising 192 feet to a gold-leafed cross at the very top.

This was the last building designed by Eero Saarinen before his untimely death. While designing this building, he wrote to the congregation, "I want to design it so that as an architect when I face St. Peter, I am able to say that this little church . . . has in it a real spirit that speaks forth to all Christians as witness to their faith."

*FIRST BAPTIST CHURCH, 1965, was designed by Harry Weese. This is a two level ensemble of brick walls topped by high pitched roofs. Set on the brow of a sloping knoll, it takes advantage of the hillside site.

*QUINCO CONSULTING CENTER, 1972, by James Stewart Polshek, is the Mental Health Consulting Center of Columbus and Bartholomew County. It is a two-storied building that spans Hawcreek, between Bartholomew County Hospital on one side and a park on the other. The main lounge is on the first floor directly over the creek, and a glassed-in balcony bridge occupies the second floor.

CUMMINS ENGINE COMPANY, Components Plant, 1973, was designed by Kevin Roche of Kevin Roche, John Dinkeloo, Associates. This building spreads out under 13.5 acres of roof, which is used for parking. Under this are two floors devoted to manufacturing and some space for offices on the two outer sides. The main floors are partially submerged to a degree depending on the slope of the lot, which falls away on the back sides. This building has been proclaimed as a prototype for future factory buildings.

11

EPILOGUE—AFTER 1975

1975 onward? To try to foretell the future may be an interesting game, but the prognostications may be far from actuality. It seems safe to say that the jet age, and in architecture the Brutal style, will go on, probably for at least 30 or 40 more years. The technology of this age seems to be firmly seated, and though there will be changes and advances, no upheaval is in sight.

Skyscrapers have probably reached their apex at 110 stories; only more conservative heights will be built. Units having 20 stories will no doubt be the norm, with 20, 40, 60, and a few of 80 floors being built in the largest cities, where land costs and intracity transportation allow. However imagine the problem of disbursing 50,000 people, the capacity of the World Trade Center in New York City, should all offices close at one time. Also to be considered are maintenance costs, plus heating and cooling, which in the steel and glass tower surpass economic limits at about the level of the fortieth floor.

However no one should base the reason for building solely on economics. The pyramids of Egypt far surpassed their economic limits; so did the Temples of Baalbek in Lebanon, Hagia Sophia in Istanbul, and the high vaultings of the cathedrals of France. But they satisfied the egos of the builders. People cannot be expected to always do the completely rational and economical thing.

Technically the skyscraper can be built a mile high and may some day do just that. It will only be necessary to find a person or corporation loaded with money and willing to spend it on a monument of that kind.

Building styles will be based on the same philosophy of forms as now, but these forms will probably be simplified. There will no doubt be bumps here and there if dictated by plan arrangement; there will be large, plain surfaces and large glass openings; it will be a very forthright style. This is what is on the drawing boards for tomorrow, and no doubt this will continue at least to the end of the century. After that, who can tell?

BIBLIOGRAPHY

GENERAL ARCHITECTURAL HISTORY

Fletcher, Sir Banister, *A History of Architecture on the Comparative Method*, Charles Scribner's Sons, New York, 1958.

Hamlin, Talbot, *Architecture Through the Ages*, Putnam's Sons, New York, 1949.

Kimball, Fiske and Edgell, George H., *A History of Architecture*, Harper, New York, 1918.

Robb, David M. and Garrison, J. J., *Art in the Western World*, Third Edition, Harper & Row, 1953.

Janson, H. W. and Janson, Dora Jane, *Key Monuments of the History of Art*, Prentice Hall, Inc., and Harry Abrams, 0000.

SPECIAL SUBJECTS IN ARCHITECTURAL HISTORY

Aalto, Alvar, *Alvar Aalto, 1963–70*, Praeger, New York, 1972.

Alsberg, Henry G. and others, *The American Guide*, 4 vols., Hastings House, 1949.

Andrews, Wayne, *Architecture, Ambition and Americans*, Harper, New York, 1955.

Andrews, Wayne, *Architecture in New England, A Photographic History*, Green Press, Brattleboro, Vermont, 1973.

Bailey, James, *New Towns in America*, John Wiley & Sons, New York, 1973.

Bastund, Knud, *Jose Luis Sert*, Praeger, New York, 1967.

Blaser, Werner, *Mies van der Rohe*, Praeger, New York, 1965.

Boesiger, Willy, *Richard Neutra, 1923–50*, Praeger, New York, 1966.

Boesiger, Willy, *Richard Neutra, 1950–60*, Praeger, New York, 1970.

Boesiger, Willy, *Richard Neutra, 1961–66*, Praeger, New York, 1974.

Boesiger, Willy and Girsberger, Hans, *Le Corbusier, 1910–65*, Praeger, New York, 1967.

Bostick, William A., Editor, *The Legacy of Albert Kahn*, Detroit Art Institute, Detroit, 1970.

Burchard, John and Bush-Brown, Albert, *Architecture of America*, Little-Brown, Boston, 1961.

Bush-Brown, Albert, *Louis Sullivan*, G. Braziller, New York, 1960.

Burton, Katherine, *The Dream Lives Forever, The Story of St. Patrick's Cathedral*, Longmans, Green and Co., New York, 1960.

Chermayeff, Ivan and Edwitt, Elliott, *Observations on American Architecture*, Viking Press, New York, 1972.

381

Christ-Janer, Albert, *Eliel Saarinen,* University of Chicago Press, Chicago, 1948.

Condit, Carl W., *The Rise of the Skyscraper,* University of Chicago Press, Chicago, 1952.

Condit, Carl W., *American Building Art in the Nineteenth Century,* Oxford University Press, New York, 1960.

Le Corbusier, *The Radiant City,* Orion Press, New York, 1964.

Le Corbusier, *Towards A New Architecture,* Payson and Clark, New York, 1927.

Creighton, Tom H., "New Sensualism," *Progressive Architecture,* October–November 1959.

Dow, Alden B., *Reflections, The Work of Alden B. Dow,* Northwood Institute, Midland, Michigan, 1970.

Downing, A. F. and Scully, Vincent, *The Architectural Heritage of Newport, Rhode Island:* 1640–1915, Second Edition, 1915.

Dulaney, Paul S., *The Architecture of Historic Richmond,* Society of Architectural Historians,

Eaton, Leonard, *Two Chicago Architects and Their Clients: Frank Lloyd Wright and Howard Van Doren Shaw,* MIT Press, Cambridge, Massachusetts, 1969.

Eaton, Leonard, *American Architecture Comes of Age,* MIT Press, Cambridge, Massachusetts, 1972.

Eberlein, Harold D. and Hubbard, Cortlandt Van D., *Colonial Interiors, Federal and Greek Revival,* Bonanza Books, New York, 1938.

Edgell, George H., *American Architecture of Today,* Scribner's Sons, New York, 1928.

Farrar, Emmie Ferguson, *Old Virginia Houses Along the James.*

Ferry, W. Hawkins, *The Buildings of Detroit,* Wayne State University Press, Detroit, 1968.

Fortune Magazine Editors, *The Exploding Metropolis,* Doubleday and Company, New York, 1958; Anchor Books (paperback), 1958.

Freeman, Donald, *Boston Architecture,* Boston Society of Architects, Boston,

Gallier, James, *Autobiography of James Gallier, Architect,* Da Capo Press, New York, 1973.

Gebhard, David and others. *A Guide to Architecture in San Francisco and Northern California,* Peregrine Press, Salt Lake City, 1973.

Gebhard, David, *Schindler,* Viking Press, New York, 1972.

Giedion, Siegfried, *Space, Time and Architecture,* Eleventh Edition, Harvard Press, Cambridge, Massachusetts, 1962.

Giedion, Siegfried, *Mechanization Takes Command,* Oxford University Press, New York, 1948.

Giedion, Siegfried, *A Decade of New Architecture,* Girsberger, Zurich, 1951.

Giedion, Siegfried, *Walter Gropius,* Reinhold, New York, 1954.

Gilchrist, Agnes A., *William Strickland,* University of Pennsylvania Press, Philadelphia, 1950.

Granger, Alfred H., *Charles Follen McKim,* Benjamin Blom, New York,

Gropius, Walter, *Scope of Total Architecture,* Harper, New York, 1955.

Gutheim, Frederick Albert, *One Hundred Years of Architecture in America,* Reinhold, New York, 1957.

Hamlin, Talbot, *Benjamin Latrobe,* Oxford University Press, New York, 1955.

Hamlin, Talbot, *Architecture, an Art for All Men,* Columbia University Press, New York, 1947.

Hamlin, Talbot, *Architecture Through the Ages,* Putnam, New York, 1953.

Hammond, Ralph, *Ante-Bellum Mansions of Alabama,* Society of Architectural Historians Guidebooks.

Harris, Frank, *A Guide to Contemporary Architecture in Southern California,* Watling, Los Angeles, 1951.

Hitchcock, Henry-Russell, Jr., *Modern Architecture, Romanticism and Reintegration,* Payson and Clark, New York, 1929.

Hitchcock, Henry-Russell, Jr., *In the Nature of Materials, The Buildings of Frank Lloyd Wright,* Durell Sloan and Pierce, New York, 1942.

Hitchcock, Henry-Russell, Jr., *Architecture, Nineteenth and Twentieth Centuries,* Penguin Books, Baltimore, Maryland, 1958.

Hitchcock, Henry-Russell, Jr., and Johnson, Philip, *The International Style,* Norton, New York, 1932.

Hoffman, Donald, *The Architecture of John Wellborn Root,* Johns Hopkins Press, Baltimore, Maryland, 1973.

Howland, Richard and Spencer, E., *The Architecture of Baltimore,* Baltimore, 1953.

Jacobus, John, *Twentieth Century Architecture, The Middle Years, 1940–65,* Praeger, New York, 1966.

Joedicke, Jurgen, *Architecture Since 1945,* Praeger, New York, 1969.

Joedicke, Jurgen, *A History of Modern Architecture,* Praeger. New York, 1969.

Jones, Cranston, *Marcel Breuer, 1921–1961,* Praeger, New York, 1962.

Kaufmann, Edgar, Jr., *Louis Sullivan and the Architecture of Free Enterprise,* Art Institute of Chicago, Chicago, 1956.

Kimball, Fiske, *Thomas Jefferson, Architect,* Second Edition, Da Capo Press, New York, 1968.

Kimball, Fiske, *Domestic Architecture of the American Colonies and of the Early Republic,* Dover, New York, 1922.

Lincoln, F. S., *Charleston Photographic Studies,* Corinthian Publications, New York, 1946.

McCall, Elizabeth, *Old Philadelphia Houses on Society Hill, 1750–1840,* Hastings House, New York, 1966.

Maass, John, *The Gingerbread Age,* Rinehard, New York, 1957.

Major, Howard, *The Domestic Architecture of the Early American Republic: The Greek Revival,* Lippincott, Philadelphia, 1926.

Manson, Grant C. *Frank Lloyd Wright to 1910,* Reinhold, New York, 1958.

Mann, Roy, *Rivers in the City,* American Institute of Architects, Washington, D.C.,

Marks, Robert W., *The Dymaxion World of Buckminster Fuller,* Reinhold, New York, 1960.

Meier, Richard, *Recent American Synagogue Architecture,* Jewish Museum, New York, 1963.

Meyer, Katherine M., Editor, *Detroit Architecture,* AIA Guide, Detroit, 1971.

Moholy-Nagy, *The New Vision, from Material to Architecture,* Norton, New York, 1938.

Moore, Charles, *Daniel H. Burnham: Architect, Planner of Cities,* Da Capo Press, New York, 1968.

Moore, Charles, *The Life and Times of Charles F. McKim,* Houghton-Mifflin, Boston, 1929.

Mock, Elizabeth, *Built in the U.S.A., 1932–1944,* Arno, New York, 1944.

Mumford, Lewis, *The Brown Decades in America, 1865–1895,* Harcourt-Brace, New York, 1931.

Mumford, Lewis, *Technics and Civilization,* Harcourt Brace, New York, 1936.

Mumford, Lewis, *The Culture of Cities,* Harcourt, Brace Jovanovich, New York, 1938.

Mumford, Lewis, *Roots of Contemporary American Architecture,* Reinhold, New York, 1952.

Mumford, Lewis, *The Highway and the City,* Harcourt Brace, New York, 1956; Mentor Books, 1956.

Museum of Modern Art, *Modern Architecture,* Museum of Modern Art, New York, 1932.

Museum of Modern Art, *What is Modern Architecture,* Museum of Modern Art, New York, 1946.

Museum of Modern Art, *Built in U.S.A. 1944–* , Simon & Schuster, New York, 1952.

Naylor, Gillian, *The Arts and Crafts Movement, A Study of Its Sources, Ideals and Influence on Design Theory,* MIT Press, Cambridge, Massachusetts, 1974.

Nelson, George, *Industrial Architecture of Albert Kahn, Inc.,* New York, 1939.

Newcomb, Rexford, *Architecture of the Old North-west Territory,* University of Chicago Press, Chicago, 1950.

O'Neal, William B., *Architecture in Virginia: An Official Guide to Four Centuries of Building in the Old Dominion,* Society of Architectural Historians Guides, Walker & Co., 1968.

Papademetrion, Peter C., Editor, *Houston, an Architectural Guide,* An Architectural Guide, American Institute of Architects, Houston, 1972.

Peter, John, *Masters of Modern Architecture,* G. Braziller, New York, 1958.

Pevsner, Nikolaus, *Pioneers of Modern Design,* Museum of Modern Art, New York, 1949.

Pratt, Dorothy and Richard, *A Guide to Early American Homes, North,* Bonanza Books, New York, 1956.

Pratt, Dorothy and Richard, *A Guide to Early American Homes, South,* Bonanza Books, New York, 1956.

Queen, Stuart A. and Carpenter, David B., *The American City,* McGraw-Hill, New York, 1953.

Rettig, Robert B., *Architecture of H. H. Richardson and His Contemporaries in Boston and Vicinity,* Society of Architectural Historians,

Redstone, Louis G. *Art in Architecture*, McGraw-Hill, New York, 1968.

Richards,, J. M. and Mock, Elizabeth B., *An Introduction to Modern Architecture*, Pelican Books, New York, 1947.

Scully, Vincent, *Modern Architecture*, G. Braziller, New York, 1961.

Scully, Vincent, *American Architecture and Urbanism*, Praeger, New York,

Sharp, Dennis, *A Visual History of Twentieth Century Architecture*, American Institute of Architects, 1973.

Siegel, Arthur, et al. *Chicago's Famous Buildings*, University of Chicago Press, Chicago, 1970.

Smith, J. Frazer, *White Pillars, the Architecture of the South.*

Stubblebine, Jo, *The Northwest Architecture of Pietro Belluschi*, F. W. Dodge, New York, 1953.

Sullivan, Louis H., *The Tall Building Artistically Considered*, Minneapolis, 1922.

Sullivan, Louis H., *Kindergarten Chats*, Wittenborn, New York, 1975.

Sullivan, Louis H.., *The Autobiography of an Idea*, Dover, New York, 1956.

Tallmadge, Thomas E., *Architecture of Old Chicago*, University of Chicago Press, Chicago, 1951.

Tallmadge, Thomas E., *The Story of Architecture in America*, Norton, New York, 1927.

Tatum, George, Penn's Great Town, University of Pennsylvania Press, Philadelphia, 1961.

Tunnard, Christopher and Reed, Henry Hope, *American Skyline: The Growth and Form of Our Cities and Towns*, Houghton Mifflin Co., New York, 1953; Mentor Books.

Upjohn, Everard M., *Richard Upjohn, Architect and Churchman*, Da Capo Press, New York, 1968.

Whiffen, Marcus, *American Architecture Since 1780: A Guide to the Styles*, MIT Press, Cambridge, Massachusetts, 1969.

White, Theodore B. and others. *Philadelphia Architecture Nineteenth Century*, University of Pennsylvania Press, Philadelphia, 1950.

Wilson, Robert H., *Philadelphia, Official Handbook for Visitors*, C. S. Hammond and Co., 1964.

Wright, Frank Lloyd, *An Autobiography*, Duell, Sloan and Pearce, New York, 1943.

Wright, Frank Lloyd, *Modern Architecture*, Princeton University Press, Princeton, New Jersey, 1931.

Wright, Frank Lloyd, *A Testament*, Horizon Press, New York, New Jersey, 1957.

Yost, Morgan L., "Greene and Greene of Pasadena, California," *S.A.H. Journal*, Vols. 7–9, 1948–1950.

LIST OF ILLUSTRATIONS

387

INDEX